PHILLIP KELLER

The Shepherd Trilogy

A SHEPHERD LOOKS AT THE 23RD PSALM

A SHEPHERD LOOKS AT THE GOOD SHEPHERD

A SHEPHERD LOOKS AT THE LAMB OF GOD

ZONDERVAN™

GRAND RAPIDS, MICHIGAN 49530 USA

ZONDERVAN™

The Shepherd Trilogy
Copyright © 1970, 1978, 1982, 1996 by W. Phillip Keller

First published in separate volumes in Great Britain as
A Shepherd Looks at the 23rd Psalm, Pickering & Inglis, 1976;
A Shepherd Looks at The Good Shephered, Pickering & Inglis, 1979;
A Shepherd Looks at the Lamb of God, Pickering & Inglis, 1983

Requests for information should be addressed to:

Zondervan, *Grand Rapids, Michigan 49530*

Phillip Keller asserts the moral right to be identified as the author of
this work.

A catalogue record for this book is available from the British Library.

ISBN 0 551 030704

Printed in the United States of America

18 19 20 /LSC/ 40 39 38 37 36

*A Shepherd Looks at
the 23rd Psalm*

Contents

Introduction   5

1 The Lord is My Shepherd   9
2 I Shall Not Want   20
3 He Maketh Me to Lie Down in Green Pastures   29
4 He Leadeth Me Beside the Still Waters   42
5 He Restoreth My Soul   51
6 He Leadeth Me in the Paths of
   Righteousness for His Name's Sake   61
7 Yea, Though I Walk Through the Valley ...   72
8 Thy Rod and Thy Staff They Comfort Me   82
9 Thou Preparest a Table Before Me ...   93
10 Thou Anointest My Head With Oil ...   103
11 Surely Goodness and Mercy Shall Follow Me ...   116
12 I Will Dwell in the House of the Lord For Ever   127

C

Introduction

To a great extent the Bible is a collection of books written by men of humble origin, who penned under the guidance of God's Spirit. Much of its terminology and teaching is couched in rural language, dealing with outdoor subjects and natural phenomena. The audience to whom these writings were originally addressed were for the most part themselves simple, nomadic folk familiar with nature and the outdoor life of the countryside about them.

Today this is not the case. Many who either read or study the Scriptures in the twentieth century come from an urban, man-made environment. City people, especially, are often unfamiliar with such subjects as livestock, crops, land, fruit, or wildlife. They miss much of the truth taught in God's Word because they are not familiar with such things as sheep, wheat, soil or grapes.

Yet divine revelation is irrevocably bound up with the basic subjects of the natural world. Our Lord Himself, when He was amongst us, continually used natural phenomena to explain supernatural truth in His parables. It is a sound, indisputable method, both scientifically and spiritually valid.

All this is understandable and meaningful when we

recognize the fact that God is author and originator of both the natural and supernatural (spiritual). The same basic laws, principles and procedures function in these two contiguous realms. Therefore it follows that to understand one is to grasp the parallel principle in the other.

It must be stated here that it is through this type of scriptural interpretation that my own understanding of the Bible has become meaningful. It explains in part, too, why truths which I shared with various audiences have been long remembered by them with great clarity.

Accordingly I make no apologies for presenting this collection of 'shepherd insights' into the well-known and loved – but often misunderstood – 23rd Psalm.

This book has been developed against a rather unique background which has perhaps given me a deeper appreciation than most men of what David had in mind when he wrote his beautiful poem. First of all I grew up and lived in East Africa, surrounded by simple native herders whose customs closely resembled those of their counterparts in the Middle East. So I am intimately acquainted with the romance, the pathos, the picturesque life of an Eastern shepherd. Secondly, as a young man, I actually made my own livelihood for about eight years as a sheep owner and sheep rancher. Consequently I write as one who has had firsthand experience with every phase of sheep management. Later, as the lay pastor of a community church, I shared the truths of this Psalm, as a shepherd, with my 'flock', every Sunday for several months.

It is, therefore, out of the variety of these firsthand experiences with sheep that the following chapters have emerged. To my knowledge this is the first time that a down-to-earth, hard-handed sheep man has ever written at length about the Shepherd's Psalm.

There is one difficulty that arises when writing a book based on a familiar portion of the Scriptures. One disillusions or disenchants the reader with some of his former notions about the Psalm. Like much spiritual teaching, the 23rd Psalm has had a certain amount of sentimental imagery wrapped around it with no sound basis in actual life. Some ideas advanced about it have, in fact, been almost ludicrous.

I would ask, then, that the reader approach the pages that follow with an open mind and an unbiased spirit. If he does, fresh truth and exciting glimpses of God's care and concern for him will flood over his being. Then he will be brought into a bold, new appreciation of the endless effort put forth by our Saviour, for His sheep. Out of this there will then emerge a growing admiration and affection for The Great Shepherd of his soul.

CHAPTER 1

The Lord is My Shepherd

The Lord! But who is the Lord? What is His character? Does He have adequate credentials to be my Shepherd – my manager – my owner?

And if He does – how do I come under His control? In what way do I become the object of His concern and diligent care?

These are penetrating, searching questions and they deserve honest and basic examination.

One of the calamities of Christianity is our tendency to talk in ambiguous generalities.

David, the author of the poem, himself a shepherd, and the son of a shepherd, later to be known as the 'Shepherd King' of Israel, stated explicitly, 'The Lord is my Shepherd.' To whom did he refer?

He referred to Jehovah, the Lord God of Israel.

His statement was confirmed by Jesus the Christ. When He was God incarnate amongst men, He declared emphatically, 'I am the good Shepherd.'

But who was this Christ?

Our view of Him is often too small – too cramped – too provincial – too human. And because it is we feel unwilling to allow Him to have authority or control – much less outright ownership of our lives.

He it was who was directly responsible for the creation of all things both natural and supernatural (see Colossians 1:15-20).

If we pause to reflect on the person of Christ – on His power and upon His achievements – suddenly like David we will be glad to state proudly, 'The Lord – *He* is my Shepherd!'

But before we do this it helps to hold clearly in mind the particular part played upon our history by God the Father, God the Son, and God the Holy Spirit.

God the Father is God the author – the originator of all that exists. It was in His mind, first, that all took shape.

God the Son, our Saviour, is God the artisan – the artist, the Creator of all that exists. He brought into being all that had been originally formulated in His Father's mind.

God the Holy Spirit is God the agent who presents these facts to both my mind and my spiritual understanding so that they become both real and relative to me as an individual.

Now the beautiful relationships given to us repeatedly in Scripture between God and man are those of a father to his children and a shepherd to his sheep. These concepts were first conceived in the mind of God our Father. They were made possible and practical through the work of Christ. They are confirmed and made real in me through the agency of the gracious Holy Spirit.

So when the simple – though sublime – statement is made by a man or woman that 'The Lord is my Shepherd', it immediately implies a profound yet practical working relationship between a human being and his Maker.

It links a lump of common clay to divine destiny – it means a mere mortal becomes the cherished object of divine diligence.

This thought alone should stir my spirit, quicken my own sense of awareness, and lend enormous dignity to myself as an individual. To think that God in Christ is deeply concerned about me as a particular person immediately gives great purpose and enormous meaning to my short sojourn upon this planet.

And the greater, the wider, the more majestic my concept is of the Christ – the more vital will be my relationship to Him. Obviously, David, in this Psalm, is speaking not as the shepherd, though he was one, but as a sheep; one of the flock. He spoke with a strong sense of pride and devotion and admiration. It was as though he literally boasted aloud, 'Look at who my shepherd is – my owner – my manager!' The Lord is!

After all, he knew from firsthand experience that the lot in life of any particular sheep depended on the type of man who owned it. Some men were gentle, kind, intelligent, brave and selfless in their devotion to their stock. Under one man, sheep would struggle, starve and suffer endless hardship. In another's care they would flourish and thrive contentedly.

So if the Lord is my Shepherd I should know something of His character and understand something of His ability.

To meditate on this I frequently go out at night to walk alone under the stars and remind myself of His majesty and might. Looking up at the star-studded sky I remember that at least 250,000,000 x 250,000,000 such bodies – each larger than our sun, one of the smallest of the stars, have been scattered across the vast spaces of the universe by His hand. I recall that the planet earth, which is my temporary home for a few short years, is so minute a speck of matter in space that if it were possible to transport our most powerful tele- scope to our nearest neighbour star, Alpha Centauri, and look back this way, the earth could not be seen, even with the aid of that powerful instrument.

All this is a bit humbling. It drains the 'ego' from a man and puts things in proper perspective. It makes me see myself as a mere mite of material in an enormous universe. Yet the staggering fact remains that Christ the Creator of such an enormous universe of over- whelming magnitude, deigns to call Himself my Shepherd and invites me to consider myself His sheep – His special object of affection and attention. Who better could care for me?

By the same sort of process I stoop down and pick up a handful of soil from the backyard or roadside. Placing it under an electron microscope I am astounded to discover it teems with billions upon billions of micro- organisms. Many of them are so complex in their own peculiar cellular structure that even a fraction of their functions in the earth are not yet properly understood.

Yes, He the Christ – the Son of God – brought all of this into being. From the most gigantic galaxy to the most minute microbe all function flawlessly in accor- dance with definite laws of order and unity which are utterly beyond the mind of finite man to master.

It is in this sense, first of all, that I am basically bound to admit that His ownership of me as a human being is legitimate – simply because it is He who brought me into being and no one is better able to understand or care for me.

I belong to Him simply because He deliberately chose to create me as the object of His own affection.

It is patently clear that most men and women refuse to acknowledge this fact. Their deliberate attempts to deny that such a relationship even exists or could exist between a man and his Maker demonstrate their abhorrence for admitting that anyone really can claim ownership or authority over them by virtue of bringing them into being.

This was of course the enormous 'risk' or 'calculated chance', if we may use the term, which God took in making man initially.

But in His usual magnanimous manner He took the second step in attempting to restore this relationship which is repeatedly breached by men who turn their backs upon Him.

Again in Christ He demonstrated at Calvary the deep desire of His heart to have men come under His benevolent care. He Himself absorbed the penalty for their perverseness, stating clearly that 'all we like sheep have gone astray, we have turned every one to his own way, and the Lord hath laid on Him the iniquity of us all' (Isaiah 53:6).

Thus, in a second very real and vital sense I truly belong to Him simply because He has bought me again at the incredible price of His own laid-down life and shed blood.

Therefore He was entitled to say, 'I am the Good Shepherd, the Good Shepherd giveth his life for the sheep.'

So there remains the moving realization that we have been bought with a price, that we are really not our own and He is well within His rights to lay claim upon our lives.

I recall quite clearly how in my first venture with sheep, the question of paying a price for my ewes was so terribly important. They belonged to me only by virtue of the fact that I paid hard cash for them. It was money earned by the blood and sweat and tears drawn from my own body during the desperate grinding years of the depression. And when I bought that first small flock I was buying them literally with my own body which had been laid down with this day in mind.

Because of this I felt in a special way that they were in very truth a part of me and I a part of them. There was an intimate identity involved which, though not apparent on the surface to the casual observer, none the less made those thirty ewes exceedingly precious to me.

But the day I bought them I also realized that this was but the first stage in a long, lasting endeavour in which from then on, I would, as their owner, have to continually lay down my life for them, if they were to flourish and prosper. Sheep do not 'just take care of themselves' as some might suppose. They require, more than any other class of livestock, endless attention and meticulous care.

It is no accident that God has chosen to call us sheep. The behaviour of sheep and human beings is similar in many ways, as will be seen in further chapters. Our mass mind (or mob instincts), our fears and timidity, our stubbornness and stupidity, our perverse habits are all parallels of profound importance.

Yet despite these adverse characteristics Christ chooses us, buys us, calls us by name, makes us His own and delights in caring for us.

It is this last aspect which is really the third reason why we are under obligation to recognize His ownership of us. He literally lays Himself out for us continually. He is ever interceding for us; He is ever guiding us by His gracious Spirit; He is ever working on our behalf to ensure that we will benefit from His care.

In fact, Psalm 23 might well be called 'David's Hymn of Praise to Divine Diligence'. For the entire poem goes on to recount the manner in which the Good Shepherd spares no pains for the welfare of His sheep.

Little wonder that the poet took pride in belonging to the Good Shepherd. Why shouldn't he?

In memory I can still see one of the sheep ranches in our district which was operated by a tenant sheepman. He ought never to have been allowed to keep sheep. His stock were always thin, weak and riddled with disease or parasites. Again and again they would come and stand at the fence staring blankly through the woven wire at the green lush pastures which my flock enjoyed. Had they been able to speak I am sure they would have said, 'Oh, to be set free from this awful owner!'

This is a picture which has never left my memory. It is a picture of pathetic people the world over who have not known what it is to belong to the Good Shepherd … who suffer instead under sin and Satan.

How amazing it is that individual men and women vehemently refuse and reject the claims of Christ on their lives. They fear that to acknowledge His ownership is to come under the rule of a tyrant.

This is difficult to comprehend when one pauses to consider the character of Christ. Admittedly there have been many false caricatures of this Person, but an unbiased look at His life quickly reveals an individual of enormous compassion and incredible integrity.

He was the most balanced and perhaps the most

beloved being ever to enter the society of men. Though born amid the most disgusting surroundings, the member of a modest working family, He bore Himself always with great dignity and assurance. Though He enjoyed no special advantages as a child, either in education or employment, His entire philosophy and outlook on life were the highest standards of human conduct ever set before mankind. Though He had no vast economic assets, political power or military might, no other person ever made such an enormous impact on the world's history. Because of Him millions of people across almost twenty centuries of time have come into a life of decency and honour and noble conduct.

Not only was He gentle and tender and true but also righteous, stern as steel, and terribly tough on phoney people.

He was magnificent in His magnanimous spirit of forgiveness for fallen folk, but a terror to those who indulged in double talk or false pretences.

He came to set men free from their own sins, their own selves, their own fears. Those so liberated loved Him with fierce loyalty.

It is this One who insists that He was the Good Shepherd, the understanding Shepherd, the concerned Shepherd who cares enough to seek out and save and restore lost men and women.

He never hesitated to make it quite clear that when an individual once came under His management and control there would be a certain new and unique relationship between Him and them. There would be something very special about belonging to this particular Shepherd. There would be a distinct mark upon the man or woman that differentiated them from the rest of the crowd.

The day I bought my first thirty ewes, my neighbour and I sat on the dusty corral rails that enclosed the sheep pens and admired the choice, strong, well-bred ewes that had become mine. Turning to me he handed me a large, sharp, killing knife and remarked tersely, 'Well, Phillip, they're yours. Now you'll have to put your mark on them.'

I knew exactly what he meant. Each sheepman has his own distinctive earmark which he cuts into one or other of the ears of his sheep. In this way, even at a distance, it is easy to determine to whom the sheep belongs.

It was not the most pleasant procedure to catch each ewe in turn and lay her ear on a wooden block then notch it deeply with the razor-sharp edge of the knife. There was pain for both of us. But from our mutual suffering an indelible lifelong mark of ownership was made that could never be erased. And from then on every sheep that came into my possession would bear my mark.

There is an exciting parallel to this in the Old Testament. When a slave in any Hebrew household chose, of his own freewill, to become a lifetime member of that home, he was subjected to a certain ritual. His master and owner would take him to his door, put his ear lobe against the door post and with an awl puncture a hole through the ear. From then on he was a man marked for life as belonging to that house.

For the man or woman who recognizes the claim of Christ and gives allegiance to His absolute ownership, there comes the question of bearing His mark. The mark of the cross is that which should identify us with Himself for all time. The question is – does it?

Jesus made it clear when He stated emphatically, 'If any man would be my disciple [follower] let him deny himself and take up his cross daily and follow me.'

Basically what it amounts to is this: A person exchanges the fickle fortunes of living life by sheer whimsy for the more productive and satisfying adventure of being guided by God.

It is a tragic truth that many people who really have never come under His direction or management claim that 'The Lord is my Shepherd'. They seem to hope that by merely admitting that He is their Shepherd somehow they will enjoy the benefits of His care and management without paying the price of forfeiting their own fickle and foolish way of life.

One cannot have it both ways. Either we belong or we don't. Jesus Himself warned us that there would come a day when many would say, 'Lord, in Your name we did many wonderful things', but He will retort that He never knew us as His own.

It is a most serious and sobering thought which should make us search our own hearts and motives and personal relationship to Himself.

Do I really belong to Him?

Do I really recognize His right to me?

Do I respond to His authority and acknowledge His ownership?

Do I find freedom and complete fulfilment in this arrangement?

Do I sense a purpose and deep contentment because I am under His direction?

Do I know rest and repose, besides a definite sense of

exciting adventure, in belonging to Him?

If so, then with genuine gratitude and exaltation I can exclaim proudly, just as David did, 'The Lord is my Shepherd!' and I'm thrilled to belong to Him, for it is thus that I shall flourish and thrive no matter what life may bring to me.

CHAPTER 2

I Shall Not Want

What a proud, positive, bold statement to make! Obviously, this is the sentiment of a sheep utterly satisfied with its owner, perfectly content with its lot in life.

Since the Lord is my Shepherd, then I shall not want. Actually the word 'want', as used here, has a broader meaning than might at first be imagined. No doubt the main concept is that of not lacking – not being deficient – in proper care, management or husbandry.

But a second emphasis is the idea of being utterly contented in the Good Shepherd's care and consequently not craving or desiring anything more.

This may seem a strange statement for a man like David to have made if we think in terms only of physical or material needs. After all, he had been hounded and harried repeatedly by the forces of his enemy Saul as well as those of his own estranged son Absalom. He was obviously a man who had known intense privation: deep personal poverty, acute hardship, and anguish of spirit.

Therefore it is absurd to assert on the basis of this statement that the child of God, the sheep in the Shepherd's care, will never experience lack or need.

It is imperative to keep a balanced view of the

Christian life. To do this it is well to consider the careers of men like Elijah, John the Baptist, our Lord Himself – and even modern men of faith such as Livingstone – to realize that all of them experienced great personal privation and adversity.

When He was among us, the Great Shepherd Himself warned His disciples before His departure for glory, that – 'In this world ye *shall* have tribulation – but be of good cheer – I have overcome the world.'

One of the fallacies that is common among Christians today is the assertion that if a man or woman is prospering materially it is a significant mark of the blessing of God upon their lives. This simply is not so.

Rather, in bold contrast we read in Revelation 3:17, 'Because thou sayest, I am rich, and increased with goods, and have need of nothing; and knowest not that thou art wretched, and miserable, and poor, and blind, and naked ...'

Or, in an equally pointed way, Jesus made clear to the rich young ruler who wished to become His follower, 'One thing thou *lackest*: go thy way, sell whatsoever thou hast, and give to the poor ... and come ... follow me' (Mark 10:21).

Based on the teachings of the Bible we can only conclude that David was not referring to material or physical poverty when he made the statement, 'I shall not want.'

For this very reason the Christian has to take a long, hard look at life. He has to recognize that as with many of God's choice people before him, he may be called on to experience lack of wealth or material benefits. He has to see his sojourn upon the planet as a brief interlude during which there may well be some privation in a physical sense. Yet amid such hardship he can still boast, 'I *shall not want ... I shall not lack* the expert care and management of my Master.'

To grasp the inner significance of this simple statement it is necessary to understand the difference between belonging to one master or another – to the Good Shepherd or to an impostor. Jesus Himself took great pains to point out to anyone who contemplated following Him that it was quite impossible to serve two masters. One belonged either to Him or to another.

When all is said and done, the welfare of any flock is entirely dependent upon the management afforded them by their owner.

The tenant sheepman on the farm next to my first ranch was the most indifferent manager I had ever met. He was not concerned about the condition of his sheep. His land was neglected. He gave little or no time to his flock, letting them pretty well forage for themselves as best they could, both summer and winter. They fell prey to dogs, cougars and rustlers.

Every year these poor creatures were forced to gnaw away at bare brown fields and impoverished pastures. Every winter there was a shortage of nourishing hay and wholesome grain to feed the hungry ewes. Shelter to safeguard and protect the suffering sheep from storms and blizzards was scanty and inadequate.

They had only polluted, muddy water to drink. There had been a lack of salt and other trace minerals needed to offset their sickly pastures. In their thin, weak and diseased condition these poor sheep were a pathetic sight.

In my mind's eye I can still see them standing at the fence, huddled sadly in little knots, staring wistfully through the wires at the rich pastures on the other side.

To all their distress, the heartless, selfish owner seemed utterly callous and indifferent. He simply did not care. What if his sheep did *want* green grass; fresh water; shade; safety or shelter from the storms? What if they did *want* relief from wounds, bruises, disease and parasites?

He ignored their needs – he couldn't care less. Why should he – they were just sheep – fit only for the slaughterhouse.

I never looked at those poor sheep without an acute awareness that this was a precise picture of those wretched old taskmasters, Sin and Satan, on their derelict ranch – scoffing at the plight of those within their power.

As I have moved among men and women from all strata of society, as both a lay pastor and as a scientist, I have become increasingly aware of one thing. It is the boss – the manager – the Master in people's lives who makes the difference in their destiny.

I have known some of the wealthiest men on this continent intimately – also some of the leading scientists and professional people. Despite their dazzling outward show of success, despite their affluence and their prestige, they remained poor in spirit, shrivelled in soul, and unhappy in life. They were joyless people held in the iron grip and heartless ownership of the wrong master.

By way of contrast, I have numerous friends among relatively poor people – people who have known hardship, disaster and the struggle to stay afloat financially. But because they belong to Christ and have recognized Him as Lord and Master of their lives, their owner and manager, they are permeated by a deep, quiet, settled peace that is beautiful to behold.

It is indeed a delight to visit some of these humble homes where men and women are rich in spirit, generous in heart, and large of soul. They radiate a serene confidence and quiet joy that surmounts all the tragedies of their time.

They are under God's care and they know it. They have entrusted themselves to Christ's control and found contentment.

Contentment should be the hallmark of the man or woman who has put his or her affairs in the hands of God. This especially applies in our affluent age. But the outstanding paradox is the intense fever of discontent among people who are ever speaking of security.

Despite an unparalleled wealth in material assets we are outstandingly insecure and unsure of ourselves and wellnigh bankrupt in spiritual values.

Always men are searching for safety beyond themselves. They are restless, unsettled, covetous, greedy for more – wanting this and that, yet never really satisfied in spirit.

By contrast the simple Christian, the humble person, the Shepherd's sheep can stand up proudly and boast.

'The Lord is my Shepherd – I shall not want.'

I am completely satisfied with His management of my life. Why? Because He is the sheepman to whom no trouble is too great as He cares for His flock. He is the rancher who is outstanding because of His fondness of sheep – who loves them for their own sake as well as His personal pleasure in them. He will, if necessary, be on the job twenty-four hours a day to see that they are properly provided for in every detail. Above all, He is very jealous of His name and high reputation as 'The Good Shepherd'.

He is the owner who delights in His flock. For Him there is no greater reward, no deeper satisfaction, than that of seeing His sheep contented, well fed, safe and flourishing under His care. This is indeed His very 'life'. He gives all He has to it. He literally lays Himself out for those who are His.

He will go to no end of trouble and labour to supply them with the finest grazing, the richest pasturage, ample winter feed, and clean water. He will spare Himself no pains to provide shelter from storms, protection from ruthless enemies and the diseases and parasites to which sheep are so susceptible.

No wonder Jesus said, 'I am the Good Shepherd – the Good Shepherd giveth his life for the sheep.' And again 'I am come that ye might have life and that ye might have it more abundantly.'

From early dawn until late at night this utterly self-less Shepherd is alert to the welfare of His flock. For the diligent sheepman rises early and goes out first thing every morning without fail to look over his flock. It is the initial, intimate contact of the day. With a practised, searching, sympathetic eye he examines the sheep to see that they are fit and content and able to be on their feet. In an instant he can tell if they have been molested during the night – whether any are ill or if there are some which require special attention.

Repeatedly throughout the day he casts his eye over the flock to make sure that all is well.

Nor even at night is he oblivious to their needs. He sleeps as it were 'with one eye and both ears open', ready at the least sign of trouble to leap up and protect his own.

This is a sublime picture of the care given to those whose lives are under Christ's control. He knows all about their lives from morning to night.

'Blessed be the Lord, who daily loadeth us with benefits – even the God of our salvation.'

'He that keepeth thee will not slumber or sleep.'

In spite of having such a master and owner, the fact remains that some Christians are still not content with His control. They are somewhat dissatisfied, always feeling that somehow the grass beyond the fence must be a little greener. These are carnal Christians – one might almost call them 'fence crawlers' or 'half Christians' who want the best of both worlds.

I once owned a ewe whose conduct exactly typified this sort of person. She was one of the most attractive sheep that ever belonged to me. Her body was beautifully proportioned. She had a strong constitution and an excellent coat of wool. Her head was clean, alert, well-set with bright eyes. She bore sturdy lambs that matured rapidly.

But in spite of all these attractive attributes she had one pronounced fault. She was restless, discontented – a fence crawler.

So much so that I came to call her 'Mrs Gadabout'.

This one ewe produced more problems for me than almost all the rest of the flock combined.

No matter what field or pasture the sheep were in, she would search all along the fences or shoreline (we lived by the sea) looking for a loophole she could crawl through and start to feed on the other side.

It was not that she lacked pasturage. My fields were my joy and delight. No sheep in the district had better grazing.

With 'Mrs Gadabout' it was an ingrained habit. She was simply never contented with things as they were. Often when she had forced her way through some such spot in a fence or found a way around the end of the wire at low tide on the beaches, she would end up feeding on bare, brown, burned-up pasturage of a most inferior sort.

But she never learned her lesson and continued to fence-crawl time after time.

Now it would have been bad enough if she was the only one who did this. It was a sufficient problem to find her and bring her back. But the further point was that she taught her lambs the same tricks. They simply followed her example and soon were as skilled at escaping as their mother.

Even worse, however, was the example she set the other sheep. In a short time she began to lead others through the same holes and over the same dangerous paths down by the sea.

After putting up with her perverseness for a summer I finally came to the conclusion that to save the rest of the flock from becoming unsettled, she would have to go. I could not allow one obstinate, discontented ewe to ruin the whole ranch operation.

It was a difficult decision to make, for I loved her in the same way I loved the rest. Her strength and beauty and alertness were a delight to the eye.

But one morning I took the killing knife in hand and butchered her. Her career of fence crawling was cut short. It was the only solution to the dilemma.

She was a sheep, who in spite of all that I had done to give her the very best care – still wanted something else.

She was not like the one who said, 'The Lord is my Shepherd – I shall not want.'

It is a solemn warning to the carnal Christian backslider – the half-Christian – the one who wants the best of both worlds.

Sometimes in short order they can be cut down.

CHAPTER 3

He Maketh Me to Lie Down in Green Pastures

The strange thing about sheep is that because of their very make-up it is almost impossible for them to be made to lie down unless four requirements are met.

Owing to their timidity they refuse to lie down unless they are free of all fear.

Because of the social behaviour within a flock sheep will not lie down unless they are free from friction with others of their kind.

If tormented by flies or parasites, sheep will not lie down. Only when free of these pests can they relax.

Lastly, sheep will not lie down as long as they feel in need of finding food. They must be free from hunger.

It is significant that to be at rest there must be a definite sense of freedom from fear, tension, aggravations and hunger. The unique aspect of the picture is that it is only the sheepman himself who can provide release from these anxieties. It all depends upon the diligence of the owner whether or not his flock is free of disturbing influences.

When we examine each of these four factors that affect sheep so severely we will understand why the part the owner plays in their management is so tremendously important. It is actually he who makes it possible for them to lie down, to rest, to relax, to be content and quiet and flourishing.

A flock that is restless, discontented, always agitated and disturbed, never does well.

And the same is true of people.

It is not generally known that sheep are so timid and easily panicked that even a stray jackrabbit suddenly bounding from behind a bush can stampede a whole flock. When one startled sheep runs in fright a dozen others will bolt with it in blind fear, not waiting to see what frightened them.

One day a friend came to call on us from the city. She had a tiny Pekinese pup along. As she opened the car door the pup jumped out on the grass. Just one glimpse of the unexpected little dog was enough. In sheer terror over 200 of my sheep which were resting nearby leaped up and rushed off across the pasture.

As long as there is even the slightest suspicion of danger from dogs, coyotes, cougars, bears or other enemies the sheep stand up ready to flee for their lives. They have little or no means of self-defence. They are helpless, timid, feeble creatures whose only recourse is to run.

When I invited friends to visit us, after the Pekinese episode, I always made it clear that dogs were to be left at home. I also had to drive off or shoot other stray dogs that came to molest or disturb the sheep. Two dogs have been known to kill as many as 292 sheep in a single night of unbridled slaughter.

Ewes, heavy in lamb, when chased by dogs or other predators, will slip their unborn lambs and lose them in abortions. A shepherd's loss from such forays can be appalling. One morning at dawn I found nine of my choicest ewes, all soon to lamb, lying dead in the field where a cougar had harried the flock during the night.

It was a terrible shock to a young man like myself just new to the business and unfamiliar with such attacks. From then on I slept with a .303 rifle and flashlight by my bed. At the least sound of the flock being disturbed I would leap from bed and calling my faithful collie, dash out into the night, rifle in hand, ready to protect my sheep.

In the course of time I came to realize that nothing so quieted and reassured the sheep as to see me in the field. The presence of their master and owner and protector put them at ease as nothing else could do, and this applied day and night.

There was one summer when sheep rustling was a common occurrence in our district. Night after night the dog and I were out under the stars, keeping watch over the flock by night, ready to defend them from the raids of any rustlers. The news of my diligence spread along the grapevine of our back country roads and the rustlers quickly decided to leave us alone and try their tactics elsewhere.

'He maketh me to lie down.'

In the Christian's life there is no substitute for the keen awareness that my Shepherd is nearby. There is nothing like Christ's presence to dispel the fear, the panic, the terror of the unknown.

We live a most uncertain life. Any hour can bring disaster, danger and distress from unknown quarters. Life is full of hazards. No one can tell what a day will produce in new trouble. We live either in a sense of anxiety, fear and foreboding, or in a sense of quiet rest. Which is it?

Generally it is the 'unknown', the 'unexpected', that produces the greatest panic. It is in the grip of fear that most of us are unable to cope with the cruel circumstances and harsh complexities of life. We feel they are foes which endanger our tranquillity. Often our first impulse is simply to get up and run from them.

Then in the midst of our misfortunes there suddenly comes the awareness that He, the Christ, the Good Shepherd, is there. It makes all the difference. His presence in the picture throws a different light on the whole scene. Suddenly things are not half so black nor nearly so terrifying. The outlook changes and there is hope. I find myself delivered from fear. Rest returns and I can relax.

This has come to me again and again as I grow older. It is the knowledge that my Master, my Friend, my Owner has things under control even when they may appear calamitous. This gives me great consolation, repose, and rest. 'Now I lay me down in peace and sleep, for Thou God keepest me.'

It is the special office work of God's gracious Spirit to convey this sense of the Christ to our fearful hearts. He comes quietly to reassure us that Christ Himself is aware of our dilemma and deeply involved in it with us.

And it is in fact in this assurance that we rest and relax.

'For God hath not given us the spirit of fear; but of power, and of love, and of a sound [disciplined] mind' (2 Timothy 1:7).

The idea of a sound mind is that of a mind at ease – at peace – not perturbed or harassed or obsessed with fear and foreboding for the future.

'I will both lay me down in peace and sleep: for thou, Lord, only makest me dwell in safety.'

The second source of fear from which the sheepman delivers his sheep is that of tension, rivalry and cruel competition within the flock itself.

In every animal society there is established an order of dominance or status within the group. In a penful of chickens it is referred to as the 'pecking order'. With cattle it is called the 'horning order'. Among sheep we speak of the 'butting order'.

Generally an arrogant, cunning and domineering old ewe will be boss of any bunch of sheep. She maintains her position of prestige by butting and driving other ewes or lambs away from the best grazing or favourite bedgrounds. Succeeding her in precise order the other sheep all establish and maintain their exact position in the flock by using the same tactics of butting and thrusting at those below and around them.

A vivid and accurate word picture of this process is given to us in Ezekiel 34:15–16 and 20–22. This is a startling example, in fact, of the scientific accuracy of the Scriptures in describing a natural phenomenon.

Because of this rivalry, tension and competition for status and self assertion, there is friction in a flock. The sheep cannot lie down and rest in contentment. Always they must stand up and defend their rights and contest the challenge of the intruder.

Hundreds and hundreds of times I have watched an austere old ewe walk up to a younger one which might have been feeding contentedly or resting quietly in some sheltered spot. She would arch her neck, tilt her head, dilate her eyes and approach the other with a stiff-legged gait. All of this was saying in unmistakable terms, 'Move over! Out of my way! Give ground or else!' And if the other ewe did not immediately leap to her feet in self-defence she would be butted unmercifully. Or if she did rise to accept the challenge one or two strong thrusts would soon send her scurrying for safety.

This continuous conflict and jealousy within the flock can be a most detrimental thing. The sheep become edgy, tense, discontented and restless. They lose weight and become irritable.

But one point that always interested me very much was that whenever I came into view and my presence attracted their attention, the sheep quickly forgot their foolish rivalries and stopped their fighting. The shepherd's presence made all the difference in their behaviour.

This, to me, has always been a graphic picture of the struggle for status in human society. There is the eternal competition 'to keep up with the Joneses' or, as it is now – 'to keep up with the Joneses' kids'.

In any business firm, any office, any family, any community, any church, any human organization or group, be it large or small, the struggle for self-assertion and self-recognition goes on. Most of us fight to be 'top sheep'. We butt and quarrel and compete to 'get ahead'. And in the process people are hurt.

It is here that much jealousy arises. This is where petty peeves grow into horrible hate. It is where ill will and contempt come into being, the place where heated rivalry and deep discontent are born. It is here that discontent gradually grows into a covetous way of life where one has to be forever 'standing up' for himself, for his rights, 'standing up' just to get ahead of the crowd.

In contrast to this, the picture in the Psalm shows us God's people lying down in quiet contentment.

One of the outstanding marks of a Christian should be a serene sense of gentle contentment.

'Godliness with contentment is great gain.'

Paul put it this way, 'I have learned in whatsoever state I am, therewith to be content', and certainly this applies to my status in society.

The endless unrest generated in the individual who is always trying to 'get ahead' of the crowd, who is attempting always to be top man or woman on the totem pole, is pretty formidable to observe.

In His own unique way, Jesus Christ, the Great Shepherd, in His earthly life pointed out that the last would be first and the first last. In a sense I am sure He meant first in the area of His own intimate affection. For any shepherd has great compassion for the poor, weak sheep that get butted about by the more domineering ones.

More than once I have strongly trounced a belligerent ewe for abusing a weaker one. Or when they butted lambs not their own I found it necessary to discipline them severely, and certainly they were not first in my esteem for their aggressiveness.

Another point that impressed me, too, was that the less aggressive sheep were often far more contented, quiet and restful. So that there were definite advantages in being 'bottom sheep'.

But more important was the fact that it was the Shepherd's presence that put an end to all rivalry. And in our human relationships when we become acutely aware of being in the presence of Christ, our foolish, selfish snobbery and rivalry will end. It is the humble heart walking quietly and contentedly in the close and intimate companionship of Christ that is at rest, that can relax, simply glad to lie down and let the world go by.

When my eyes are on my Master they are not on those around me. This is the place of peace.

And it is good and proper to remind ourselves that in the end it is He who will decide and judge what my status really is. After all, it is His estimation of me that is of consequence. Any human measurement at best is bound to be pretty unpredictable, unreliable, and far from final.

To be thus, close to Him, conscious of His abiding Presence, made real in my mind, emotions and will by the indwelling gracious Spirit, is to be set free from fear of my fellow man and whatever he might think of me.

I would much rather have the affection of the Good Shepherd than occupy a place of prominence in society … especially if I had attained it by fighting, quarrelling and bitter rivalry with my fellow human beings.

'Blessed [happy, to be envied] are the merciful: for they shall obtain mercy' (Matthew 5:7).

As is the case with freedom from fear of predators or friction within the flock, the freedom of fear from the torment of parasites and insects is essential to the contentment of sheep. This aspect of their behaviour will be dealt with in greater detail later in the Psalm. But it is nevertheless important to mention it here.

Sheep, especially in the summer, can be driven to absolute distraction by nasal flies, bot flies, warble flies and ticks. When tormented by these pests it is literally impossible for them to lie down and rest. Instead they are up and on their feet, stamping their legs, shaking their heads, ready to rush off into the bush for relief from the pests.

Only the diligent care of the owner who keeps a constant lookout for these insects will prevent them from annoying his flock. A good shepherd will apply various types of insect repellant to his sheep. He will see that they are dipped to clear their fleeces of ticks. And he will see that there are shelter belts of trees and bush available where they can find refuge and release from their tormentators.

This all entails considerable extra care. It takes time and labour and expensive chemicals to do the job thoroughly. It means, too, that the sheepman must be amongst his charges daily, keeping a close watch on their behaviour. As soon as there is the least evidence that they are being disturbed he must take steps to provide them with relief. Always uppermost in his mind is the aim of keeping his flock quiet, contented and at peace.

Similarly in the Christian life there are bound to be many small irritations. There are the annoyances of petty frustrations and ever-recurring disagreeable experiences. In modem terminology we refer to these upsetting circumstances or people as 'being bugged'.

Is there an antidote for them?

Can one come to the place of quiet contentment despite them?

The answer, for the one in Christ's care, is definitely 'Yes!'

This is one of the main functions of the gracious Holy Spirit. In Scripture He is often symbolized by oil – by that which brings healing and comfort and relief from the harsh and abrasive aspects of life.

The gracious Holy Spirit makes real in me the very presence of the Christ. He brings quietness, serenity, strength and calmness in the face of frustrations and futility.

When I turn to Him and expose the problem to Him, allowing Him to see that I have a dilemma, a difficulty, a disagreeable experience beyond my control, He comes to assist. Often a helpful approach is simply to say aloud, 'O Master, this is beyond me – I can't cope with it – it's bugging me – I can't rest – please take over!'

Then it is He does take over in His own wondrous way. He applies the healing, soothing, effective anti-dote of His own person and presence to my particular problem. There immediately comes into my conscious-ness the awareness of His dealing with the difficulty in a way I had not anticipated. And because of the assurance that He has become active on my behalf, there steals over me a sense of quiet contentment. I am then able to lie down in peace and rest. All because of what He does.

Finally, to produce the conditions necessary for a sheep to lie down there must be freedom from the fear of hunger. This of course is clearly implied in the state-ment, 'He maketh me to lie down in green pastures.'

It is not generally recognized that many of the great sheep countries of the world are dry, semi-arid areas. Most breeds of sheep flourish best in this sort of terrain. They are susceptible to fewer hazards of health or para-sites where the climate is dry. But in those same regions it is neither natural nor common to find green pastures. For example, Palestine, where David wrote this Psalm and kept his father's flocks, especially near Bethlehem, is a dry, brown, sunburned wasteland.

Green pastures did not just happen by chance. Green pastures were the product of tremendous labour, time, and skill in land use. Green pastures were the result of clearing rough, rocky land; of tearing out brush and roots and stumps; of deep ploughing and careful soil preparation; of seeding and planting special grains and legumes; of irrigating with water, and husbanding with care the crops of forage that would feed the flocks.

All of this represented tremendous toil and skill and time for the careful shepherd. If his sheep were to enjoy green pastures amid the brown, barren hills it meant he had a tremendous job to do.

But green pastures are essential to success with sheep. When lambs are maturing and the ewes need green, succulent feed for a heavy milk flow, there is no substitute for good pasturage. No sight so satisfies the sheep owner as to see his flock well and quietly fed to repletion on rich green forage, able to lie down to rest, ruminate and gain.

In my own ranching operations one of the keys to the entire enterprise lay in developing rich, lush pastures for my flock. On at least two ranches there were old, worn out, impoverished fields that were either bare or infested with inferior forage plants. By skilful management and scientific land use these were soon converted into flourishing fields knee deep in rich green grass and legumes. On such forage it was common to have lambs reach a hundred pounds in weight within a hundred days from birth.

The secret to this was that the flock could fill up quickly, then lie down quietly to rest and ruminate.

A hungry, ill-fed sheep is ever on its feet, on the move, searching for another scanty mouthful of forage to try and satisfy its gnawing hunger. Such sheep are not contented, they do not thrive, they are no use to themselves nor to their owners. They languish and lack vigour and vitality.

In the Scriptures the picture portrayed of the Promised Land, to which God tried so hard to lead Israel from Egypt, was that of a 'land flowing with milk and honey'. Not only is this figurative language but also essentially scientific terminology. In agricultural terms we speak of a 'milk flow' and 'honey flow'. By this we mean the peak season of spring and summer when pastures are at their most productive stages. The livestock that feed on the forage and the bees that visit the blossoms are said to be producing a corresponding 'flow' of milk or honey. So a land flowing with milk and honey is a land of rich, green, luxuriant pastures.

And when God spoke of such a land for Israel He also foresaw such an abundant life of joy and victory and contentment for His people.

For the child of God, the Old Testament account of Israel moving from Egypt into the Promised Land, is a picture of us moving from sin into the life of overcoming victory. We are promised such a life. It has been provided for us and is made possible by the unrelenting effort of Christ on our behalf.

How He works to clear the life of rocks of stoney unbelief. How He tries to tear out the roots of bitterness. He attempts to break up the hard, proud human heart that is set like sun-dried clay. He then sows the seed of His own precious Word, which, if given half a chance to grow, will produce rich crops of contentment and peace. He waters this with the dews and rain of His own presence by the Holy Spirit. He tends and cares and cultivates the life, longing to see it become rich and green and productive.

It is all indicative of the unrelenting energy and industry of an owner who wishes to see his sheep satisfied and well fed. It all denotes my Shepherd's desire to see my best interests served. His concern for my care is beyond my comprehension, really. At best all I can do is to enjoy and revel in what He has brought into effect.

This life of quiet overcoming; of happy repose; of rest in His presence, of confidence in His management is something few Christians ever fully enjoy.

Because of our own perverseness we often prefer to feed on the barren ground of the world around us. I used to marvel how some of my sheep actually chose inferior forage at times.

But the Good Shepherd has supplied green pastures for those who care to move onto them and there find peace and plenty.

CHAPTER 4

℃

He Leadeth Me Beside the Still Waters

Although sheep thrive in dry, semi-arid country, they still require water. They are not like some of the African gazelles which can survive fairly well on the modest amount of moisture found in natural forage.

It will be noticed that here again the key or the clue to where water can be obtained lies with the shepherd. It is he who knows where the best drinking places are. In fact, very often he is the one who, with much effort and industry, has provided the watering places. And it is to these spots that he leads the flock.

But before thinking about the water sources themselves, we do well to understand the role of water in the animal body and why it is so essential for its well-being. The body of an animal such as a sheep is composed of about 70 per cent water, on an average. This fluid is used to maintain normal body metabolism; it is a portion of every cell, contributing to its turgidity and normal life functions. Water determines the vitality, strength and vigour of the sheep and is essential to its health and general well-being.

If the supply of water for an animal drops off, bodily desiccation sets in. This dehydration of the tissues can result in serious damage to them. It can also mean that the animal becomes weak and impoverished.

Any animal is made aware of water lack by thirst. Thirst indicates the need of the body to have its water supply replenished from a source outside itself.

Now, just as the physical body has a capacity and need for water, so Scripture points out to us clearly that the human personality, the human soul has a capacity and need for the water of the Spirit of the eternal God.

When sheep are thirsty they become restless and set out in search of water to satisfy their thirst. If not led to the good water supplies of clean, pure water, they will often end up drinking from the polluted pot holes where they pick up such internal parasites as nematodes, liver flukes or other disease germs.

And in precisely the same manner Christ, our Good Shepherd, made it clear that thirsty souls of men and women can only be fully satisfied when their capacity and thirst for spiritual life is fully quenched by drawing on Himself.

In Matthew 5:6 He said, 'Blessed are they which do hunger and thirst after righteousness: for they shall be filled [satisfied] .'

At the great feast in Jerusalem He declared boldly, 'If any man thirst, let him come unto me and drink.'

'To drink' in spiritual terminology simply means 'take in' – or 'to accept' – or 'to believe'. That is to say, it implies that a person accepts and assimilates the very life of God in Christ to the point where it becomes a part of him.

The difficulty in all of this is that men and women who are 'thirsty' for God (who do have a deep inner sense of searching and seeking; who are in quest of that which will completely satisfy) often are unsure of where to look or really what they are looking for. Their inner spiritual capacity for God and divine life is desiccated, and in their dilemma they will drink from any dirty pool to try to satisfy their thirst for fulfilment.

Saint Augustine of Africa summed it up so well when he wrote, 'O God! Thou hast made us for Thyself and our souls are restless, searching, till they find their rest in Thee.'

All the long and complex history of earth's religions, pagan worship and human philosophy is bound up with this insatiable thirst for God.

David, when he composed Psalm 23, knew this. Looking at life from the standpoint of a sheep he wrote, 'He [the Good Shepherd] leadeth me beside the still waters.' In other words, He alone knows where the still, quiet, deep, clean, pure water is to be found that alone can satisfy His sheep and keep them fit and strong.

Generally speaking, water for the sheep came from three main sources ... dew on the grass ... deep wells ... or springs and streams.

Most people are not aware that sheep can go for months on end, especially if the weather is not too hot, without actually drinking, if there is heavy dew on the grass each morning. Sheep, by habit, rise just before dawn and start to feed. Or if there is bright moonlight they will graze at night. The early hours are when the vegetation is drenched with dew, and sheep can keep fit on the amount of water taken in with their forage when they graze just before and after dawn.

Of course, dew is a clear, clean, pure source of water. And there is no more resplendent picture of still waters than the silver droplets of the dew hanging heavy on leaves and grass at break of day.

The good shepherd, the diligent manager, makes sure that his sheep can be out and grazing on this dew-drenched vegetation. If necessary it will mean he himself has to rise early to be out with his flock. On the home ranch or afield he will see to it that his sheep benefit from this early grazing.

In the Christian life it is of more than passing significance to observe that those who are often the most serene, most confident and able to cope with life's complexities are those who rise early each day to feed on God's Word. It is in the quiet, early hours of the morning that they are led beside the quiet, still waters where they imbibe the very life of Christ for the day. This is much more than mere figure of speech. It is practical reality. The biographies of the great men and women of God repeatedly point out how the secret of the success in their spiritual life was attributed to the 'quiet time' of each morning. There, alone, still, waiting for the Master's voice, one is led gently to the place where, as the old hymn puts it, 'The still dews of His Spirit can be dropped into my life and soul.'

One comes away from these hours of meditation, reflection and communion with Christ refreshed in mind and spirit. The thirst is slaked and the heart is quietly satisfied.

In my mind's eye I can see my flock again. The gentleness, stillness and softness of early morning always found my sheep knee deep in dew-drenched grass. There they fed heavily and contentedly. As the sun rose and its heat burned the dewdrops from the leaves, the flock would retire to find shade. There, fully satisfied and happily refreshed, they would lie down to rest and ruminate through the day. Nothing pleased me more.

A Shepherd Looks at the 23rd Psalm

I am confident this is precisely the same reaction in My Master's heart and mind when I meet the day in the same way. He loves to see me contented, quiet, at rest and relaxed. He delights to know my soul and spirit have been refreshed and satisfied.

But the irony of life, and tragic truth for most Christians, is that this is not so. It is often the case that they try, instead, to satisfy their thirst by pursuing almost every other sort of substitute.

For their minds and intellects they will pursue knowledge, science, academic careers, vociferous reading or off-beat companions. But somehow they are always left panting and dissatisfied.

Some of my friends have been among the most learned and highly respected scientists and professors in the country. Yet, often, about them there is a strange yearning, an unsatisfied thirst which all their learning, all their knowledge, all their achievements have not satisfied.

To appease the craving of their souls and emotions men and women will turn to the arts, to culture, to music, to literary forms, trying to find fulfilment. And again, so often these are amongst the most jaded and dejected of people.

Amongst my acquaintances are some outstanding authors and artists. Yet it is significant that to many of them life is a mockery. They have tried drinking deeply from the wells of the world only to turn away unsatisfied – unquenched in their soul's thirst.

There are those who, to quench this thirst in their parched lives, have attempted to find refreshment in all sorts of physical pursuits and activities.

They try travel. Or they participate feverishly in sports. They attempt adventures of all sorts, or indulge in social activities. They take up hobbies or engage in community efforts. But when all is said and everything has been done they find themselves facing the same haunting, hollow, empty, unfilled thirst within.

The ancient prophet Jeremiah put it very bluntly when he declared, 'My people ... they have forsaken me, the fountain of living waters, and hewed them out cisterns, broken cisterns, that can hold no water' (Jeremiah 2:13).

It is a compelling picture. It is an accurate portrayal of broken lives – of shattered hopes – of barren souls that are dried up and parched and full of the dust of despair.

Among young people, especially the 'beat' generation, the recourse to drugs, to alcohol, to sexual adventure in a mad desire to assuage their thirst is classic proof that such sordid indulgences are no substitute for the Spirit of the living God. These poor people are broken cisterns. Their lives are a misery. I have yet to talk to a truly happy 'hippie'. Their faces show the desperation within.

And amid all this chaos of a confused, sick society, Christ comes quietly as of old, and invites us to come to Him. He invites us to follow Him. He invites us to put our confidence in Him. For He it is who best knows how we can be satisfied. He knows the human heart, the human personality, the human soul with its amazing capacity, for God can never be satisfied with a substitute. Only the Spirit and life of Christ Himself will satisfy the thirsting soul.

Now, strange as it may appear on the surface, the deep wells of God from which we may drink are not always necessarily the delightful experiences we may imagine them to be.

I recall so clearly standing under the blazing equatorial sun of Africa and watching the native herds being led to their owner's water wells. Some of these were enormous, hand-hewn caverns cut from the sandstone formation along the sandy rivers. They were like great rooms chiselled out of the rocks with ramps running down to the water trough at the bottom. The herds and flocks were led down into these deep cisterns where cool, clear, clean water awaited them.

But down in the well, stripped naked, was the owner bailing water to satisfy the flock. It was hard, heavy, hot work. Perspiration poured off the body of the bailer whose skin glistened under the strain and heat of his labour.

As I stood there watching the animals quench their thirst at the still waters I was again immensely impressed by the fact that everything hinged and depended upon the diligence of the owner, the shepherd. Only through his energy, his efforts, his sweat, his strength could the sheep be satisfied.

In the Christian life exactly the same applies. Many of the places we may be led into will appear to us as dark, deep, dangerous and somewhat disagreeable. But it simply must be remembered that He is there with us in it. He is very much at work in the situation. It is His energy, effort and strength expended on my behalf that even in this deep, dark place is bound to produce a benefit for me.

It is there that I will discover He only can really satisfy me. It is He who makes sense and purpose and meaning come out of situations which otherwise would be but a mockery to me. Suddenly life starts to have significance. I discover I am the object of His special care and attention. Dignity and direction come into the events of my life and I see them sorting themselves out into a definite pattern of usefulness. All of this is refreshing, stimulating, invigorating. My thirst for reality in life is assuaged and I discover that I have found that satisfaction in my Master.

Of course there is always a percentage of perverse people who will refuse to allow God to lead them. They insist on running their own lives and following the dictates of their own wills. They insist they can be masters of their own destinies even if ultimately such destinies are destructive. They don't want to be directed by the Spirit of God – they don't want to be led by Him – they want to walk in their own ways and drink from any old source that they fancy might satisfy their whims.

They remind me very much of a bunch of sheep I watched one day which were being led down to a magnificent mountain stream. The snow-fed waters were flowing pure and clear and crystal clean between lovely banks of trees. But on the way several stubborn ewes and their lambs stopped, instead, to drink from small, dirty, muddy pools beside the trail. The water was filthy and polluted not only with the churned up mud from the passing sheep but even with the manure and urine of previous flocks that had passed that way. Still these stubborn sheep were quite sure it was the best drink obtainable.

The water itself was filthy and unfit for them. Much more, it was obviously contaminated with nematodes and liver fluke eggs that would eventually riddle them with internal parasites and disease of destructive impact.

People often try this pursuit or that with the casual comment, 'So, what? I can't see that it's going to do any harm!' Little do they appreciate that often there is a delayed reaction and that considerable time may elapse before the full impact of their misjudgement strikes home. Then suddenly they are in deep trouble and wonder why.

To offset these dangers and guard against them God invites us to allow ourselves to be led and guided by His own gracious Spirit. Much of the emphasis and teaching of the Pauline Epistles in the New Testament is that the child of God should not end up in difficulty. Galatians 5 and Romans 8 bring this out very clearly.

Jesus' own teaching to His twelve disciples just before His death, given to us in John 14 to 17, points out that the gracious Holy Spirit was to be given to lead us into truth. He would come as a guide and counsellor. Always He would lead us into the things of Christ. He would make us see that the life in Christ was the only truly satisfying life. We would discover the delight of having our souls satisfied with His presence. It would be He who would become to us very meat and drink – that as His resurrection, overcoming life was imparted to me by His Spirit each day I would be refreshed and satisfied.

CHAPTER 5

℃

He Restoreth My Soul

In studying this Psalm it must always be remembered that it is a sheep in the Good Shepherd's care who is speaking. It is essentially a Christian's claim of belonging in the family of God. As such he boasts of the benefits of such a relationship.

This being the case, one might well ask, 'Why then this statement … "He restoreth my soul"?' Surely it would be assumed that anyone in the Good Shepherd's care could never become so distressed in soul as to need restoration.

But the fact remains that this does happen.

Even David, the author of the Psalm, who was much loved of God, knew what it was to be cast down and dejected. He had tasted defeat in his life and felt the frustration of having fallen under temptation. David was acquainted with the bitterness of feeling hopeless and without strength in himself.

In Psalm 42:11 he cries out, 'Why art thou cast down, O my soul? And why art thou disquieted within me? Hope thou in God …'

Now there is an exact parallel to this in caring for sheep. Only those intimately acquainted with sheep and their habits understand the significance of a 'cast' sheep or a 'cast down' sheep.

51

This is an old English shepherd's term for a sheep that has turned over on its back and cannot get up again by itself.

A 'cast' sheep is a very pathetic sight. Lying on its back, its feet in the air, it flays away frantically struggling to stand up, without success. Sometimes it will bleat a little for help, but generally it lies there lashing about in frightened frustration.

If the owner does not arrive on the scene within a reasonably short time, the sheep will die. This is but another reason why it is so essential for a careful sheepman to look over his flock every day, counting them to see that all are able to be up and on their feet. If one or two are missing, often the first thought to flash into his mind is, *One of my sheep is cast somewhere. I must go in search and set it on its feet again.*

One particular ewe that I owned in a flock of Cheviots was notorious for being a cast sheep. Every spring when she became heavy in lamb it was not uncommon for her to become cast every second or third day. Only my diligence made it possible for her to survive from one season to the next. One year I had to be away from the ranch for a few days just when she was having her problems. So I called my young son aside and told him he would be responsible for her well-being while I was absent. If he managed to keep her on her feet until I came home he would be well paid for his efforts. Every evening after school he went out to the fields faithfully and set up the old ewe so she could survive. It was quite a task but she rewarded us with a fine pair of twin lambs that spring.

It is not only the shepherd who keeps a sharp eye for cast sheep, but also the predators. Buzzards, vultures, dogs, coyotes and cougars all know that a cast sheep is easy prey and death is not far off.

This knowledge that any 'cast' sheep is helpless, close to death and vulnerable to attack, makes the whole problem of cast sheep serious for the manager.

Nothing seems so to arouse his constant care and diligent attention to the flock as the fact that even the largest, fattest, strongest and sometimes healthiest sheep can become cast and be a casualty. Actually it is often the fat sheep that are the most easily cast.

The way it happens is this. A heavy, fat or longfleeced sheep will lie down comfortably in some little hollow or depression in the ground. It may roll on its side slightly to stretch out or relax. Suddenly the centre of gravity in the body shifts so that it turns on its back far enough that the feet no longer touch the ground. It may feel a sense of panic and start to paw frantically. Frequently this only makes things worse. It rolls over even further. Now it is quite impossible for it to regain its feet.

As it lies there struggling, gases begin to build up in the rumen. As these expand they tend to retard and cut off blood circulation to extremities of the body, especially the legs. If the weather is very hot and sunny a cast sheep can die in a few hours. If it is cool and cloudy and rainy it may survive in this position for several days.

If the cast sheep is a ewe with lambs, of course, it is a multiple loss to the owner. If the lambs are unborn they, too, perish with her. If they are young and suckling they become orphans. All of which adds to the seriousness of the situation.

So it will be seen why a sheepman's attention is always alert for this problem.

During my own years as a keeper of sheep, perhaps

some of the most poignant memories are wrapped around the commingled anxiety of keeping a count of my flock and repeatedly saving and restoring cast sheep. It is not easy to convey on paper the sense of this ever present danger. Often I would go out early and merely cast my eye across the sky. If I saw the black-winged buzzards circling overhead in their long slow spirals anxiety would grip me. Leaving everything else I would immediately go out into the rough wild pastures and count the flock to make sure every one was well and fit and able to be on its feet.

This is part of the pageantry and drama depicted for us in the magnificent story of the ninety and nine sheep with one astray. There is the Shepherd's deep concern; his agonizing search; his longing to find the missing one; his delight in restoring it not only to its feet but also to the flock as well as to himself.

Again and again I would spend hours searching for a single sheep that was missing. Then more often than not I would see it at a distance, down on its back, lying helpless. At once I would start to run towards it – hurrying as fast as I could – for every minute was critical. Within me there was a mingled sense of fear and joy: fear it might be too late; joy that it was found at all.

As soon as I reached the cast ewe my very first impulse was to pick it up. Tenderly I would roll the sheep over on its side. This would relieve the pressure of gases in the rumen. If she had been down for long I would have to lift her onto her feet. Then, straddling the sheep with my legs, I would hold her erect, rubbing her limbs to restore the circulation to her legs. This often took quite a little time. When the sheep started to walk again she often just stumbled, staggered and collapsed in a heap once more.

All the time I worked on the cast sheep I would talk to it gently, 'When are you going to learn to stand on your own feet?' – 'I'm so glad I found you in time – you rascal!'

And so the conversation would go. Always couched in language that combined tenderness and rebuke; compassion and correction.

Little by little the sheep would regain its equilibrium. It would start to walk steadily and surely. By and by it would dash away to rejoin the others, set free from its fears and frustrations, given another chance to live a little longer.

All of this pageantry is conveyed to my heart and mind when I repeat the simple statement, 'He restoreth my soul!'

There is something intensely personal, intensely tender, intensely endearing, yet intensely fraught with danger in the picture. On the one hand there is the sheep so helpless, so utterly immobilized though otherwise strong, healthy and flourishing; while on the other hand there is the attentive owner quick and ready to come to its rescue – ever patient and tender and helpful.

At this point it is important to point out that similarly in the Christian life there is an exciting and comforting parallel here.

Many people have the idea that when a child of God falls, when he is frustrated and helpless in a spiritual dilemma, God becomes disgusted, fed-up and even furious with him.

This simply is not so.

One of the great revelations of the heart of God given to us by Christ is that of Himself as our Shepherd. He has the same identical sensations of anxiety, concern and compassion for cast men and women as I had for cast sheep. This is precisely why He looked on people with such pathos and compassion. It explains His magnanimous dealing with down-and-out individuals for whom even human society had no use. It reveals why He wept over those who spurned His affection. It discloses the depth of His understanding of undone people to whom He came eagerly and quickly, ready to help, to save, to restore.

When I read the life story of Jesus Christ and examine carefully His conduct in coping with human need, I see Him again and again as the Good Shepherd picking up 'cast' sheep. The tenderness, the love, the patience that He used to restore Peter's soul after the terrible tragedy of his temptations is a classic picture of the Christ coming to restore one of His own.

And so He comes quietly, gently, reassuringly to me no matter when or where or how I may be cast down.

In Psalm 56:13 we are given an accurate commentary on this aspect of the Christian's life in these words, '... Thou has delivered my soul from death: wilt not Thou deliver my feet from falling, that I may walk before God in the light of the living.'

We have to be realistic about the life of the child of God and face facts as they really are. Most of us, though we belong to Christ and desire to be under His control and endeavour to allow ourselves to be led by Him, do on occasion find ourselves cast down.

We discover that often when we are most sure of ourselves we stumble and fall. Sometimes when we appear to be flourishing in our faith we find ourselves in a situation of utter frustration and futility.

Paul in writing to the Christians at Corinth warned

them of this danger. 'Wherefore let him that thinketh he standeth take heed lest he fall' (1 Corinthians 10:12).

Admittedly this may appear as one of the paradoxes and enigmas of our spiritual lives. When we examine it carefully, however, we will not find it too difficult to understand.

As with sheep, so with Christians, some basic principles and parallels apply which will help us to grasp the way in which a man or woman can be 'cast'.

There is, first of all, the idea of looking for a soft spot. The sheep that choose the comfortable, soft, rounded hollows in the ground in which to lie down very often become cast. In such a situation it is so easy to roll over on their backs.

In the Christian life there is great danger in always looking for the easy place, the cosy corner, the comfortable position where there is no hardship, no need for endurance, no demand upon self-discipline.

The time when we think 'we have it made', so to speak, is actually when we are in mortal danger. There is such a thing as the discipline of poverty and privation which can be self-imposed to do us worlds of good. Jesus suggested this to the rich young man who mistakenly assumed he was in a safe position when in truth he was on the verge of being cast down.

Sometimes if, through self-indulgence, I am unwilling to forfeit or forgo the soft life, the easy way, the cosy corner, then the Good Shepherd may well move me to a pasture where things aren't quite so comfortable – not only for my own good but also His benefit as well.

There is the aspect, too, of a sheep simply having too much wool. Often when the fleece becomes very long, and heavily matted with mud, manure, burrs and other debris, it is much easier for a sheep to become cast, literally weighed down with its own wool.

Wool in Scripture depicts the old self-life in the Christian. It is the outward expression of an inner attitude, the assertion of my own desire and hopes and aspirations. It is the area of my life in which and through which I am continually in contact with the world around me. Here is where I find the clinging accumulation of things, of possessions, of worldly ideas beginning to weigh me down, drag me down, hold me down.

It is significant that no high priest was ever allowed to wear wool when he entered the Holy of Holies. This spoke of self, of pride, of personal preference – and God could not tolerate it.

If I wish to go on walking with God and not be forever cast down, this is an aspect of my life which He must deal with drastically.

Whenever I found that a sheep was being cast because it had too long and heavy a fleece, I soon took swift steps to remedy the situation. In short order I would shear it clean and so forestall the danger of having the ewe lose her life. This was not always a pleasant process. Sheep do not really enjoy being sheared and it represents some hard work for the shepherd, but it must be done.

Actually when it is all over both sheep and owner are relieved. There is no longer the threat of being cast down, while for the sheep there is the pleasure of being set free from a hot, heavy coat. Often the fleece is clogged with filthy manure, mud, burrs, sticks and ticks. What a relief to be rid of it all!

And similarly in dealing with our old self-life, there will come a day when the Master must take us in hand and apply the keen cutting edge of His Word to our lives. It may be an unpleasant business for a time. No doubt we'll struggle and kick about it. We may get a few cuts and wounds. But what a relief when it is all over. Oh, the pleasure of being set free from ourselves! What a restoration!

The third chief cause of cast sheep is simply that they are too fat. It is a well-known fact that over-fat sheep are neither the most healthy nor the most productive. And certainly it is the fattest that most often are cast. Their weight simply makes it that much harder for them to be agile and nimble on their feet.

Of course once a sheepman even suspects that his sheep are becoming cast for this reason he will take long-range steps to correct the problem. He will put the ewes on a more rigorous ration; they will get less grain and the general condition of the flock will be watched very closely. It is his aim to see that the sheep are strong, sturdy and energetic, not fat, flabby and weak.

Turning to the Christian life we are confronted with the same sort of problem. There is the man or woman, who because they may have done well in business or their careers or their homes, feel that they are flourishing and have 'arrived'. They may have a sense of well-being and self-assurance which in itself is dangerous. Often when we are most sure of ourselves we are the most prone to fall flat.

In His warning to the church in Revelation 3:17 God points out that though some considered themselves rich and affluent, they were actually in desperate danger. The same point was made by Jesus in His account of the wealthy farmer who intended to build more and bigger barns, but who, in fact, faced utter ruin.

Material success is no measure of spiritual health. Nor is apparent affluence any criteria of real godliness. And it is well for us that the Shepherd of our souls sees through this exterior and takes steps to set things right.

He may well impose on us some sort of 'diet' or 'discipline' which we may find a bit rough and unpalatable at first. But again we need to reassure ourselves that it is for our own good, because He is fond of us, and for His own reputation as the Good Shepherd.

In Hebrews 12 we read how God chooses to discipline those He loves. At the time it may prove a tough routine. But the deeper truth is that afterwards it produces a life of repose and tranquillity free from the fret and frustration of being cast down like a helpless sheep.

The toughness it takes to face life and the formidable reverses which it brings to us can come only through the discipline of endurance and hardship. In His mercy and love our Master makes this a part of our programme. It is part of the price of belonging to Him.

We may rest assured that He will never expect us or ask us to face more than we can stand (1 Corinthians 10:13). But what He does expose us to will strengthen and fortify our faith and confidence in His control. If He is the Good Shepherd we can rest assured that He knows what He is doing. This in and of itself should be sufficient to continually refresh and restore my soul. I know of nothing which so quiets and enlivens my own spiritual life as the knowledge that – 'God knows what He is doing with me!'

CHAPTER 6

❦

He Leadeth Me in the Paths of Righteousness for His Name's Sake

Sheep are notorious creatures of habit. If left to themselves they will follow the same trails until they become ruts; graze the same hills until they turn to desert wastes; pollute their own ground until it is corrupt with disease and parasites. Many of the world's finest sheep ranges have been ruined beyond repair by over-grazing, poor management and indifferent or ignorant sheep owners.

One need only travel through areas like Spain, Greece, Mesopotamia, North Africa and even parts of the western United States and New Zealand or Australia to see the havoc wrought by sheep on the land. Some areas in these countries which were formerly productive grasslands have gradually been reduced to ravaged wastelands. Too many sheep over too many years under poor management have brought nothing but poverty and disaster in their wake.

A commonly held, but serious misconception, about sheep is that they can just 'get along anywhere'. The truth is quite the reverse. No other class of livestock requires more careful handling, more detailed direction, than do

61

sheep. No doubt David, as a shepherd himself, had learned this firsthand from touch experience. He knew beyond dispute that if the flock was to flourish and the owner's reputation was to be held in high esteem as a good manager, the sheep had to be constantly under his meticulous control and guidance.

The first sheep farm I purchased as a young man was a piece of derelict land that had been 'sheeped to death'. An absentee owner had rented the place to a tenant. The latter simply loaded the ranch with sheep, then left them pretty much to their own ways. The result was utter desolation. Fields became so overgrazed and impoverished they would grow little but poverty grass. Little sheep trails had deteriorated into great gullies. Erosion on the slopes was rampant and the whole place was ravaged almost beyond repair.

All of this happened simply because the sheep, instead of being managed and handled with intelligent care, had been left to struggle for themselves – left to go their own way, left to the whims of their own destructive habits.

The consequence of such indifference is that the sheep gnaw the grass to the very ground until even the roots are damaged. I have seen places in Africa where grass roots were pawed out of the soil, leaving utter barrenness behind. Such abuse means loss of fertility and the exposure of the land to all the ravages of erosion.

Because of the behaviour of sheep and their preference for certain favoured spots, these well-worn areas become quickly infested with parasites of all kinds. In a short time a whole flock can thus become infected with worms, nematodes and scab. The final upshot is that both land and owner are ruined while the sheep become thin, wasted and sickly.

The intelligent shepherd is aware of all this. Not only just for the welfare of his sheep and the health of his land, but also for his own sake and reputation as a rancher, he must take the necessary precautions to safeguard against these adverse animal traits. Such habits, in themselves, comprise very serious hazards.

The greatest single safeguard which a shepherd has in handling his flock is to keep them on the move. That is to say, they dare not be left on the same ground too long. They must be shifted from pasture to pasture periodically. This prevents over-grazing of the forage. It also avoids the rutting of trails and erosion of land from over-use. It forestalls the reinfestation of the sheep with internal parasites or disease, since the sheep move off the infested ground before these organisms complete their life cycles.

In a word – there must be a pre-determined plan of action, a deliberate, planned rotation from one grazing ground to another in line with right and proper principles of sound management. This is precisely the sort of action and the idea David had in mind when he spoke of being led in paths of righteousness.

In this following of a precise plan of operation lies the secret for healthy flocks and healthy land. Here is the key to successful sheep husbandry. The owner's entire name and reputation depend on how effectively and efficiently he keeps his charges moving onto wholesome, new, fresh forage. The one who directs his flock along this course is sure of success.

Casting my mind's eye back over the years that I kept sheep, no other single aspect of the ranch operations commanded more of my careful attention than this moving of the sheep. It literally dominated all my decisions. Not a day went by but what I would walk over the pasture in which the sheep were feeding to observe the balance between its growth and the grazing pressure upon it. As soon as the point was reached where I felt the maximum benefit for both sheep and land was not being met, the sheep were moved to a fresh field. On the average this meant they were put onto new ground almost every week. In very large measure the success I enjoyed in sheep ranching must be attributed to this care in managing my flock.

A similar procedure applies to flocks of sheep taken out on summer range in the hills by itinerant herders. They deliberately lead or drive their sheep onto fresh range almost every day. A pattern of grazing is worked out carefully in advance so that the sheep do not feed over the same ground too long or too frequently. Some shepherds set up a base camp and fan out from it in wide circles, like the lobes of a clover leaf, covering new pasturage each day, returning to camp at night.

Coupled with this entire concept of management, there is of course the owner's intimate knowledge of his pastures. He has been all over this ground again and again. He knows its every advantage and every drawback. He knows where his flock will thrive and he is aware of where the feed is poor. So he acts accordingly.

A point worthy of mention here is that whenever the shepherd opens a gate into a fresh pasture the sheep are filled with excitement. As they go through the gate even the staid old ewes will often kick up their heels and leap with delight at the prospect of finding fresh feed. How they enjoy being led onto new ground.

Now as we turn to the human aspect of this theme we will be astonished at some of the parallels. As mentioned earlier, it is no mere whim on God's part to call us sheep. Our behaviour patterns and life habits are so much like that of sheep it is well nigh embarrassing.

First of all Scripture points out that most of us are a stiff-necked and stubborn lot. We prefer to follow our own fancies and turn to our own ways. 'All we like sheep have gone astray; we have turned every one to his own way' (Isaiah 53:6). And this we do deliberately, repeatedly, even to our own disadvantage. There is something almost terrifying about the destructive self-determination of a human being. It is inexorably interlocked with personal pride and self-assertion. We insist we know what is best for us even though the disastrous results may be self-evident.

Just as sheep will blindly, habitually, stupidly follow one another along the same little trails until they become ruts that erode into gigantic gullies, so we humans cling to the same habits that we have seen ruin other lives.

Turning to 'my own way' simply means doing what I want. It implies that I feel free to assert my own wishes and carry out my own ideas. And this I do in spite of every warning.

We read in Proverbs 14:12 and 16:25, 'There is a way which seemeth right unto a man, *but* the end thereof is the way of death.'

In contrast to which Christ the Good Shepherd comes gently and says, 'I am the way, the truth and the life: no man cometh unto the Father, but by me' (John 14:6). 'I am come that they might have life, and that they might have it more abundantly' (John 10:10).

The difficult point is that most of us don't want to come. We don't want to follow. We don't want to be led in the paths of righteousness. Somehow it goes against our grain. We actually prefer to turn to our own way, even though it may take us straight into trouble.

The stubborn, self-willed, proud, self-sufficient sheep that persists in pursuing its old paths and grazing on its old polluted ground will end up a bag of bones on ruined land. The world we live in is full of such folk. Broken homes, broken hearts, derelict lives and twisted personalities remind us everywhere of men and women who have gone their own way. We have a sick society struggling to survive on beleaguered land. The greed and selfishness of mankind leaves behind a legacy of ruin and remorse.

Amid all this chaos and confusion Christ the Good Shepherd comes and says, If any man will follow me, let him deny himself daily and take up his cross and follow me (Mark 8:34). But most of us, even as Christians, simply don't want to do this. We don't want to deny ourselves, give up our right to make our own decisions – we don't want to follow; we don't want to be led.

Of course, most of us, if confronted with this charge, would deny it. We would assert vehemently that we are 'led of the Lord'. We would insist that we would follow wherever He leads. We sing songs to this effect and give mental assent to the idea. But as far as actually being led in paths of righteousness is concerned, precious few of us follow that path.

Actually this is the pivot point on which a Christian either 'goes on' with God or at which point he 'goes back' from following on.

There are many wilful, wayward, indifferent, self-interested Christians who cannot really be classified as followers of Christ. There are relatively few diligent disciples who forsake all to follow the Master.

Jesus never made light of the cost involved in following Him. In fact He made it painfully clear that it was a rugged life of rigid self-denial. It entailed a whole new set of attitudes. It was not the natural, normal way a person would ordinarily live, and this is what made the price so prohibitive to most people.

In brief, seven fresh attitudes have to be acquired. They are the equivalent of progressive forward movements onto new ground with God. If one follows them they will discover fresh pasturage; new, abundant life; and increased health, wholesomeness and holiness, in their walk with God. Nothing will please Him more, and most certainly no other activity on our part will or can result in as great benefit to other lives around us.

1   Instead of loving myself most I am willing to love Christ best and others more than myself.

Now love in a scriptural sense is not a soft, sentimental emotion. It is a deliberate act of my will. It means that I am willing to lay down my life, lay myself out, put myself out on behalf of another. This is precisely what God did for us in Christ. 'Hereby perceive [understand] we the love of God, because he laid down his life for us' (1 John 3:16).

The moment I deliberately do something definite either for God or others that costs me something, I am expressing love. Love is 'self-lessness' or 'self-sacrifice' in contradistinction to 'selfishness'. Most of us know little of living like this or being 'led' in this right way. But once a person discovers the delight of doing something for others, he has started through the gate being led into one of God's green pastures.

2   Instead of being one of the crowd I am willing to be singled out, set apart from the gang.

Most of us, like sheep, are pretty gregarious. We want to belong. We don't want to be different in a deep, distinctive way, though we may wish to be different in minor details that appeal to our selfish egos.

But Christ pointed out that only a few would find His way acceptable. And to be marked as one of His would mean a certain amount of criticism and sarcasm from a cynical society. Many of us don't want this. Just as He was a man of sorrows and acquainted with grief, so we may be. Instead of adding to the sorrows and sadness of society we may be called on to help bear some of the burdens of others, to enter into the suffering of others. Are we ready to do this?

3   Instead of insisting on my rights I am willing to forgo them in favour of others.

Basically this is what the Master meant by denying one's self. It is not easy, nor normal, nor natural to do this. Even in the loving atmosphere of the home, self-assertion is pretty evident and the powerful exercise of individual rights is always apparent.

But the person who is willing to pocket his pride, to take a back seat, to play second fiddle without a feeling of being abused or put upon has gone a long way onto new ground with God.

There is a tremendous emancipation from 'self' in this attitude. One is set free from the shackles of personal pride. It's pretty hard to hurt such a person. He who has no sense of self-importance cannot be offended or deflated. Somehow such people enjoy a wholesome outlook of carefree abandon that makes their Christian lives contagious with contentment and gaiety.

4 Instead of being 'boss' I am willing to be at the bottom of the heap. Or to use sheep terminology, instead of being 'Top Ram' I'm willing to be a 'tail-ender'.

When the desire for self-assertion, self-aggrandizement, self-pleasing gives way to the desire for simply pleasing God and others, much of the fret and strain is drained away from daily living.

A hallmark of the serene soul is the absence of 'drive', at least, 'drive' for self-determination. The person who is prepared to put his personal life and personal affairs in the Master's hands for His management and direction has found the place of rest in fresh fields each day. These are the ones who find time and energy to please others.

5 Instead of finding fault with life and always asking 'Why?' I am willing to accept every circumstance of life in an attitude of gratitude.

Human beings, being what they are, somehow feel entitled to question the reasons for everything that happens to them. In many instances life itself becomes a continuous criticism and dissection of one's circumstances and acquaintances. We look for someone or something on which to pin the blame for our misfortunes. We are often quick to forget our blessings, slow to forget our misfortunes.

But if one really believes his affairs are in God's hands, every event, no matter whether joyous or tragic, will be taken as part of God's plan. To know beyond doubt that He does all for our welfare is to be led into a wide area of peace and quietness and strength for every situation.

6 Instead of exercising and asserting my will, I learn

to co-operate with His wishes and comply with His will.

It must be noted that all the steps outlined here involve the will. The saints from earliest times have repeatedly pointed out that nine-tenths of religion, of Christianity, of becoming a true follower, a dedicated disciple, lies in the will.

When a man or woman allows his or her will to be crossed out, cancelling the great 'I' in their decisions, then indeed the Cross has been applied to that life. This is the meaning of taking up one's cross daily to go to one's own death – no longer my will in the matter but His will be done.

7 Instead of choosing my own way I am willing to choose to follow in Christ's way: simply to do what He asks me to do.

This basically is simple, straightforward obedience. It means I just do what He asks me to do. I go where He invites me to go. I say what He instructs me to say. I act and re-act in the manner He maintains is in my own best interest as well as for His reputation (if I'm His follower).

Most of us possess a formidable amount of factual information on what the Master expects of us. Precious few have either the will, intention or determination to act on it and comply with His instructions. But the person who decides to do what God asks him has moved onto fresh ground which will do both him and others a world of good. Besides, it will please the Good Shepherd no end.

God wants us all to move on with Him. He wants us to walk with Him. He wants it not only for our welfare but for the benefit of others as well as His own dear reputation.

Perhaps there are those who think He expects too much of us. Maybe they feel the demands are too drastic. Some may even consider His call impossible to carry out.

It would be if we had to depend on self-determination, or self-discipline to succeed. But if we are in earnest about wanting to do His will, and to be led, *He makes this possible* by His own gracious Spirit who is given to those who *obey* (Acts 5:32). For it is He who works in us *both* to *will* and *to do* of His good pleasure (Philippians 2:13).

CHAPTER 7

𝒞

Yea, Though I Walk Through the Valley ...

From a shepherd's point of view this statement marks the halfway stage in the Psalm. It is as though up to this point the sheep has been boasting to its unfortunate neighbour across the fence about the excellent care it received from its owner on the 'home' ranch through the winter and spring.

Now it turns to address the shepherd directly. The personal pronouns *I* and *Thou* enter the conversation. It becomes a most intimate discourse of deep affection.

This is natural and normal. The long treks into the high country with their summer range begin here. Left behind are the neglected sheep on the other side of the fence. Their owner knows nothing of the hill country – the mountain meadows to which these sheep will be led. Their summer will be spent in the close companionship and solitary care of the good shepherd.

Both in Palestine and on our western sheep ranches, this division of the year is common practice. Most of the efficient sheepmen endeavour to take their flocks onto distant summer ranges during summer. This often entails long 'drives'. The sheep move along slowly, feeding as they go, gradually working their way up the mountains behind the receding snow. By late summer they are well up on the remote alpine meadows above the timberline.

With the approach of autumn, early snow settles on the highest ridges, relentlessly forcing the flock to withdraw back down to lower elevations. Finally, towards the end of the year as autumn passes, the sheep are driven home to the ranch headquarters where they will spend the winter. It is this segment of the yearly operations that is described in the last half of the poem.

During this time the flock is entirely alone with the shepherd. They are in intimate contact with him and under his most personal attention day and night. That is why these last verses are couched in such intimate first-person language. And it is well to remember that all of this is done against a dramatic background of wild mountains, rushing rivers, alpine meadows and high rangelands.

David, the psalmist, of course knew this type of terrain first hand. When Samuel was sent of God to anoint him king over Israel, he was not at home with his brothers on the 'home' ranch. Instead he was high up on the hills tending his father's flock. They had to send for him to come home. It is no wonder he could write so clearly and concisely of the relationship between a sheep and its owner.

He knew from firsthand experience about all the difficulties and dangers, as well as the delights, of the treks into high country. Again and again he had gone up into the summer range with his sheep. He knew this wild but wonderful country like the palm of his own strong hand. Never did he take his flock where he had not already been before.

Always he had gone ahead to look over the country with care.

All the dangers of rampaging rivers in flood; avalanches; rock slides; poisonous plants; the ravages of predators that raid the flock, or the awesome storms of sleet and hail and snow were familiar to him. He had handled his sheep and managed them with care under all these adverse conditions. Nothing took him by surprise. He was fully prepared to safeguard his flock and tend them with skill under every circumstance.

All of this is brought out in the beautiful simplicity of the last verses. Here is a grandeur, a quietness, an assurance that sets the soul at rest. 'I will not fear, for thou art with me ...' – with me in every situation, in every dark trial, in every dismal disappointment, in every distressing dilemma.

In the Christian life we often speak of wanting 'to move onto higher ground with God'. How we long to live above the lowlands of life. We want to get beyond the common crowd, to enter a more intimate walk with God. We speak of mountaintop experiences and we envy those who have ascended the heights and entered into this more sublime sort of life.

Often we get an erroneous idea about how this takes place. It is as though we imagined we could be 'air lifted' onto higher ground. On the rough trail of the Christian life this is not so. As with ordinary sheep management, so with God's people, one only gains higher ground by climbing up through the valleys.

Every mountain has its valleys. Its sides are scarred by deep ravines and gulches and draws. And the best route to the top is always along these valleys.

Any sheepman familiar with the high country knows this. He leads his flock gently, but persistently, up the paths that wind through the dark valleys. It should be noticed that the verse states, 'Yea, though *I walk through* the valley of the shadow of death.' It does not say 'I die there', or 'stop there' – but rather 'I walk through'.

It is customary to use this verse as a consolation to those who are passing through the dark valley of death. But even here, for the child of God, death is not an end but merely the door into a higher and more exalted life of intimate contact with Christ. Death is but the dark valley opening out into an eternity of delight with God. It is not something to fear, but an experience through which one passes on the path to a more perfect life.

The Good Shepherd knows this. It is one reason why He has told us, 'Lo, I am with you alway' – yes, even in the valley of death. What a comfort and what a cheer.

I was keenly aware of this consolation when my wife went to 'higher ground'. For two years we had walked through the dark valley of death watching her beautiful body being destroyed by cancer. As death approached I sat by her bed, her hand in mine. Gently we 'passed' through the valley of death. Both of us were quietly aware of Christ's presence. There was no fear – *just a going on to higher ground.*

For those of us who remain on earth, there is still a life to live here and now. There are still valleys to walk through during our remaining days. These need not be 'dead end' streets. The disappointments, the frustrations, the discouragements, the dilemmas, the dark, difficult days, though they be shadowed valleys, need not be disasters. They can be the road to higher ground in our walk with God.

A Shepherd Looks at the 23rd Psalm

After all, when we pause to think about it a moment, we must realize that even our modern mountain highways follow the valleys to reach the summit of the passes they traverse. Similarly the ways of God lead upward through the valleys of our lives.

Again and again I remind myself, 'O God, this seems terribly tough, but I know for a fact that in the end it will prove to be the easiest and gentlest way to get me onto higher ground.' Then when I thank Him for the difficult things, the dark days, I discover that He is there with me in my distress. At that point my panic, my fear, my misgivings give way to calm and quiet confidence in His care. Somehow, in a serene quiet way I am assured all will turn out well for my best because He is with me in the valley and things are under His control.

To come to this conviction in the Christian life is to have entered into an attitude of quiet acceptance of every adversity. It is to have moved onto higher ground with God. Knowing Him in this new and intimate manner makes life much more bearable than before.

There is a second reason why sheep are taken to the mountain tops by way of the valleys. Not only is this the way of the gentlest grades, but also it is the well watered route. Here one finds refreshing water all along the way. There are rivers, streams, springs and quiet pools in the deep defiles.

During the summer months long drives can be hot and tiresome. The flocks experience intense thirst. How glad they are for the frequent watering places along the valley route where they can be refreshed.

I recall one year when an enormous flock of over 10,000 sheep was being taken through our country *en route* to their summer range. The owners came asking permission to water their sheep at the river that flowed by our ranch. Their thirsty flocks literally ran to the water's edge to quench their burning thirst under the blazing summer sun. Only in our valley was there water for their parched flesh. How glad we were to share the water with them.

As Christians we will sooner or later discover that it is in the valleys of our lives that we find refreshment from God Himself. It is not until we have walked with Him through some very deep troubles that we discover He can lead us to find our refreshment in Him right there in the midst of our difficulty. We are thrilled beyond words when there comes restoration to our souls and spirits from His own gracious Spirit.

During my wife's illness and after her death I could not get over the strength, solace and serene outlook imparted to me virtually hour after hour by the presence of God's gracious Spirit Himself.

It was as if I was being repeatedly refreshed and restored despite the most desperate circumstances all around me. Unless one has actually gone through such an experience it may seem difficult to believe. In fact there are those who claim they could not face such a situation. But for the man or woman who walks with God through these valleys, such real and actual refreshment is available.

The corollary to this is that only those who have been through such dark valleys can console, comfort or encourage others in similar situations. Often we pray or sing the hymn requesting God to make us an inspiration to someone else. We want, instinctively, to be a channel of blessing to other lives. The simple fact is that just as water can only flow in a ditch or channel or valley – so in the Christian's career, the life of God can only flow in blessing through the valleys that have been carved and cut into our own lives by excruciating experiences.

For example, the one best able to comfort another in bereavement is the person who himself has lost a loved one. The one who can best minister to a broken heart is one who has known a broken heart.

Most of us do not want valleys in our lives. We shrink from them with a sense of fear and foreboding. Yet in spite of our worst misgivings God can bring great benefit and lasting benediction to others through those valleys. Let us not always try to avoid the dark things, the distressing days. They may well prove to be the way of greatest refreshment to ourselves and those around us.

A third reason why the rancher chooses to take his flock into the high country by way of the valleys is that this is generally where the richest feed and best forage is to be found along the route.

The flock is moved along gently – they are not hurried. There are lambs in the flock which have never been this way before. The shepherd wants to be sure there will not only be water but also the best grazing available for the ewes and their lambs. Generally the choicest meadows are in these valleys along the stream banks. Here the sheep can feed as they move towards the high country.

Naturally these grassy glades are often on the floor of steep-walled canyons and gulches. There may be towering cliffs above them on either side. The valley floor itself may be in dark shadow, with the sun seldom reaching the bottom except for a few hours around noon.

The shepherd knows from past experience that

predators like coyotes, bears, wolves or cougars can take cover in these broken cliffs, and from their vantage point prey on his flock. He knows these valleys can be subject to sudden storms and flash floods that send walls of water rampaging down the slopes. There could be rock slides, mud or snow avalanches and a dozen other natural disasters that would destroy or injure his sheep. But in spite of such hazards he also knows that this is still the best way to take his flock to the high country. He spares himself no pains or trouble or time to keep an eye out for any danger that might develop.

One of the most terrible threats are the sudden chilling storms of sleet, rain and snow that can sweep down through the valleys from the mountain peaks. If sheep become soaked and chilled with a freezing rain, the exposure can kill them in a very short time. They are thin-skinned creatures, easily susceptible to colds, pneumonia and other respiratory complications.

I recall one storm I went through in the foothills of the Rockies in early summer. The morning had been bright and clear. Suddenly around noon enormous dark, black, forbidding clouds began to sweep down over the hills from the north. A chilling wind accompanied the approaching storm. The sky grew blacker by the hour. Suddenly in mid-afternoon long streamers of rain and sleet began to sweep across the valley. I ran to take shelter in a clump of stunted, wind-blown spruce. The rain soaked me through. As it fell it cooled the whole country. The rain turned to sleet, then to commingled snow and hail. In a short time the whole mountain slope (in mid July!) was white and frozen. Ominous darkness shrouded the whole scene. The sheep sensed the storm approaching. Perhaps the flock would have perished if they had not raced away to find shelter in the steep cliffs at the edge of the canyon.

But in these valleys was where the grass grew best and it was the route to the high country.

Our Shepherd knows all of this when He leads us through the valleys with Himself. He knows where we can find strength, and sustenance and gentle grazing despite every threat of disaster about us.

It is a most reassuring and re-enforcing experience to the child of God to discover that there is, even in the dark valley, a source of strength and courage to be found in God. It is when he can look back over life and see how the Shepherd's hand has guided and sustained him in the darkest hours that renewed faith is engendered.

I know of nothing which so stimulates my faith in my Heavenly Father as to look back and reflect on His faithfulness to me in every crisis and every chilling circumstance of life. Over and over He has proved His care and concern for my welfare. Again and again I have been conscious of the Good Shepherd's guidance through dark days and deep valleys.

All of this multiplies my confidence in Christ. It is this spiritual, as well as emotional and mental, exposure to the storms and adversities of life that puts stamina into my very being. Because He has led me through without fear before, He can do it again, and again, and again. In this knowledge fear fades and tranquillity of heart and mind takes it place.

Let come what may. Storms may break about me, predators may attack, the rivers of reverses may threaten to inundate me. But because He is in the situation with me, I shall not fear.

To live thus is to have taken some very long treks

towards the high country of holy, calm, healthy living with God.

Only the Christian who learns to live this way is able to encourage and inspire the weaker ones around him. Too many of us are shaken up, frightened and panicked by the storms of life. We claim to have confidence in Christ but when the first dark shadows sweep over us and the path we tread looks gloomy we go into a deep slump of despair. Sometimes we just feel like lying down to die. This is not as it should be.

The person with a powerful confidence in Christ; the one who has proved by past experience that God is with him in adversity; the one who walks through life's dark valleys without fear, his head held high, is the one who in turn is a tower of strength and a source of inspiration to his companions.

There are going to be some valleys in life for all of us. The Good Shepherd Himself assured us that 'in this world ye shall have tribulation: but be of good cheer; I have overcome the world' (John 16:33).

The basic question is not whether we have many or few valleys. It is not whether those valleys are dark or merely dim with shadows. The question is, how do I react to them? How do I go through them? How do I cope with the calamities that come my way?

With Christ I face them calmly.

With His gracious Spirit to guide me I face them fearlessly.

I know of a surety that only through them can I possibly travel on to higher ground with God. In this way not only shall I be blessed but in turn I will become a benediction to others around me who may live in fear.

CHAPTER 8

C

Thy Rod and Thy Staff
They Comfort Me

When the shepherd is afield with his flock in the high country, it is customary for him to carry a minimum of equipment. This was especially true in olden times where the sheepman did not have the benefit of mechanized equipment to transport camp supplies across the rough country. Even today the so-called 'shepherd shacks' or 'cabooses' in which the herder spends his lonely summers with the sheep are equipped with only the barest essentials.

But during the hours that he is actually in the field the sheepman carries only a rifle slung over his shoulder and a long slender staff in his hand. There will be a small knapsack in which are packed his lunch, a bottle of water and perhaps a few simple first-aid remedies for his flock.

In the Middle East the shepherd carries only a rod and staff. Some of my most vivid boyhood recollections are those of watching the African herdsmen shepherding their stock with only a long slender stick and a rough *knob-kerrie* in their hands. These are the common and universal equipment of the primitive sheepman.

Each shepherd boy, from the time he first starts to

tend his father's flock, takes special pride in the selection of a rod and staff exactly suited to his own size and strength. He goes into the bush and selects a young sapling which is dug from the ground. This is carved and whittled down with great care and patience. The enlarged base of the sapling, where its trunk joins the roots, is shaped into a smooth, rounded head of hard wood. The sapling itself is shaped to exactly fit the owner's hand. After he completes it, the shepherd boy spends hours practising with this club, learning how to throw it with amazing speed and accuracy. It becomes his main weapon of defence for both himself and his sheep.

I used to watch the native lads having competitions to see who could throw his rod with the greatest accuracy across the greatest distance. The effectiveness of these crude clubs in the hands of skilled shepherds was a thrill to watch. The rod was, in fact, an extension of the owner's own right arm. It stood as a symbol of his strength, his power, his authority in any serious situation. The rod was what he relied on to safeguard both himself and his flock in danger. And it was, furthermore, the instrument he used to discipline and correct any wayward sheep that insisted on wandering away.

There is an interesting sidelight on the word, 'rod', which has crept into the colloquial language of the West. Here the slang term 'rod' has been applied to hand-guns such as pistols and revolvers which were carried by cowboys, and other western rangemen. The connotation is exactly the same as that used in this Psalm.

The sheep asserts that the owner's rod, his weapon of power, authority and defence, is a continuous comfort to him. For with it the manager is able to carry out effective control of his flock in every situation.

It will be recalled how when God called Moses, the desert shepherd, and sent him to deliver Israel out of Egypt from under Pharaoh's bondage, it was his rod that was to demonstrate the power vested in him. It was always through Moses' rod that miracles were made manifest, not only to convince Pharaoh of Moses divine commission, but also to reassure the people of Israel.

The rod speaks, therefore, of the spoken Word, the expressed intent, the extended activity of God's mind and will in dealing with men. It implies the authority of divinity. It carries with it the convicting power and irrefutable impact of '*Thus saith the Lord*'.

Just as for the sheep of David's day, there was comfort and consolation in seeing the rod in the shepherd's skilful hands, so in our day there is great assurance in our own hearts as we contemplate the power, veracity and potent authority vested in God's Word. For, in fact, the Scriptures are His rod. They are the extension of His mind and will and intentions to mortal man.

Living as we do in an era when numerous confused voices and strange philosophies are presented to people, it is reassuring to the child of God to turn to the Word of God and know it to be His Shepherd's hand of authority. What a comfort to have this authoritative, clear-cut, powerful instrument under which to conduct ourselves. By it we are kept from confusion amid chaos. This in itself brings into our lives a great sense of quiet serenity which is precisely what the psalmist meant when he said, '… thy rod … comfort[s] me.'

There is a second dimension in which the rod is used

by the shepherd for the welfare of his sheep – namely that of discipline. If anything, the club is used for this purpose perhaps more than any other.

I could never get over how often, and with what accuracy, the African herders would hurl their *knob-kerries* at some recalcitrant beast that misbehaved. If the shepherd saw a sheep wandering away on its own, or approaching poisonous weeds, or getting too close to danger of one sort or another, the club would go whistling through the air to send the wayward animal scurrying back to the bunch.

As has been said of the Scripture so often, 'This Book will keep you from sin!' It is the Word of God that comes swiftly to our hearts, that comes with surprising suddenness to correct and reprove us when we go astray. It is the Spirit of the Living God, using the living Word, that convicts our conscience of right conduct. In this way we are kept under control by Christ, who wants us to walk in the ways of righteousness.

Another interesting use of the rod in the shepherd's hand was to examine and count the sheep. In the terminology of the Old Testament this was referred to as passing 'under the rod' (Ezekiel 20:37). This meant not only coming under the owner's control and authority, but also to be subject to his most careful, intimate and firsthand examination. A sheep that passed 'under the rod' was one which had been counted and looked over with great care to make sure all was well with it.

Because of their long wool it is not always easy to detect disease, wounds or defects in sheep. For example, at a sheep show an inferior animal can be clipped and shaped and shown so as to appear a perfect specimen. But the skilled judge will take his rod and part the sheep's wool to determine the condition of the skin, the cleanliness of the fleece and the conformation of the body. In plain language, 'One just does not pull the wool over his eyes.'

In caring for his sheep, the good shepherd, the careful manager, will from time to time make a careful examination of each individual sheep. The picture is a very poignant one. As each animal comes out of the corral and through the gate, it is stopped by the shepherd's outstretched rod. He opens the fleece with the rod; he runs his skilful hands over the body; he feels for any sign of trouble; he examines the sheep with care to see that all is well. This is a most searching process entailing every intimate detail. It is, too, a comfort to the sheep, for only in this way can its hidden problems be laid bare before the shepherd.

This is what was meant in Psalm 139:23, 24 when the psalmist wrote, 'Search me, O God, and know my heart: try me, and know my thoughts: and see if there be any wicked way in me, and lead me in the way everlasting.'

If we will allow it, if we will submit to it, God by His Word will search us. There will be no 'pulling the wool over His eyes'. He will get below the surface, behind the front of our old self life and expose things that need to be made right.

This is a process from which we need not shrink. It is not something to avoid. It is done in concern and compassion for our welfare. The Great Shepherd of all our souls has our own best interests at heart when He so searches us. What a comfort this should be to the child of God, who can trust in God's care.

Wool in Scripture speaks of the self-life, self-will, self-assertion, self-pride. God has to get below this and do a deep work in our wills to right the wrongs which are often bothering us beneath the surface. So often we put on a fine front and brave, bold exterior when really deep down below there needs to be some remedy applied.

Finally the shepherd's rod is an instrument of protection both for himself and his sheep when they are in danger. It is used both as a defence and a deterrent against anything that would attack.

The skilled shepherd uses his rod to drive off predators like coyotes, wolves, cougars or stray dogs. Often it is used to beat the brush, discouraging snakes and other creatures from disturbing the flock. In extreme cases, such as David recounted to Saul, the psalmist no doubt used his rod to attack the lion and the bear that came to raid his flocks.

Once in Kenya photographing elephants, I was being accompanied by a young Masai herder who carried a club in his hand. We came to the crest of a hill from which we could see a herd of elephants in the thick bush below us. To drive them out into the open we decided to dislodge a boulder and roll it down the slope. As we heaved and pushed against the great rock, a cobra, coiled beneath it, suddenly came into view ready to strike. In a split second the alert shepherd boy lashed out with his club killing the snake on the spot. The weapon had never left his hand even while we worked on the rock.

'Thy rod ... comfort[s] me.' In that instant I saw the meaning of this phrase in a new light. It was the rod ever ready in the shepherd's hand that had saved the day for us.

It was the rod of God's Word that Christ, our Good Shepherd, used in His own encounter with that serpent

– Satan – during His desert temptation. It is the same Word of God which we can count on again and again to counter the assaults and attacks of Satan. And it matters not whether the guise He assumes is that of a subtle serpent or a roaring lion that desires to destroy us.

There is no substitute for the Scriptures in coping with the complexities of our social order. We live in an ever-more involved and difficult milieu. We are part of a world of men and women whose code of conduct is contrary to all that Christ has advocated. To live with such people is to be ever exposed to enormous temptations of all sorts. Some people are very subtle, very smooth, very sophisticated. Others are capable of outright, violent, vituperative attacks against the children of God.

In every situation and under every circumstance there is comfort in the knowledge that God's Word can meet and master the difficulty if we will rely on it.

We turn now to discuss and consider the shepherd's staff. In a sense the staff, more than any other item of his personal equipment, identifies the shepherd as a shepherd. No one in any other profession carries a shepherd's staff. It is uniquely an instrument used for the care and management of sheep – and only sheep. It will not do for cattle, horses or hogs. It is designed, shaped and adapted especially to the needs of sheep. And it is used only for their benefit.

The staff is essentially a symbol of the concern, the compassion that a shepherd has for his charges. No other single word can better describe its function on behalf of the flock than that it is for their *comfort.*

Whereas the rod conveys the concept of authority, of power, of discipline, of defence against danger, the word 'staff' speaks of all that is longsuffering and kind.

The shepherd's staff is normally a long, slender stick, often with a crook or hook on one end. It is selected with care by the owner; it is shaped, smoothed and cut to best suit his own personal use.

Some of the most moving memories I carry with me from Africa and the Middle East are of seeing elderly shepherds in the twilight of life, standing silently at sunset, leaning on their staves, watching their flocks with contented spirits. Somehow the staff is of special comfort to the shepherd himself. In the tough tramps and during the long weary watches with his sheep he leans on it for support and strength. It becomes to him a most precious comfort and help in his duties.

Just as the rod of God is emblematic of the Word of God, so the staff of God is symbolic of the Spirit of God. In Christ's dealings with us as individuals there is the essence of the sweetness, the comfort and consolation, the gentle correction brought about by the work of His gracious Spirit.

There are three areas of sheep management in which the staff plays a most significant role. The first of these lies in drawing sheep together into an intimate relationship. The shepherd will use his staff to gently lift a newborn lamb and bring it to its mother if they become separated. He does this because he does not wish to have the ewe reject her offspring if it bears the odour of his hands upon it. I have watched skilled shepherds moving swiftly with their staffs amongst thousands of ewes that were lambing simultaneously. With deft but gentle strokes the newborn lambs are lifted with the staff and placed side by side with their dams. It is a touching sight that can hold one spellbound for hours.

But in precisely the same way, the staff is used by the

shepherd to reach out and catch individual sheep, young or old, and draw them close to himself for intimate examination. The staff is very useful this way for the shy and timid sheep that normally tend to keep at a distance from the shepherd.

Similarly in the Christian life we find the gracious Holy Spirit, 'The Comforter', drawing folks together into a warm, personal fellowship with one another. It is also He who draws us to Christ, for as we are told in Revelation, 'The Spirit and the bride say, Come.'

The staff is also used for guiding sheep. Again and again I have seen a shepherd use his staff to guide his sheep gently into a new path or through some gate or along dangerous, difficult routes. He does not use it actually to beat the beast. Rather, the tip of the long slender stick is laid gently against the animal's side and the pressure applied guides the sheep in the way the owner wants it to go. Thus the sheep is reassured of its proper path.

Sometimes I have been fascinated to see how a shepherd will actually hold his staff against the side of some sheep that is a special pet or favourite, simply so that they 'are in touch'. They will walk along this way almost as though it were 'hand-in-hand'. The sheep obviously enjoys this special attention from the shepherd and revels in the close, personal, intimate contact between them. To be treated in this special way by the shepherd is to know comfort in a deep dimension. It is a delightful and moving picture.

In our walk with God we are told explicitly by Christ Himself that it would be His Spirit who would be sent to guide us and to lead us into all truth (John 16:13). This same gracious Spirit takes the truth of God, the Word of God, and makes it plain to our hearts and minds and spiritual understanding. It is He who gently, tenderly, but persistently says to us, 'This is the way – walk in it.' And as we comply and co-operate with His gentle promptings a sense of safety, comfort and well-being envelops us.

It is He, too, who comes quietly but emphatically to make the life of Christ, my Shepherd, real and personal and intimate to me. Through Him I am 'in touch' with Christ. There steals over me the keen awareness that I am His and He is mine. The gracious Spirit continually brings home to me the acute consciousness that I am God's child and He is my Father. In all of this there is enormous comfort and a sublime sense of 'oneness', of 'belonging', of 'being in His care', and hence the object of His special affection.

The Christian life is not just one of subscribing to certain doctrines or believing certain facts. Essential as all of this confidence in the Scriptures may be, there is, as well, the actual reality of experiencing and knowing first-hand the feel of His touch – the sense of His Spirit upon my spirit. There is for the true child of God that intimate, subtle, yet magnificent experience of sensing the Comforter at his side. This is not imagination – it is the genuine, bona-fide reality of everyday life. There is a calm, quiet repose in the knowledge that He is there to direct even in the most minute details of daily living. He can be relied on to assist us in every decision, and in this there lies tremendous comfort for the Christian.

Over and over I have turned to Him and in audible, open language asked for His opinion on a problem. I have asked, 'What would you do in this case?', or I have said, 'You are here now. You know all the complexities; tell me precisely what is the best procedure at this point.'

And the thrilling thing is He does just that. He actually conveys the mind of Christ in the matter to my mind. Then the right decisions are made with con-fidence.

It is when I do not do this that I end up in difficulty. It is then that I find myself in a jam of some sort. And here again the gracious Spirit comes to my rescue, just as the shepherd rescues his sheep out of the situations into which their own stupidity leads them.

Being stubborn creatures sheep often get into the most ridiculous and preposterous dilemmas. I have seen my own sheep, greedy for one more mouthful of green grass, climb down steep cliffs where they slipped and fell into the sea. Only my long shepherd's staff could lift them out of the water back onto solid ground again. One winter day I spent several hours rescuing a ewe that had done this very thing several times before. Her stubbornness was her undoing.

Another common occurrence was to find sheep stuck fast in labyrinths of wild roses or brambles where they had pushed in to find a few stray mouthfuls of green grass. Soon the thorns were so hooked in their wool they could not possibly pull free, tug as they might. Only the use of a staff could free them from their entanglement.

Likewise with us. Many of our jams and impasses are of our own making. In stubborn, self-willed, self-assertion we keep pushing into a situation where we cannot extricate ourselves. Then in tenderness, compassion and care our Shepherd comes to us. He draws near and in tenderness lifts us by His Spirit out of the difficulty and dilemma. What patience God has with us! What longsuffering and compassion! What forgiveness!

Thy staff comforts me! Your Spirit, O Christ, is my consolation!

CHAPTER 9

۷

Thou Preparest a Table Before Me ...

In thinking about this statement it is well to bear in mind that the sheep are approaching the high mountain country of the summer ranges. These are known as alplands or tablelands, so much sought after by sheepmen.

In some of the finest sheep country of the world, especially in the western United States and southern Europe, the high plateaux of the sheep ranges are always referred to as 'mesas' – the Spanish word for 'tables'.

Oddly enough, the Kiswahili (African) word for a table is also 'mesa'. Presumably this had its origin with the first Portuguese explorers to touch the East African coast. In fact the use of this word is not uncommon in referring to the high, flat-topped plateaux of the continent. The classic example, of course, is Table Mountain, near Cape Town, which is world renowned.

So it may be seen that what David referred to as a table was actually the entire high summer range. Though these 'mesas' may have been remote and hard to reach, the energetic and aggressive sheep owner takes the time and trouble to ready them for the arrival of his flocks.

Early in the season, even before all the snow has been melted by spring sunshine, he will go ahead and make preliminary survey trips into this rough, wild country. He will look it over with great care, keeping ever in mind its best use for his flock during the coming season.

Then just before the sheep arrive he will make another expedition or two to prepare the tableland for them. He takes along a supply of salt and minerals to be distributed over the range at strategic spots for the benefit of the sheep during the summer. The intelligent, careful manager will also decide well ahead of time where his camps will be located so the sheep have the best bed grounds. He goes over the range carefully to determine how vigorous the grass and upland vegetation is. At this time he decides whether some glades and basins can be used only lightly, whereas other slopes and meadows may be grazed more heavily.

He will check to see if there are poisonous weeds appearing, and if so, he will plan his grazing programme to avoid them, or take drastic steps to eradicate them.

Unknown to me the first sheep ranch I owned had a rather prolific native stand of both blue and white cammas. The blue cammas were a delightful sight in the spring when they bloomed along the beaches. The white cammas, though a much less conspicuous flower, were also quite attractive but a deadly menace to sheep. If lambs, in particular, ate or even just nibbled a few of the lily-like leaves as they emerged in the grass sward during spring, it would spell certain death. The lambs would become paralysed, stiffen up like blocks of wood and simply succumb to the toxic poisons from the plants.

My youngsters and I spent days and days going over the ground plucking out these poisonous plants. It was a recurring task that was done every spring before the sheep went on these pastures. Though tedious and tiring with all of the bending, it was a case of 'preparing the table in the presence of mine enemies'. And if my sheep were to survive it simply had to be done.

A humorous sidelight on this chore was the way I hit on the idea of making up animal stories to occupy the children's minds as we worked together this way for long hours, often down on our hands and knees. They would become so engrossed in my wild fantasies about bears and skunks and raccoons that the hours passed quite quickly. Sometimes both of them would roll in the grass with laughter as I added realistic action to enliven my tales. It was one way to accomplish an otherwise terribly routine task.

All of this sort of thing was in the back of David's mind as he penned these lines. I can picture him walking slowly over the summer range ahead of his flock. His eagle eye is sharp for any signs of poisonous weeds which he would pluck before his sheep got to them. No doubt he had armfuls to get rid of for the safety of his flock.

The parallel in the Christian life is clear. Like sheep, and especially lambs, we somehow feel that we have to try everything that comes our way. We have to taste this thing and that, sampling everything just to see what it's like. And we may very well know that some things are deadly. They can do us no good. They can be most destructive. Still somehow we give them a whirl anyway.

To forestall our getting into grief of this sort, we need

to remember our Master has been there ahead of us, coping with every situation which would otherwise undo us.

A classic example of this was the incident when Jesus warned Peter that Satan desired to tempt him and sift him like wheat. But Christ pointed out that He had prayed that Peter's faith might not fail during the desperate difficulty he would encounter. And so it is even today. Our great Good Shepherd is going ahead of us in every situation, anticipating what danger we may encounter, and praying for us that in it we might not succumb.

Another task the attentive shepherd takes on in the summer is to keep an eye out for predators. He will look for signs and spoor of wolves, coyotes, cougars and bears. If these raid or molest the sheep he will have to hunt them down or go to great pains to trap them so that his flock can rest in peace.

Often what actually happens is that these crafty ones are up on the rimrock watching every movement the sheep make, hoping for a chance to make a swift, sneaking attack that will stampede the sheep. Then one or other of the flock is bound to fall easy prey to the attacker's fierce teeth and claws.

The picture here is full of drama, action, suspense – and possible death. Only the alertness of the sheepman who tends his flock on the tableland in full view of possible enemies can prevent them from falling prey to attack. It is only his preparation for such an eventuality that can possibly save the sheep from being slaughtered and panicked by their predators.

And again we are given a sublime picture of our Saviour who knows every wile, every trick, every treachery of our enemy Satan and his companions. Always we are in danger of attack. Scripture sometimes refers to him as 'a roaring lion' who goes about seeking whom he may devour.

It is rather fashionable in some contemporary Christian circles to discredit Satan. There is a tendency to try and write him off, or laugh him off, as though he was just a joke. Some deny that such a being as Satan even exists. Yet we see evidence of his merciless attacks and carnage in a society where men and women fall prey to his cunning tactics almost every day. We see lives torn and marred and seared by his assaults though we may never see him personally.

It reminds me of my encounters with cougars. On several occasions these cunning creatures came in among my sheep at night, working terrible havoc in the flock. Some ewes were killed outright, their blood drained and livers eaten. Others were torn open and badly clawed. In these cases the great cats seemed to chase and play with them in their panic like a housecat would chase a mouse. Some had huge patches of wool torn from their fleeces. In their frightened stampede some had stumbled and broken bones or rushed over rough ground, injuring legs and bodies.

Yet despite the damage, despite the dead sheep, despite the injuries and fear instilled in the flock, I never once actually saw a cougar on my range. So cunning and so skilful were their raids they defy description.

At all times we would be wise to walk a little closer to Christ. This is one sure place of safety. It was always the distant sheep, the roamers, the wanderers, which were picked off by the predators in an unsuspecting moment. Generally the attackers are gone before the shepherd is alerted by their cry for help. Some sheep, of course, are utterly dumb with fear under attack; they will not even give a plaintive bleat before their blood is spilled.

The same is true of Christians. Many of us get into deep difficulty beyond ourselves; we are stricken dumb with apprehension, unable even to call or cry out for help; we just crumple under our adversary's attack.

But Christ is too concerned about us to allow this to happen. Our Shepherd wants to forestall such a calamity. He wants our summer sojourn to be in peace. Our Lord wants our mountaintop times to be tranquil interludes. And they will be if we just have the common sense to stay near Him where He can protect us. Read His Word each day. Spend some time talking to Him. We should give Him opportunity to converse with us by His Spirit as we contemplate His life and work for us as our Shepherd.

There is another chore which the sheepman takes care of on the tableland. He clears out the water holes, springs and drinking places for his stock. He has to clean out the accumulated debris of leaves, twigs, stones and soil which may have fallen into the water source during the autumn and winter. He may need to repair small earth dams he has made to hold water. And he will open the springs that may have become overgrown with grass and brush and weeds. It is all his work, his preparation of the table for his own sheep in summer.

The parallel in the Christian life is that Christ, our great Good Shepherd, has Himself already gone before us into every situation and every extremity that we might encounter. We are told emphatically that He was tempted in all points like we are. We know He entered fully and completely and very intimately into the life of men upon our planet. He has known our sufferings, experienced our sorrows and endured our struggles in this life; He was a man of sorrows and acquainted with grief.

Because of this He *understands* us, He has totally *identified* Himself with humanity. He has, therefore, a care and compassion for us beyond our ability to grasp. No wonder He makes every possible provision to ensure that when we have to cope with Satan, sin or self, the contest will not be one-sided. Rather, we can be sure He has been in that situation before; He is in it now again with us and because of this the prospects of our preservation are excellent.

It is this attitude of rest in Him, of confidence in His care, of relaxation as we realize His presence in the picture that can make the Christian's life one of calm and quiet confidence. The Christian walk can thus become a mountaintop experience – a tableland trip – simply because we are in the care and control of Christ, who has been over all this territory before us and prepared the 'table' for us in plain view of our enemies who would demoralize and destroy us if they could.

It is encouraging to know that just as in any other aspect of life where there are lights and shadows, so in the Christian life there are valleys and mountaintops. Too many people assume that once one becomes a Christian, automatically life becomes one glorious garden of delight. This is simply not the case. It may well become a garden of sorrow just as our Saviour went through the garden of Gethsemane. As was pointed out previously, you do not have mountains without valleys, and even on the mountaintop there can be some tough experiences.

Just because the shepherd has gone ahead and made every possible provision for the safety and welfare of his sheep while they are on the summer range does not mean they will not have problems there. Predators can still attack; poisonous weeds can still grow; storms and gales can still come swirling up over the peaks; and a dozen other hazards can haunt the high country.

Yet, in His care and concern for us Christ still ensures that we shall have some gladness with our sadness; some delightful days as well as dark days; some sunshine as well as shadow.

It is not always apparent to us what tremendous personal cost it has been for Christ to prepare the table for His own. Just as the lonely, personal privation of the sheepman who prepares the summer range for his stock entails a sacrifice, so the lonely agony of Gethsemane, of Pilate's hall, of Calvary, have cost my Master much.

When I come to the Lord's Table and partake of the communion service, which is a feast of thanksgiving for His love and care, do I fully appreciate what it has cost Him to prepare this table for me?

Here we commemorate the greatest and deepest demonstration of *true love* the world has ever known. For God looked down upon sorrowing, struggling, sinning humanity and was moved with compassion for the contrary, sheep-like creatures He had made. In spite of the tremendous personal cost it would entail to Himself to deliver them from their dilemma, He chose deliberately to descend and live amongst them that He might deliver them.

This meant laying aside His splendour, His position,

His prerogatives as the perfect and faultless One. He knew He would be exposed to terrible privation, to ridicule, to false accusations, to rumour, gossip and malicious charges that branded Him as a glutton, drunkard, friend of sinners and even an imposter. It entailed losing His reputation. It would involve physical suffering, mental anguish and spiritual agony.

In short, His coming to earth as the Christ, as Jesus of Nazareth, was a straightforward case of utter self-sacrifice that culminated in the cross of Calvary. The laid-down life, the poured-out blood were the supreme symbols of total selflessness. This was *love*. This was *God*. This was *divinity* in action, delivering men from their own utter selfishness, their own stupidity, their own suicidal instincts as lost sheep unable to help themselves.

In all of this there is an amazing mystery. No man will ever be able fully to fathom its implications. It is bound up inexorably with the concept of God's divine love of self-sacrifice, which is so foreign to most of us who are so self-centred. At best we can only grasp feebly the incredible concept of a perfect person, a sinless one being willing actually to be made sin that we who are so full of faults, selfish self-assertion and suspicion might be set free from sin and self to live a new, free, fresh, abundant life of righteousness.

Jesus told us Himself that He had come that we might have life and have it more abundantly. Just as the sheepman is thrilled beyond words to see his sheep thriving on the high, rich summer range (it is one of the highlights of his whole year), so my Shepherd is immensely pleased when He sees me flourish on the tablelands of a noble, lofty life that He has made possible for me.

Part of the mystery and wonder of Calvary, of God's love to us in Christ, is bound up too with the deep desire of His heart to have me live on a higher plane. He longs to see me living above the mundane level of common humanity. He is so pleased when I walk in the ways of holiness, of selflessness, of serene contentment in His care, aware of His presence and enjoying the intimacy of His companionship.

To live thus is to live richly.
To walk here is to walk with quiet assurance.
To feed here is to be replete with good things.
To find this tableland is to have found something
    of my Shepherd's love for me.

CHAPTER 10

Thou Anointest My Head With Oil ...

As one meditates on this magnificent poem it is helpful to keep in mind that the poet is recounting the salient events of the full year in a sheep's life. He takes us with him from the home ranch where every need is so carefully supplied by the owner, out into the green pastures, along the still waters, up through the mountain valleys to the high tablelands of summer.

Here, now, where it would appear the sheep are in a sublime setting on the high meadows; where there are clear running springs; where the forage is fresh and tender; where there is the intimate close contact with the shepherd; suddenly we find 'a fly in the ointment', so to speak.

For in the terminology of the sheepman, 'summer time is fly time'. By this, reference is made to the hordes of insects that emerge with the advent of warm weather. Only those people who have kept livestock or studied wildlife habits are aware of the serious problems for animals presented by insects in the summer.

To name just a few parasites that trouble stock and make their lives a misery: there are warble flies, bot flies, heel flies, nose (nasal) flies, deer flies, black flies, mosquitoes, gnats and other minute, winged parasites that proliferate at this time of year. Their attacks on animals can readily turn the golden summer months into a time of torture for sheep and drive them almost to distraction.

Sheep are especially troubled by the nose fly, or nasal fly, as it is sometimes called. These little flies buzz about the sheep's head, attempting to deposit their eggs on the damp, mucous membranes of the sheep's nose. If they are successful the eggs will hatch in a few days to form small, slender, worm-like larvae. They work their way up the nasal passages into the sheep's head; they burrow into the flesh and there set up an intense irritation accompanied by severe inflammation.

For relief from this agonizing annoyance sheep will deliberately beat their heads against trees, rocks, posts or brush. They will rub them in the soil and thrash around against woody growth. In extreme cases of intense infestation a sheep may even kill itself in a frenzied endeavour to gain respite from the aggravation. Often advanced stages of infection from these flies will lead to blindness.

Because of all this, when the nose flies hover around the flock, some of the sheep become frantic with fear and panic in their attempt to escape their tormentors. They will stamp their feet erratically and race from place to place in the pasture, trying desperately to elude the flies. Some may run so much they will drop from sheer exhaustion. Others may toss their heads up and down for hours. They will hide in any bush or woodland that offers shelter. On some occasions they may refuse to graze in the open at all.

All this excitement and distraction has a devastating

affect on the entire flock. Ewes and lambs rapidly lose condition and begin to drop in weight. The ewes will go off milking and their lambs will stop growing gainfully. Some sheep will be injured in their headlong rushes of panic; others may be blinded and some even killed outright.

Only the strictest attention to the behaviour of the sheep by the shepherd can forestall the difficulties of 'fly time'. At the very first sign of flies among the flock he will apply an antidote to their heads. I always preferred to use a homemade remedy composed of linseed oil, sulphur and tar which was smeared over the sheep's nose and head as a protection against nose flies.

What an incredible transformation this would make among the sheep! Once the oil had been applied to the sheep's head there was an immediate change in behaviour. Gone was the aggravation; gone the frenzy; gone the irritability and the restlessness. Instead, the sheep would start to feed quietly again, then soon lie down in peaceful contentment.

This, to me, is the exact picture of irritations in my own life. How easy it is for there to be a fly in the ointment of even my most lofty spiritual experience! So often it is the small, petty annoyances that ruin my repose. It is the niggling distractions that become burning issues that can wellnigh drive me round the bend or up the wall. At times some tiny, tantalizing thing torments me to the point where I feel I am just beating my brains out. And so my behaviour as a child of God degenerates to a most disgraceful sort of frustrated tirade.

Just as with the sheep there must be continuous and renewed application of oil to forestall the 'flies' in my life, there must be a continuous anointing of God's gracious Spirit to counteract the ever-present aggravations of personality conflicts. Only one application of oil, sulphur and tar was not enough for the entire summer. It was a process that had to be repeated. The fresh application was the effective antidote.

There are those who contend that in the Christian life one need only have a single, initial anointing of God's Spirit. Yet the frustrations of daily dilemmas demonstrate that one must have Him come continuously to the troubled mind and heart to counteract the attacks of one's tormentors.

This is a practical and intimate matter between myself and my Master. In Luke 11:13 Christ Himself, our Shepherd, urges us to ask for the Holy Spirit to be given to us by the Father.

It is both a logical and legitimate desire for us to have the daily anointing of God's gracious Spirit upon our minds. God alone can form in us the mind of Christ. The Holy Spirit alone can give to us the attitudes of Christ. He alone makes it possible for us to react to aggravations and annoyances with quietness and calmness.

When people or circumstances or events beyond our control tend to 'bug' us, it is possible to be content and serene when these 'outside' forces are counteracted by the presence of God's Spirit. In Romans 8:1-2, we are told plainly it is the law of the Spirit of life in Christ Jesus that makes us free from the law of sin and death.

It is this daily anointing of God's gracious Spirit upon my mind which produces in my life such personality traits as joy, contentment, love, patience, gentleness and peace. What a contrast this is to the tempers, frustration and irritableness which mars the daily conduct of so many of God's children.

What I do in any given situation is to expose it to my Master, my Owner, Christ Jesus, and say simply, 'O Lord, I can't cope with these petty, annoying, peevish problems. Please apply the oil of Your Spirit to my mind. Both at the conscious and sub-conscious levels of my thought-life enable me to act and react just as You would.' And He will. It will surprise you how promptly He complies with such a request made in deadly earnest.

But summertime for the sheep is more than just flytime. It is also 'scab-time'. Scab is an irritating and highly contagious disease common among sheep the world over. Caused by a minute, microscopic parasite that proliferates in warm weather, 'scab' spreads throughout a flock by direct contact between infected and non-infected animals.

Sheep love to rub heads in an affectionate and friendly manner. Scab is often found most commonly around the head. When two sheep rub together the infection spreads readily from one to the other.

In the Old Testament when it was declared that the sacrificial lambs should be without blemish, the thought uppermost in the writer's mind was that the animal should be free of scab. In a very real and direct sense scab is significant of contamination, of sin, of evil.

Again as with flies, the only effective antidote is to apply linseed oil, sulphur and other chemicals that can control this disease. In many sheep-rearing countries dips are built and the entire flock is put through the dip. Each animal is completely submerged in the solution until its entire body is soaked. The most difficult part to do is the head. The head has to be plunged under repeatedly to ensure that scab there will be controlled. Some sheepmen take great care to treat the head by hand.

Only once did my sheep become infected by scab. I had purchased a few extra ewes from another rancher to increase the flock. It so happened they had, unknown to me, a slight infection of scab which quickly began to spread through the entire healthy flock. It meant I had to purchase a huge dipping tank and install it in my corrals. At great expense, to say nothing of the time and heavy labour involved, I had to put the entire flock, one by one, through the dipping solution to clear them of the disease. It was a tremendous task and one which entailed special attention to their heads. So I know precisely what David meant when he wrote, 'Thou anointest my head with oil.' Again it was the only antidote for scab.

Perhaps it should be mentioned that in Palestine the old remedy for this disease was olive oil mixed with sulphur and spices. This home remedy served equally well in the case of flies that came to annoy the flocks.

In the Christian life, most of our contamination by the world, by sin, by that which would defile and disease us spiritually comes through our minds. It is a case of mind meeting mind to transmit ideas, concepts and attitudes which may be damaging.

Often it is when we 'get our heads together' with someone else who may not necessarily have the mind of Christ, that we come away imbued with concepts that are not Christian.

Our thoughts, our ideas, our emotions, our choices, our impulses, drives and desires are all shaped and moulded through the exposure of our minds to other people's minds. In our modern era of mass communication, the danger of the 'mass mind' grows increasingly grave. Young people in particular, whose minds are so malleable, find themselves being moulded under the subtle pressures and impacts made on them by television, radio, magazines, newspapers, and fellow classmates, to say nothing of their parents and teachers.

Often the mass media which are largely responsible for shaping our minds are in the control of men whose characters are not Christlike: who in some cases are actually anti-Christian.

One cannot be exposed to such contacts without coming away contaminated. The thought patterns of people are becoming increasingly abhorrent. Today we find more tendency to violence, hatred, prejudice, greed, cynicism, and increasing disrespect for that which is noble, fine, pure or beautiful.

This is precisely the opposite of what Scripture teaches us. In Philippians 4:8 we are instructed emphatically in this matter, '... whatsoever things are true, whatsoever things are honest, whatsoever things are just, whatsoever things are pure, whatsoever things are lovely, whatsoever things are of good report; if there be any virtue, and if there be any praise, think on these things'! Here again, the only possible, practical path to attaining such a mind free of the world's contamination is to be conscious daily, hourly of the purging presence of God's Holy Spirit, applying Himself to my mind.

There are those who seem unable to realize His control of their minds and thoughts. It is a simple matter of faith and acceptance. Just as one asks Christ to come into the life initially to assure complete control of one's conduct, so one invites the Holy Spirit to come into one's conscious and subconscious mind to monitor one's thought-life. Just as by faith we believe and know and accept and thank Christ for coming into our lives, so by simple faith and confidence in the same Christ, we believe and know and accept with thanks the coming (or anointing) of His gracious Spirit upon our minds. Then having done this, we simply proceed to live and act and think as He directs us.

The difficulty is that some of us are not in dead earnest about it. Like a stubborn sheep we will struggle, kick, and protest when the Master puts His hand upon us for this purpose. Even if it is for our own good, we still rebel and refuse to have Him help us when we need it so desperately.

In a sense we are a stiff-necked lot and were it not for Christ's continuing compassion and concern for us, most of us would be beyond hope or help. Sometimes I am quite sure Christ comes to us and applies the oil of His own Spirit to our minds in spite of our own objections. Were this not so, where would most of us be? Surely every gracious thought that enters my mind had its origin in Him.

Now as summer, in the high country, moves gradually into autumn, subtle changes occur both in the countryside and in the sheep. The nights become cooler; there are the first touches of frost; the insects begin to disappear and are less a pest; the foliage on the hills turns to crimson, gold and bronze; mist and rain begin to fall and the earth prepares for winter.

In the flock there are also subtle changes. This is the season of the rut, of mating, of great battles between the rams for possession of the ewes. The necks of the monarchs swell and grow strong. They strut proudly across the pastures and fight furiously for the favours of the ewes. The crash of heads and thud of colliding bodies can be heard through the hours of day and night.

The shepherd knows all about this. He knows that some of the sheep will and can actually kill, injure and maim each other in these deadly combats. So he decides on a very simple remedy. At this season of the year he will catch his rams and smear their heads with grease. I used to apply generous quantities of axle grease to the head and nose of each ram. Then when they collided in their great crashing battles the lubricant would make them glance off each other in such a ludicrous way they stood there feeling rather stupid and frustrated. In this way much of the heat and tension was dissipated and little damage done.

Among God's people there is a considerable amount of knocking each other. Somehow if we don't see eye to eye with the other person, we persist in trying to assert ourselves and become 'top sheep'. A good many become badly bruised and hurt this way.

In fact I found as a pastor that much of the grief, the wounds, the hurts, the ill will, the unforgiven things in people's lives could usually be traced back to old rivalries or jealousies or battles that had broken out between believers. Scores of sceptical souls will never enter a church simply because away back in their experience someone had battered them badly.

To forestall and prevent this sort of thing from happening among His people our Shepherd loves to apply the precious ointment of the presence of His gracious Spirit to our lives. It will be recalled that just before His crucifixion, our Lord in dealing with His twelve disciples, who, even then, were caught up in jealous bickering and rivalry for prestige, told of the coming of the Comforter – the Spirit of Truth. Because of His being sent to them, He said, they would know peace. He went on to say that His people would be known everywhere for their love for one another.

But too often this simply is not true among God's own people. They hammer and knock each other, stiff-necked with pride and self-assertion. They are intolerant, dogmatic and uncharitable with other Christians.

Yet when the gracious Holy Spirit invades a man or woman, when He enters that life and is in control of the personality, the attributes of peace, joy, longsuffering and generosity become apparent. It is then that suddenly one becomes aware of how ridiculous are all the petty jealousies, rivalries and animosities which formerly motivated their absurd assertions. This is to come to a place of great contentment in the Shepherd's care. And it is then the cup of contentment becomes real in the life. As the children of God, the sheep in the Divine Shepherd's care, we should be known as the most contented people on earth. A quiet, restful contentment should be the hallmark of those who call Christ their Master.

If He is the One who has all knowledge and wisdom and understanding of my affairs and management; if He is able to cope with every situation, good or bad, that I encounter, then surely I should be satisfied with His care. In a wonderful way my cup, or my lot in life, is a happy one that overflows with benefits of all sorts.

The trouble is most of us just don't see it this way. Especially when troubles or disappointments come along, we are apt to feel forgotten by our Shepherd. We act as though He had fallen down on the job.

Actually He is never asleep. He is never lax or careless. He is never indifferent to our well-being. Our Shepherd always has our best interests in mind.

Because of this we are actually under obligation to be a thankful, grateful, appreciative people. The New Testament instructs us clearly to grasp the idea that the cup of our life is full and overflowing with good, with the life of Christ Himself and with the presence of His gracious Spirit. And because of this we should be joyous, grateful and serene.

This is the overcoming Christian life. It is the life in which a Christian can be content with whatever comes his way – *even trouble* (Hebrews 13:5). Most of us are glad when things go well. How many of us can give thanks and praise when things go wrong?

Looking again at the round of the year through which the sheep pass in the shepherd's care, we see summer moving into autumn. Storms of sleet and hail and early snow begin to sweep over the high country. Soon the flocks will be driven from the alplands and tablelands. They will turn again towards the home ranch for the long, quiet winter season.

These autumn days can be golden under Indian summer weather. The sheep have respite now from flies and insects and scab. No other season finds them so fit and well and strong. No wonder David wrote, 'My cup runneth over.'

But at the same time, unexpected blizzards can blow up or sleet storms suddenly shroud the hills. The flock and their owner can pass through appalling suffering together.

It is here that I grasp another aspect altogether of the meaning of a cup that overflows. There is in every life a cup of suffering. Jesus Christ referred to His agony in the Garden of Gethsemane and at Calvary as His cup. And had it not overflowed with His life poured out for men, we would have perished.

In tending my sheep I carried a bottle in my pocket containing a mixture of brandy and water. Whenever a ewe or lamb was chilled from undue exposure to wet, cold weather I would pour a few spoonfuls down its throat. In a matter of minutes the chilled creature would be on its feet and full of renewed energy. It was especially cute the way the lambs would wiggle their tails with joyous excitement as the warmth from the brandy spread through their bodies.

The important thing was for me to be there on time, to find the frozen, chilled sheep before it was too late. I had to be in the storm with them, alert to every one that was in distress. Some of the most vivid memories of my sheep ranching days are wrapped around the awful storms my flock and I went through together. I can see again the grey-black banks of storm clouds sweeping in off the sea; I can see the sleet and hail and snow sweeping across the hills; I can see the sheep racing for shelter in the tall timber; I can see them standing there soaked, chilled and dejected. Especially the young lambs went through appalling misery without the benefit of a full, heavy fleece to protect them. Some would succumb and lie down in distress, only to become more cramped and chilled.

Then it was that my mixture of brandy and water came to their rescue. I'm sure the Palestinian shepherds must have likewise shared their wine with their chilled and frozen sheep.

What a picture of my Master, sharing the wine, the very life blood of His own suffering from His over-flowing cup, poured out at Calvary for me. He is there with me in every storm. My Shepherd is alert to every approaching disaster that threatens His people. He has been through the storms of sufferings before. He bore our sorrows and was acquainted with our grief.

And now no matter what storms I face, His very life and strength and vitality is poured into mine. It over-flows so the cup of my life runs over with His life ... often with great blessing and benefit to others who see me stand up so well in the midst of trials and suffering.

❦

CHAPTER 11

Surely Goodness and Mercy Shall Follow Me ...

Throughout the study of this Psalm continuous emphasis has been put upon the care exercised by the attentive sheepman. It has been stressed how essential to the welfare of the sheep is the rancher's diligent effort and labour. All the benefits enjoyed by a flock under skilled and loving management have been drawn in bold lines.

Now all of this is summed up here by the Psalmist in one brave but simple statement: 'Surely goodness and mercy shall follow me all the days of my life'!

The sheep with such a shepherd knows of a surety that his is a privileged position. No matter what comes, at least and always he can be perfectly sure that goodness and mercy will be in the picture. He reassures himself that he is ever under sound, sympathetic, intelligent ownership. What more need he care about? Goodness and mercy will be the treatment he receives from his master's expert, loving hands.

Not only is this a bold statement, but it is somewhat of a boast, an exclamation of implicit confidence in the One who controls his career and destiny.

How many Christians actually feel this way about

Christ? How many of us are truly concerned that no matter what occurs in our lives we are being followed by goodness and mercy? Of course it is very simple to speak this way when things are going well. If my health is excellent; my income is flourishing; my family is well; and my friends are fond of me, it is not hard to say 'Surely goodness and mercy shall follow me all the days of my life.'

But what about when one's body breaks down? What do I say when I stand by helpless, as I have had to do, and watch a life partner die by degrees under appalling pain? What is my reaction when my job folds up and there is no money to meet bills? What happens if my children can't make their grades in school, or get caught running with the wrong gang? What do I say when suddenly, without good grounds, friends prove false and turn against me?

These are the sort of times that test a person's confidence in the care of Christ. These are the occasions during which the chips are down and life is more than a list of pious platitudes. When my little world is falling apart and the dream castles of my ambitions and hopes crumble into ruins can I honestly declare 'Surely – yes – surely – goodness and mercy shall follow me all the days of my life'? Or is this sheer humbug and a maddening mockery?

In looking back over my own life, in the light of my own love and care for my sheep, I can see again and again a similar compassion and concern for me in my Master's management of my affairs. There were events which at the time seemed like utter calamities; there were paths down which He led me that appeared like blind alleys; there were days He took me through which were well nigh black as night itself. But all in the end turned out for my benefit and my well-being.

With my limited understanding as a finite human being I could not always comprehend His management executed in infinite wisdom. With my natural tendencies to fear, worry and ask 'why?', it was not always simple to assume that He really did know what He was doing with me. There were times I was tempted to panic, to bolt and to leave His care. Somehow I had the strange, stupid notion I could survive better on my own. Most men and women do.

But despite this perverse behaviour I am so glad He did not give me up. I am so grateful He did follow me in goodness and mercy. The only possible motivation was His own love, His care and concern for me as one of His sheep. And despite my doubts, despite my misgivings about His management of my affairs, He has picked me up and borne me back again in great tenderness.

As I see all of this in retrospect I realize that for the one who is truly in Christ's care, no difficulty can arise, no dilemma emerge, no seeming disaster descend on the life without eventual good coming out of the chaos. This is to see the goodness and mercy of my Master in my life. It has become the great foundation of my faith and confidence in Him.

I love Him because He first loved me.

His goodness and mercy and compassion to me are new every day. And my assurance is lodged in these aspects of His character. My trust is in His love for me as His own. My serenity has as its basis an implicit, unshakable reliance on His ability to do the right thing, the best thing in any given situation.

This to me is the *supreme* portrait of my Shepherd.

Continually there flows out to me His goodness and His mercy, which, even though I do not deserve them, come unremittingly from their source of supply – His own great heart of love.

Herein is the essence of all that has gone before in this Psalm.

All the care, all the work, all the alert watchfulness, all the skill, all the concern, all the self-sacrifice are born of His love – the love of One who loves His sheep, loves His work, loves His role as a Shepherd.

'I am the good shepherd: the good shepherd giveth his life for the sheep.'

'Hereby perceive we the love of God, because he laid down his life for us' (1 John 3:16).

With all this in view it is then proper to ask myself, 'Is this outflow of goodness and mercy for me to stop and stagnate in my life? Is there no way in which it can pass on through me to benefit others?'

Yes, there is a way.

And this aspect is one which eludes many of us.

There is a positive, practical aspect in which my life in turn should be one whereby goodness and mercy follow in my footsteps for the well-being of others.

Just as God's goodness and mercy flow to me all the days of my life, so goodness and mercy should follow me, should be left behind me, as a legacy to others, wherever I may go.

It is worth reiterating at this point that sheep can, under mismanagement, be the most destructive livestock. In short order they can ruin and ravage land almost beyond remedy. But in bold contrast they can, on the other hand, be the most beneficial of all livestock if properly managed.

Their manure is the best balanced of any produced by domestic stock. When scattered efficiently over the pastures it proves of enormous benefit to the soil. The sheep's habit of seeking the highest rise of ground on which to rest ensures that the fertility from the rich low land is re-deposited on the less productive higher ground. No other livestock will consume as wide a variety of herbage. Sheep eat all sorts of weeds and other undesirable plants which might otherwise invade a field. For example, they love the buds and tender tips of Canada thistle which, if not controlled, can quickly become a most noxious weed. In a few years a flock of well-managed sheep will clean up and restore a piece of ravaged land as no other creature can do.

In ancient literature sheep were referred to as 'those of the golden hooves' – simply because they were regarded and esteemed so highly for their beneficial effect on the land.

In my own experience as a sheep rancher I have, in just a few years, seen two derelict ranches restored to high productivity and usefulness. More than this, what before appeared as depressing eyesores became beautiful, park-like properties of immense worth. Where previously there had been only poverty and pathetic waste, there now followed flourishing fields and rich abundance.

In other words, goodness and mercy had followed my flocks. They left behind them something worth-while, productive, beautiful and beneficial to both themselves, others and me. Where they had walked there followed fertility and weed-free land. Where they had lived there remained beauty and abundance.

The question now comes to me pointedly, is this true of my life?

Do I leave a blessing and benediction behind me?

Lord Alfred Tennyson wrote in one of his great classic poems, 'The good men do lives after them.'

On one occasion two friends spent a few days in our home while passing through *en route* to some engagements in the East. They invited me to go along. After several days on the road one of the men missed his hat. He was sure it had been left in our home. He asked me to write to my wife to find it and kindly send it on to him.

Her letter of reply was one I shall never forget. One sentence in particular made an enormous impact on me. 'I have combed the house from top to bottom and can find no trace of the hat. The only thing those men left behind was a great blessing!'

Is this the way people feel about me?

Do I leave a trail of sadness or of gladness behind?

Is my memory, in other people's minds, entwined with mercy and goodness, or would they rather forget me altogether?

Do I deposit a blessing behind me or am I a bane to others? Is my life a pleasure to people or a pain?

In Isaiah 52:7 we read, 'How beautiful upon the mountains are the feet of [them] that bringeth good tidings, that publisheth peace ...'

Sometimes it is profitable to ask ourselves such simple questions as –

'Do I leave behind peace in lives – or turmoil?'

'Do I leave behind forgiveness – or bitterness?'

'Do I leave behind contentment – or conflict?'

'Do I leave behind flowers of joy – or frustration?'

'Do I leave behind love – or rancour?'

Some people leave such a sorry mess behind them

wherever they go that they prefer to cover their tracks.

For the true child of God, the one under the Shepherd's care, there should never be any sense of shame or fear in going back to where they have lived or been before. Why? Because there they have left a legacy of uplift, encouragement and inspiration to others.

In Africa, where I spent so many years, one of the greatest marks left by any man was that of David Livingstone. No matter where his footsteps took him through the bush and plains of the great continent there remained the impact of his love. Natives, whose language he never learned, long years after, remembered him as the kindly, tender doctor whom goodness and mercy had followed all the days of his life.

There remains in my own mind boyhood recollections of the first stories I was told about Jesus Christ as a man amongst us. His life was summed up in the simple, terse, but deeply profound statement: 'He went about, doing good!' It was as though this was the loftiest, noblest, most important thing on which He could possibly spend His few short years.

But I also was deeply impressed by the fact that His good and kindly acts were always commingled with mercy. Where so often other human beings were rude and harsh and vindictive of one another, His compassion and tenderness was always apparent.

Even the most flagrant sinners found forgiveness with Him, whereas at the hands of their fellow men they knew only condemnation, censure and cruel criticism.

And again I have to ask myself, is this my attitude to other people? Do I sit up on my pedestal of self-pride and look with contempt upon my contemporaries, or do I get down and identify myself with them in their dilemma and there extend a small measure of the goodness and mercy given to me by my Master?

Do I see sinners with the compassion of Christ or with the critical eye of censure?

Am I willing to overlook faults and weaknesses in others and extend forgiveness as God has forgiven me my failings?

The only real, practical measure of my appreciation for the goodness and mercy of God to me is the extent to which I am, in turn, prepared to show goodness and mercy to others.

If I am unable to forgive and extend friendship to fallen men and women, then it is quite certain I know little or nothing in a practical sense of Christ's forgiveness and mercy to me.

It is this lack of love among Christians which today makes the Church an insipid, lukewarm institution. People come to find affection and are turned off by our tepidity.

But the man or woman who knows firsthand about the goodness and mercy of God in his own life, will be warm and affectionate with goodness and mercy to others. This is to be a benefit to them, but equally important, it is to be a blessing to God.

Yes, a blessing to God!

Most of us think only God can bring a blessing to us. The Christian life is a two-way proposition.

Nothing pleased me more than to see my flock flourish and prosper. It delighted *me* personally, no end, to feel compensated for the care I had given them. To see them content was wonderful. To see the land benefiting was beautiful. And the two together made me a happy man. It enriched my own life; it was a reward for my efforts and energy. In this experience I received full compensation for all that I had poured into the endeavour.

Most of us forget that our Shepherd is looking for some satisfaction as well. We are told that He looked upon the travail of His soul and was satisfied.

This is the benefit we can bring to Him.

He looks on my life in tenderness for He loves me deeply. He sees the long years during which His goodness and mercy have followed me without slackening. He longs to see some measure of that same goodness and mercy not only passed on to others by me but also passed back to Him with joy.

He longs for love – my love.

And I love Him – only and because He first loved me.

Then He is satisfied.

CHAPTER 12

I Will Dwell in the House of the Lord For Ever

This psalm opened with the proud, joyous statement, 'The Lord is my Shepherd.'

Now it closes with the equally positive, buoyant affirmation, 'And I will dwell in the house of the Lord for ever.'

Here is a sheep so utterly satisfied with its lot in life, so fully contented with the care it receives, so much 'at home' with the shepherd that there is not a shred of desire for a change.

Stated in simple, direct, rather rough ranch language it would be put like this, 'Nothing will ever make me leave this outfit – it's great!'

Conversely on the shepherd's side there has developed a great affection and devotion to his flock. He would never think of parting with such a sheep. Healthy, contented, productive sheep are his delight and profit. So strong now are the bonds between them that it is in very truth – for ever.

The word 'house' used here in the poem has a wider meaning than most people could attach to it. Normally we speak of the house of the Lord as the sanctuary or church or meeting place of God's people. In one sense

David may have had this in mind. And, of course, it is pleasant to think that one would always delight to be found in the Lord's house.

But it must be kept in mind always, that the Psalmist, writing from the standpoint of a sheep, is reflecting on and recounting the full round of the year's activities for the flock.

He has taken us from the green pastures and still waters of the home ranch, up through the mountain passes onto the high tablelands of the summer range. Fall has come with its storms and rain and sleet that drives the sheep down the foothills and back to the home ranch for the long, quiet winter. In a sense this is coming home. It is a return to the fields and corrals and barns and shelters of the owner's home. During all seasons of the year, with their hazards, dangers and disturbances, it is the rancher's alertness, care and energetic management that has brought the sheep through satisfactorily.

It is with a sublime feeling of both composure and contentment that this statement, 'I will dwell in the house of the Lord for ever', is made.

Actually what is referred to by 'house' is the family or household or flock of the Good Shepherd. The sheep is so deeply satisfied with the flock to which it belongs, with the ownership of this particular shepherd, that it has no wish to change whatever.

It is as if it had finally come home again and was now standing at the fence, bragging to its less fortunate neighbours on the other side. It boasts about the wonderful year it has had and its complete confidence in its owner.

Sometimes I feel we Christians should be much more

like this. We should be proud to belong to Christ. Why shouldn't we feel free to boast to others of how good our Shepherd is? How glad we should be to look back and recall all the amazing ways in which He has provided for our welfare. We should delight to describe, in detail, the hard experiences through which He has brought us. And we should be eager and quick to tell of our confidence in Christ. We should be bold to state fearlessly that we are so glad we are His. By the contentment and serenity of our lives we should show what a distinct advantage it is to be a member of His 'household', of His flock.

I can never meditate on this last phrase in the Psalm without there welling up in my memory vivid scenes from some of the early days on my first sheep ranch.

As winter, with its cold rains and chilling winds, came on, my neighbour's sickly sheep would stand huddled at the fence, their tails to the storm, facing the rich fields in which my flock flourished. Those poor, abused, neglected creatures under the ownership of a heartless rancher had known nothing but suffering most of the year. With them there had been gnawing hunger all summer. They were thin and sickly with disease and scab and parasites. Tormented by flies and attacked by predators, some were so weak and thin and wretched that their thin legs could scarcely bear their scanty frames.

Always there seemed to lurk in their eyes the slender, faint hope that perhaps with a bit of luck they could break through the fence or crawl through some hole to free themselves. Occasionally this used to happen, especially around Christmas. This was the time of extreme tides when the sea retreated far out beyond the end of the fence lines which ran down to it. The neighbour's emaciated, dissatisfied, hungry sheep would wait for this to happen. Then at the first chance they would go down on the tidal flats; slip around the end of the fence and come sneaking in to gorge themselves on our rich green grass.

So pitiful and pathetic was their condition that the sudden feast of lush feed, to which they were unaccustomed, often proved disastrous. Their digestive systems would begin to scour and sometimes this led to death. I recall clearly coming across three of my neighbour's ewes lying helpless under a fir tree near the fence one drizzly day. They were like three old, limp, grey, sodden sacks collapsed in a heap. Even their bony legs would no longer support them.

I loaded them into a wheelbarrow and wheeled them back to their heartless owner. He simply pulled out a sharp killing knife and slit all three of their throats. He couldn't care less.

What a picture of Satan who holds ownership over so many.

Right there the graphic account Jesus portrayed of Himself as being the door and entrance by which sheep were to enter His fold flashed across my mind.

Those poor sheep had not come into my ranch through the proper gate. I had never let them in. They had never really become mine. They had not come under my ownership or control. If they had, they would not have suffered so. Even starting out under my management they would have been given very special care. First they would have been put on dry, limited rations, then they would gradually have been allowed green feed until they were adjusted to the new diet and mode of life.

In short, they tried to get in on their own. It simply spelled disaster. What made it doubly sad was that they were doomed anyway. On the old impoverished ranch they would have starved to death that winter.

Likewise with those apart from Christ. The old world is a pretty wretched ranch and Satan is a heartless owner. He cares not a wit for men's souls or welfare. Under his tyranny there are hundreds of hungry, discontented hearts who long to enter into the household of God – who ache for His care and concern.

Yet there is only one way into this fold. That way is through the owner, Christ Himself – the Good Shepherd. He boldly declared, 'I am the door: by me if any man enter in, he shall be saved, and shall go in and out, and find pasture' (John 10:9).

Almost every day I am literally rubbing shoulders with men and women 'on the other side of the fence'. What is my impact upon them? Is my life so serene, so satisfying, so radiant because I walk and talk and live with God, that they become envious? Do they see in me the benefits of being under Christ's control? Do they see something of Himself reflected in my conduct and character? Does my life and conversation lead them to Him – and thus into life everlasting?

If so, then I may be sure some of them will also long to dwell in the house of the Lord for ever. And there is no reason why this cannot happen if they come under His proper ownership.

There is one other beautiful and final sense in which the psalmist was speaking as a sheep. It is brought out in the Amplified Old Testament where the meaning of this last phrase is, 'I will dwell in the "presence" of the Lord for ever.'

My personal conviction is that this is the most significant sentiment that David had in his heart as he ended this hymn of praise to divine diligence.

Not only do we get the idea of an ever-present Shepherd on the scene, but also the concept that the sheep wants to be in full view of his owner at all times.

This theme has run all through our studies. It is the alertness, the awareness, the diligence of a never-tiring master which alone assures the sheep of excellent care. And from the sheep's standpoint it is knowing that the shepherd is there; it is the constant awareness of his presence nearby that automatically eliminates most of the difficulties and dangers while at the same time providing a sense of security and serenity.

It is the sheep owner's presence that guarantees there will be no lack of any sort; that there will be abundant green pastures; that there will be still, clean waters; that there will be new paths into fresh fields; that there will be safe summers on the high tablelands; that there will be freedom from fear; that there will be antidotes for flies and disease and parasites; that there will be quietness and contentment.

In our Christian lives and experience precisely the same idea and principle apply. For when all is said and done on the subject of a successful Christian walk, it can be summed up in one sentence: 'Live ever aware of God's presence.'

There is the 'inner' consciousness, which can be very distinct and very real, of Christ's presence in my life, made evident by His gracious Holy Spirit within.

It is He who speaks to us in distinct and definite ways about our behaviour. For our part it is a case of being sensitive and responsive to that inner voice.

There can be an habitual awareness of Christ within me, empowering me to live a noble and richly rewarding life in co-operation with Himself. As I respond to Him and move in harmony with His wishes I discover life becomes satisfying and worthwhile. It acquires great serenity and is made an exciting adventure of fulfilment as I progress in it. This is made possible as I allow His gracious Spirit to control, manage and direct my daily decisions. In fact, I should deliberately ask for His direction even in minute details.

Then there is the wider but equally thrilling awareness of God all around me. I live surrounded by His presence. I am an open person, an open individual, living life open to His scrutiny. He is conscious of every circumstance I encounter. He attends me with care and concern because I belong to Him. And this will continue through eternity. What an assurance!

I shall dwell in the presence (in the care of) the Lord for ever.

Bless His Name.

*A Shepherd Looks at
the Good Shepherd*

To
Sidney Waterman
my friend, brother, and fellow adventurer
under God

Contents

Acknowledgements 137
Preface to the original edition 139
Setting the Stage 141

PARABLE I   JOHN 10:1–5 CHRIST IN ME

1 *The Sheepfold* 147
2 *The Shepherd's Entry* 155
3 *The Shepherd's Voice* 164
4 *The Shepherd Puts Forth His Sheep* 176
5 *The Sheep Follow* 184
6 *A Stranger They Will Not Follow* 194

PARABLE II   JOHN 10:7–18 ME IN CHRIST

7 *The Doorway for the Sheep* 207
8 *Entering Into a New Life* 218
9 *The Abundant Life* 228
10 *The Hireling* 236
11 *The Shepherd Knows His Sheep*
   and They Know Him 246
12 *One Flock of One Shepherd* 257
13 *Christ Lays Down and*
   Takes Up His Own Life 266

PARABLE III   JOHN 10:25–30
CHRIST IN ME AND ME IN CHRIST

14 *To Believe in Christ is to Belong to Christ*   277
15 *Eternal Life in the Hand of the Shepherd*   286
16 *The Good Shepherd is God!*   295

Acknowledgements

This is to express my genuine gratitude to my church for recording the messages upon which this work has been based. Those tapes, together with my own detailed study notes, comprise the background material for the book.

A note of appreciation is due also to my courageous wife, Ursula. She has taken great pains to type the manuscript carefully, correcting my wild spelling and making helpful suggestions. She, too, has encouraged me in my writing, when at times the pressure of so many responsibilities seemed almost too great to bear. I am grateful for her good cheer.

Lastly, I must thank Zondervan for their patience in waiting several years for this book to appear. May it be used in the hand of God to enrich and inspire those who read it quietly.

W. Phillip Keller

C

Preface
to the original edition

It was at the special request of the publishers that I undertook the writing of this book. It is intended as a companion piece to my previous work, *A Shepherd Looks at the 23rd Psalm*.

That book has been used of God to enrich and inspire thousands of hearts and homes all over the world. It is my deep desire that the same may be true of this volume.

As with *A Shepherd Looks at the 23rd Psalm*, this book also has first been shared in an extended series of lay lectures with my own congregation. In simple yet sincere studies the truths contained in John 10 have been passed on to seeking souls week after week. And out of those sessions our Lord has been pleased to bring enormous benefit to His people.

The fact that the Word of God first 'comes alive' in the midst of people in public, reassures the writer that it can likewise 'come alive' on the printed page for the reader in private. It was our great Shepherd Himself who stated emphatically, 'The words that I speak unto you, they are spirit, and they are life' (John 6:63).

As with the book on Psalm 23, here, too, the

Scriptures are explained from the standpoint of one who has been a sheep owner and sheep rancher. But beyond this they are examined by one who has enjoyed the care and companionship of the Good Shepherd, Christ our Lord, for many years.

It is the author's earnest prayer that these pages will open for the reader new vistas and wider horizons of understanding what God our Father, through Christ, by His gracious Spirit intends for His followers – the sheep of His care.

Setting the Stage

Before we begin our study of this section of Scripture it is essential to set the stage in which our Lord stated the three parables contained in John 10. Only in this way can we comprehend clearly the truths He was teaching.

His own contemporaries, those to whom He addressed these ideas, were totally baffled by them. In fact, His hearers were so bewildered that some accused Him of being mad, or under the control of an evil spirit. They insisted that such statements as He made deserved death by stoning.

On the other hand there were those who, having just seen Him restore sight to the young man born blind, felt sure that what He said contained truth. It was bound to, since He could perform such miracles.

So it was that a storm of controversy raged around Christ. People were polarized by His parables. Some said He deserved to die. Others hailed Him as a Saviour.

Down the long centuries of time since that desperate day in which He declared Himself to be the Good Shepherd, the controversy has continued over what He really meant. Scholars, teachers, theologians, academics, and preachers have all applied themselves to this passage of Scripture. Commentaries and books of various kinds have dealt with these parables. The diversity of views, and explanations given, leave one almost as perplexed as the people of Jesus' own time.

Consequently it is no easy thing to be invited to do a book on John 10. Yet it has been undertaken in humility and with the full knowledge of what others have written previously. It is not intended to discredit what has been drawn from these parables by other teachers. They are fully entitled to their views. But it should be said at the outset that the approach which I have taken is a very distinct, personal one. It is based, not on the concept of the nation Israel, referred to in the Old Testament as God's flock, the people of His fold; nor on the New Testament emphasis of the church being Christ's little flock; but rather on my simply belonging to Him as an individual.

The reasons for this are neither theological nor doctrinal. They are the practical realities of the setting and events in which these statements were made by Christ. And if, with open minds and gently receptive spirits we look at what transpired during the days immediately preceding this passage, it will be seen that the personal approach is valid.

Jesus was nearing the end of His public life. An increasing hostility was building up against Him from the ecclesiastical élite of His time. The religious leaders of His day felt threatened by His enormous popularity and appeal to the common people. The plain people applauded Him openly. His winsome words drew them with magnetic and positive power.

This continuous polarization around Christ created a constant storm centre of controversy. The Scribes, Sadducees, and Pharisees tried every tactic to attack Him whenever He appeared in public. The masses on the other hand came to love Him with great affection. His healing, helping, and heartening life had restored and lifted so many of them.

He entered Jerusalem to celebrate the Feast of Tabernacles, or Booths, with His men. It was a festival commemorating Jehovah's care of His people during their long wilderness wanderings after their exodus from Egypt. The Master immediately came under attack. In John 7 we see some claiming Him to be a 'good man'; others insisting He was a 'deceiver'. And they would have lynched Him, if they could, but His hour of arrest had not yet come.

Then, on the last day of the feast He was assailed again. Some asserted He was truly 'the Christ'. His antagonists on the other hand claimed that Christ could not possibly come from Galilee. Officers were sent to arrest Him but failed to do so, declaring instead, 'never man spake like this man!' So once more He was spared from the clutches of His opponents.

On the next day He returned to the city and was confronted by the Scribes and Pharisees with a young woman caught in an illicit sexual relationship. She was to be stoned, but to bait Jesus the frightened girl was brought to Him. Instead of condemning her, He forgave her but instructed her to go and sin no more.

The girl's accusers were furious. They engaged in a dreadful diatribe with Jesus in which He insisted upon His oneness with the Father. For this they again determined to stone Him to death. Yet He eluded them and escaped. All of this is described in John 8.

Later He was met by a man blind from birth. In a remarkable manner He touched the sightless eyes and the blind man saw when he went to bathe them in the pool of Siloam, as instructed. Out of deep gratitude the healed man gave glory and praise to his benefactor. This precipitated another angry controversy with the religious sceptics and leaders.

Because he believed in the Christ the poor fellow was excommunicated from the religious life of his people. Jesus met him again and declared His own identity. The healed man was ecstatic and overwhelmed with adoration.

But to the Pharisees our Lord declared bluntly that they were both blind and steeped in sin and self-righteousness. All their religiosity had done them not one bit of good.

It is on this pathetic theme that John 9 concludes.

In blazing, bold contrast, Christ had personally touched and entered both the lives of the young adulteress and this supposedly sinful, blind man. He had brought them into an intimate, new relationship of abundant living with Himself.

Put into the language of the New Testament, these two individuals had discovered what is meant by 'Christ in me,' and 'I in Christ.' They had both entered into that dynamic new dimension of living which Christ Himself later referred to as '[Abiding] in me, and I in you.'

To depict and dramatize this remarkable relationship with Himself He then proceeded to tell the three parables of the Shepherd and His sheep in the next chapter.

By contrast, in Psalm 23, David the author writes from the standpoint of a sheep speaking about its owner. In John 10 the approach is the opposite. Our Lord, Jesus the Christ, here speaks as the Good Shepherd. He describes His relationship to His sheep; we, the common people, who have come into His ownership and under His care.

Christ in Me

CHAPTER 1

ℰ

The Sheepfold

Verily, verily I say unto you, He that entereth not by the door into the sheepfold, but climbeth up some other way, the same is a thief and a robber.

(John 10:1)

What is a sheepfold?

It is an enclosure open to the wind.

It is an enclosure open to the scrutiny of the owner.

It is an enclosure *not* covered in, roofed over, or shielded from the eyes of the shepherd.

It is not a barn, shed, or closed-in structure.

Its walls, open to the sun, the sky, stars, rain, and wind may be made of rough-laid stones, sun-dried bricks, timber, mud and wattle, or even tightly packed thorn brush, called a corral in some places, a kraal in others, and a boma in parts of Africa.

The main purpose of the sheepfold is to provide protection for the sheep – especially at night and in stormy weather. Its high thick walls are a barrier that prevents thieves or, to use a modern parlance, rustlers from invading the flock to plunder the defenceless sheep.

The enclosing walls are also a safeguard for the sheep

against all sorts of predators. These vary, depending upon the country in which the sheep are kept. In some areas it is a case of keeping out wolves or jackals. In others, especially parts of Africa, lions, leopards, and even hyenas are guarded against.

Even then, despite the barricade of thorn brush, there are occasions when predators will prowl around a sheepfold stealthily searching for some spot where they can leap over the enclosure to capture and kill their prey. This produces panic among the flock. The carnage is terrifying and the losses among the flock can be enormous. For the sheep owner the raids on his sheep represent serious financial reverses which may take years to recover.

I had a neighbour whose flock was raided one night by a cougar. By daybreak more than thirty of his finest ewes lay dead on the ground. Fences and walls had been cleared by the powerful predator without it ever passing through a gate or open door.

'Sheepfold,' besides being the name for an enclosure where sheep are generally kept at night, is also a term for managing sheep. In sheep countries we often speak freely of 'folding' sheep. By that we mean the much wider sense in which a flock of sheep are said to be 'enfolded' by a certain owner or sheepman. The sheep come under his special management and his direct control continuously. He folds his flock exactly as he sees fit in order that they will flourish and prosper under his care.

Folding sheep is another way of saying a shepherd is managing his flock with maximum skill. It is to say that he handles them with expertise, moving them from field to field, pasture to pasture, range to range in order to benefit them as much as he can, as well as to enhance his own land.

So a sheepfold conveys the idea of the special relationship a sheep has to the ownership and care of a certain shepherd. And when our Lord, who referred to Himself as the Good Shepherd, spoke these parables, He saw the overall picture of the unique relationship between Himself and His followers – between Himself and those who had come under His good hand for the management of their lives.

He begins this first parable by asserting that anyone who forces a way into the 'sheepfold' other than by the proper doorway or entrance may be a thief or robber. In other words, He is saying that my life is a sheepfold to which He alone, the Good Shepherd, is the rightful owner.

Within the fold of my life there are all kinds of people who come in and out. There are the members of my immediate family circle, my wife, children, grandchildren, cousins, or more distant relatives. Then there are friends, neighbours, business associates, schoolmates or strangers who from time to time pass in and out of the circle of my life.

In reality none of our lives is totally closed in, roofed over, and so completely sealed and safeguarded as to forestall the entry of others. Each of us is a sheepfold in our own private, individual way. We are within a fold, a circle, a life, which really cannot be roofed over.

It is true some of us may have high walls of self-defence erected around us. We may even go so far as to try and enclose ourselves completely to forestall invasion from others, and we may feel we have actually succeeded in this. However, we may fool ourselves into believing that we can withdraw into our own secluded little domain where we are exempt from the entrance and intrusion of others.

Christ's assertion is that in fact this is simply not possible. It is true I am in an enclosure. It is true I live within a limited circle which, however, is shared by others who enter it. But over and beyond this my life is surrounded and enfolded by the encircling care and provision of a providential God. Nor is it closed off from His loving care and concern. It is in fact wide open to the wind – the wind of His gracious Spirit. There is no way He can be kept out, any more than the wind blowing across the countryside can be kept out of an open sheepfold.

The truth that there is no one anywhere who can escape or elude the coming of God's Spirit, is portrayed in exquisite detail in Psalm 139. There is no way known to man in which he can prevent the gracious presence of God's Spirit from making an impact on the fold of his life. We are surrounded by Him; we are found by Him; we are touched by Him. His impact is upon us. We are beneath the influence of His hand … His person … His presence!

O Lord, thou hast searched me, and known me.
Thou knowest my downsitting and mine uprising,
    thou understandest my thought afar off.
Thou compassest my path and my lying down,
    and art acquainted with all my ways.
For there is not a word in my tongue, but,
    lo, O Lord, thou knowest it altogether.
Thou hast beset me behind and before,
    and laid thine hand upon me.

Such knowledge is too wonderful for me;
>   it is high, I cannot attain unto it.
Whither shall I go from thy spirit?
>   or whither shall I flee from thy presence?
If I ascend up into heaven, thou art there:
>   if I make my bed in hell, behold, thou art there.
If I take the wings of the morning, and dwell
>   in the uttermost parts of the sea;
Even there shall thy hand lead me,
>   and thy right hand shall hold me.
If I say, Surely the darkness shall cover me;
>   even the night shall be light about me.
Yea, the darkness hideth not from thee;
>   but the night shineth as the day:
The darkness and the light are both alike to thee.

>   (Psalm 139:1–12)

In the light of all this we must conclude quietly that though we may be able to exclude others from our lives, to a degree, we cannot do this with Christ. He comes to us again and again seeking entry.

He does not force His way in. He does not gatecrash my life or yours. He chooses to enter by the proper entrance which is really His privilege. Yet He is so gracious in requesting our co-operation in this.

Still, in fear and apprehension we often exclude Him, while at the same time, unknowingly, we are invaded by adversaries.

Many who force their way into my life, who slip in by means that are cunning, who impose themselves by devious and destructive tactics, often are bent on deceiving and destroying me. They are thieves and predators who are determined to plunder and exploit me as a person for their own selfish ends.

We live in a world and society rife with those who hold and propagate false teachings, false philosophies, false ideologies, false concepts, false values, and false standards of behaviour. We are approached on every side by those who would penetrate our lives to pillage them if they could. Their aim is to exploit us. They would rob us of the rich benefits which could be ours as the sheep of God's pasture.

Sad to say that in many lives they have actually succeeded. People have been pillaged. Countless lives have been robbed by the enemy posing as proper owners. Yet in those same lives, in those very sheepfolds, the door has never been opened to the Good Shepherd who really does have the right to enter, and who in truth is entitled to their ownership and care.

This is one of the enduring enigmas of human behaviour that is so baffling. We human beings will allow all kinds of strange ideologies and philosophies to permeate our thinking. We will allow humanistic standards and materialistic concepts to actually rob us of the finest values that would otherwise enrich us. We permit false aims and ambitions to penetrate our thinking and dominate our desires, scarcely aware that in so doing we are forfeiting the richest values our Good Shepherd intended for us.

On every side we see people robbed, not necessarily of materialistic possessions, but of the much more enduring assets of eternal worth and duration.

The simple solution to this whole dilemma is to discover for ourselves that in truth the only One who really has a right to manage the fold of my life is not myself, but God.

Most of us labour under the delusion that we have every right to our lives; that we have the right to go where we wish, do as we please, live as we choose, and decide our own destiny. We do not. We belong to God. He made us for Himself. He chose us in Christ out of love, from before the foundation of the earth to be His own. He has bought us twice over, both through His generous death and also by His amazing resurrection life.

Every faculty I possess in my body, mind, emotions, will, disposition, and spirit has been entrusted to me as a gift, bestowed by the bounty of a generous, gracious, self-giving, self-sharing God in Christ. There is no such thing as a 'self-made' man or woman. To assert this is colossal conceit of the first magnitude. It is an affront to the living Lord who alone has a rightful claim on me.

Even the total earth environment, the biota, of which I am a part, and which sustains me during my brief earth sojourn is God's doing. Only at His pleasure is it maintained in perfect balance and poise. It provides the precise support mechanisms which insure my survival upon this sphere in space.

Now Christ is the visible expression of the invisible God. He was born before creation began, for it was through him that everything was made, whether heavenly or earthly, seen or unseen. Through him, and for him, also, were created power and dominion, ownership and authority. In fact, all things were created through, and for, him. He is both the first principle and the upholding principle of the whole scheme of creation.

(Colossians 1:15–17, *Phillips*)

153

In view of the fact that all of life originates with Christ we should be able to see the reasonableness of admitting His ownership of us. We ought to discern the inescapable conclusion that He is entitled to enfold us with His loving care and concern. We should recognize the fact that He is fully and uniquely qualified to manage us with a skill and understanding far surpassing our own.

In spite of all this He does not insist on imposing Himself upon us. He does not override our wills. He refuses to rush into our experience by gate-crashing His way over our decisions. Having made us in His own likeness, freewill agents able to choose as we wish, whether or not we shall be His sheep, enfolded in His care, is ultimately up to us. This is a staggering decision facing each individual.

The amazing generosity of Christ in so approaching us stills our spirits and awes our souls before Him. Yet at the same time He insists anyone else who attempts to invade my life as an imposter, a counterfeit shepherd, is in truth none other than a thief and a robber ... a plunderer of my life who will impoverish and cripple me.

CHAPTER 2

𝒞

The Shepherd's Entry

But he that entereth in by the door is the shepherd of the sheep. To him the porter openeth.

(John 10:2–3a)

Because the sheepfold belongs to the shepherd who constructed it, he has the right to use and enter it as he wishes. The sheep who occupy it belong to him. The sheepfold is an integral part of his complete sheep operation. The flock move in and out through the entrance either to find security by night or fresh fields for grazing by day.

Whenever the shepherd comes to the fold it is for the benefit of the sheep. Unlike the rustlers or predators who come to raid or rob the livestock within, he always comes with beneficial intentions. The sheep do not fear him. They do not flee in panic or rush about in bewildered confusion, trampling and maiming each other in blind excitement.

In fact, some of my most winsome recollections of handling livestock during my long life are wrapped around those poignant moments of watching an owner come to his stock. Some come with gentle calls. They alert the sheep that they are approaching. Others whistle gaily as they near the gate so as to set the sheep at ease. Some sheepmen and sheepherders in Africa love to sing soft plaintive tunes as they come to the corral or sheepfold.

All of these approaches are diametrically opposite to the sly, subtle tactics of the predators or prowlers who attempt to pounce on their prey by surprise. They want to catch the sheep off-guard and capture them amid their confusion. It is a crafty, cunning part of their plan of attack.

And when the shepherd reaches the entrance it is customary to tap on the gate, or rattle the latch, or knock on the door loud enough so that all within the enclosure are alerted to the fact that he is outside, ready to enter. More than this, he expects to enter.

When we apply this concept to our own lives we see the striking parallels. So often in our past we have seen our lives exploited by those who had only their own selfish interests at heart. They were not in the least concerned what happened to us as long as their own insidious, greedy ends were gained. They used and abused their prey to promote their own designs, no matter how much destruction they wrought.

By contrast there is none of this in Christ, the great Good Shepherd. Because of His care and concern for us, because of His self-giving love and conduct He comes to us always with peaceable intentions. All through the long and painful history of the human race we see God coming to wilful, wayward men in peace.

Always His words of introduction to us are: 'Peace be with you'; 'Peace be unto you!'; 'Be not afraid, it is I'; 'Peace, good will toward men!'; 'Peace I leave with you … not as the world giveth, give I unto you!'

He does not come to men to plunder or prey upon

them. God has never exploited any person. Not once has He extracted anything from anyone for His own ends. There is not even a hint of grasping greed regarding the Good Shepherd who approaches us only with our best interests in mind. He does not use people for some selfish pleasure of His own.

And because He comes to us in generous good will He comes gently and graciously. He is Jesus the Christ; 'The perfect Gentleman!' He refuses to force His way into our lives. In His magnanimity He created us in His own image with free wills, able to act independently in determining our own decisions.

He stands outside our lives, entreating us gently to grant Him admission. The generosity of such an approach overwhelms us when we pause to reflect that in truth He really has every right to enter.

The enormous pathos of this appeal by Christ to our human hearts is portrayed vividly by the aged and beloved John writing in the third chapter of Revelation. There God's Spirit speaks to us,

See, I am now standing at the door and knocking. If any one listens to My voice and opens the door, I will come in to him and feast (share life) with him, and he shall feast with Me.

(Revelation 3:20, *Weymouth*)

This One who so entreats us to open our lives to His entrance is none other than God very God, the Christ, who in the second parable of John 10 declares emphatically 'I am the good shepherd . . . I am come that they might have life, and that they might have it more abundantly!'

He comes to us anticipating an entrance. He is entitled to enter and has that privilege because He is our rightful owner. This will be explained later in this chapter.

There is a gross misunderstanding among many as to what God's intentions may be in expecting entry into our lives. They assume He will make enormous demands upon them which cannot be fulfilled. They imagine they will be deprived of pleasures or practices which will leave them poorer people. Beleaguered by such misconceptions they are reluctant to grant Him admission.

Yet, the opposite is true of the Good Shepherd. He seeks entry to enrich us. He desires to put at our disposal all of His wondrous resources. He wants to inject an exciting new dimension of dynamic living into our days. He intends to share His very life with us. Out of that life imparted to me as an individual can come all the noble qualities of a fine and wholesome life which are uniquely His. These are made real in me, by His presence. They are further transmitted through me to touch other lives bringing blessing and benefit to those around me.

Why then are we still so loath to let Him in?

There are various reasons, of which two far transcend all the others.

The first of these is fear. Almost all of us have at some time or other allowed people into our lives who took unfair advantage of us. They have hurt and wounded us. Sometimes they have abused us callously and with great cruelty. We started out trusting them to a degree, and ended up torn and mutilated by the encounter.

The end result is that we begin to build high walls of

self-defence and self-preservation around ourselves. We want to protect ourselves from the onslaught of outsiders. If perchance we have been injured repeatedly we become even more wary, cautious, and unwilling to open ourselves to anyone whom we regard as an intruder.

We bluntly warn people, 'I don't want you in my life!'; 'Please stay away, I don't want you interfering in my affairs'; 'Just keep out of my business and mind your own'; 'Live your life and let me live mine.'

And though we may not say so in actual words, we entertain the same attitude toward Christ when He comes to call at the doorway of our hearts (i.e., our wills). We subconsciously attribute to Him the same selfish motives and ulterior designs which characterize selfish human beings.

This is, of course, unfair to God. But it also demonstrates that we really do not know or understand Him, for His thoughts toward us are always good.

For I know the thoughts that I think toward you, saith the Lord, thoughts of peace, and not of evil, to give you an expected end.

(Jeremiah 29:11)

And the ultimate end He has in mind for me is that my will should be aligned with His; my life moving in harmony with His; together sharing in the magnificent plans and purposes He has for His people. To so live is to enter a powerful, positive adventure of selfless giving of ourselves for the good of all. This is the great dynamic of the love of God at work throughout the whole cosmos. It is the divine energy that drives the universe!

Yet most of us will not respond to His overtures. We prefer to draw back, to close ourselves off from Christ, to withdraw within the closely confining circle of our selfish little lives. There we feel more secure and self-assured. It is comfortable and we prefer this confinement – even if we are cramped within the constricting walls of our own making and choice.

The second reason why people will not open up their lives to the Good Shepherd is much more subtle and insidious. It is an integral part of our lifelong conditioning and culture to assume that I, Me, My, are entitled to absolute priority in our thinking, planning, and conduct.

From earliest childhood we insist on having our own way, indulging our own desires, doing our own thing, going our own way with our wishes always paramount. We become veritable little 'kings in our own castles,' or even worse, 'little gods in the temples of our own lives.' We resent anyone who dares to enter our domain. We even naively assume at times we can be 'the shepherd in our own fold.'

There is no doubt in our minds that we are entitled to make all our own decisions, no matter how disastrous the consequences. We are sure we can solve all our dilemmas even though they lead us deeper and deeper into despair. We are determined to run our own lives even if we run them into the ground, ending up in absolute ruin.

In all of this we are positive no one else can manage our affairs nor control our conduct any better than we can. In pride and self-will we view outsiders, God included, as intruders, imposters who dare to try and usurp control. And we adamantly refuse them entrance.

As I sometimes say to people who take up this forti-fied position, 'You have not only erected high walls around your life; you have dug a deep moat outside and drawn up the drawbridge lest anyone ever come in.'

In spite of our indifference, our fear, our pride, our determined refusal to let Him in, Christ is very patient and compassionate with us. He keeps coming. He keeps speaking. He keeps standing at the door. He keeps knocking. He keeps rattling the latch.

In the case of a few lives the door is finally opened. Our Lord made the unusual comment that it was really the 'porter,' the doorkeeper who opens the door. And it may well be asked, 'Who is the porter? Who is this One who for the sake and welfare of the sheep opens up the sheepfold to the Good Shepherd?'

He is none other than the gracious Spirit of God Himself. It is He who, unbeknown to us, and long before we are conscious of the presence of Christ, comes to us quietly to begin His gentle work within. It is He who gradually prevails upon our spirits to respond. It is He who, even in our wilful waywardness, is at work within us turning us toward the One who stands outside the fold of our lives. It is He who gradually overcomes our fears, our deep subconscious inhibi-tions toward Christ. He is able in His own wondrous way to pulverize our pride, to lead us gently to see the enormous folly of our self-centredness. He generates within our wills the active faith needed to comply with and respond to the voice of the Good Shepherd.

It is then and only then that the door is opened to Christ. It is then that the guard, so to speak, is let down. Then the One outside is granted entry. For some this is an act of great apprehension. It involves a definite movement within the will. Yet it is God who works within us to will and to do of His good pleasure. (See Philippians 2:13.)

In his autobiography C. S. Lewis tells how he had long resisted the gentle overtures of Christ to enter his life. One day, while riding atop a double-decker bus to the zoo in London, he sensed he could no longer keep the Lord out of his life. By a definite, deliberate act of his will he literally unfastened the defences within which he had enclosed himself for so long. Then the presence and the person of Christ moved quietly, but wondrously, into his soul. He was instantly 'surprised by joy.' And this phrase is the title of his book.

When Christ enters He brings not only joy, peace, and reassurance to the opened heart; He brings also the divine resources of love, life, light, and fullness of character which are uniquely His. These are essential to the new life style He initiates. It is He who assumes control. It is He who begins to manage the sheep. It is He who begins to give direction and purpose to all that happens to them.

Of course it can be asked, 'Is He really entitled to do this?' 'Is He my rightful owner?' 'Does He have the credentials to determine what shall be done with my life?' To each of these the emphatic reply is yes!

First of all, we must be reminded that it is He who made us. The amazing intricacy of our bodies; the incredible potential of our minds and memories; the enormous capacities of our emotions; the unmeasurable impact of our wills; the unplumbed depths of our spirits ... each and all are glorious gifts bestowed upon us in generosity by God. We did not fashion or form them. They belong rightfully to Him. They are simply entrusted to us for wise use under His direction for the brief duration of our days on earth.

Secondly, though all of us in wilful, self-centred waywardness have gone our way to do as we want, we are invited to return to Him and to come under His care. To make this possible, He has brought us back with His own life, given in sacrifice for us. So in reality He has redeemed us, brought us back, made it possible to be accepted again as His own.

Thirdly, He continues ever to intercede on our behalf. He suffers in our stead. He entreats us to become wholly His in glad abandon.

So it is that on this basis it is both reasonable and proper that, as His own people, the sheep of His pasture, we have every obligation to throw open wide the door of our lives, allowing Him to enter gladly as our Lord, our Shepherd.

CHAPTER 3

𝒞

The Shepherd's Voice

And the sheep hear his voice: and he calleth his own sheep by name, and leadeth them out.

(John 10:3b)

The relationship which rapidly develops between a shepherd and the sheep under his care is to a definite degree dependent upon the use of the shepherd's voice. Sheep quickly become accustomed to their owner's particular voice. They are acquainted with its unique tone. They know its peculiar sounds and inflections. They can distinguish it from that of any other person.

If a stranger should come among them, they would not recognize nor respond to his voice in the same way they would to that of the shepherd. Even if the visitor should use the same words and phrases as that of their rightful owner they would not react in the same way. It is a case of becoming actually conditioned to the familiar nuances and personal accent of their shepherd's call.

It used to amaze and intrigue visitors to my ranches to discover that my sheep were so indifferent to their voices. Occasionally I would invite them to call my sheep using the same words and phrases which I habitually employed. But it was to no avail. The ewes and lambs, and even the rams, would simply stand and stare at the newcomers in rather blank bewilderment, as if to say, 'Who are you?'

This is simply because over a period of time sheep come to associate the sound of the shepherd's voice with special benefits. When the shepherd calls to them it is for a specific purpose that has their own best interests in mind. It is not something he does just to indulge himself or to pass the time away.

His voice is used to announce his presence; he is there. It is to allay their fears and timidity. Or it is to call them to himself so they can be examined and counted carefully. He wants to make sure that they are all well, fit, and flourishing. Sometimes the voice is used to announce that fresh feed is being supplied, or salt, minerals, or water. He might call them up to lead them into fresh pastures or into some shelter from an approaching storm. But always the master's call conveys to the sheep a positive assurance that he cares for them and is acting in their best interests.

When my children were young they saved up their few dollars to purchase their own pet ewes. And it was a delight to watch them go out to the fields and call up their own sheep. Quickly these ewes came to recognize the voice of their owners. When they were called they would come running to be given some special little hand-out of grain or green grass. They would be hugged and cuddled and caressed with childish delight. It was something which both the sheep and the owners enjoyed.

In all of this the key to the contentment of the sheep lies in recognizing the owner's voice. When the sheep hear that voice they know it is their master and respond at once. And the response is much more than one of mere recognition. They actually run toward the shepherd. They come to him for they know he has something good for them.

In examining the Christian life we discover powerful parallels. We find that at some time or other most of us have heard God's voice. We knew the Good Shepherd was calling. As our Lord Himself said so often when He was here among men, 'If any man hear my voice,' then certain things would happen.

But first the question may well be asked, 'How does one hear God's voice?' 'Is it possible for Him to communicate with me?' The simple answer is Yes; definitely.

He may speak to me clearly through His Word, whereby He has chosen to articulate Himself. His own gracious Spirit will impress upon my spirit His intentions and purposes for me as a person.

He may do this privately in the quiet seclusion of my own home, in the stillness of my devotions. He may, on the other hand, do it through some message spoken from a church pulpit, through a radio broadcast or a television programme.

Christ may come and speak to me through a devout and godly friend, neighbour, or family member. He may call to me clearly through some magazine, periodical, or book I have read. An ever-deepening conviction and awareness that this or that is what I 'ought to do,' may come to me. This great 'I ought to' or 'I ought not' is the growing compulsion of His inner voice speaking to me in unmistakable accents by His Spirit.

The Lord has chosen to articulate Himself also through the splendour and beauty of His created universe. The psalmist portrays this for us in exquisite poetry.

The heavens declare the glory (character) of God; and the firmament sheweth his handiwork. Day unto day uttereth speech, and night unto night sheweth knowledge. There is no speech nor language, where their voice is not heard. Their line is gone out through all the earth, and their words to the end of the world.

(Psalm 19:1–4)

He also communicates with me clearly through the wondrous character, conduct, and conversation of Christ Himself. He, 'the Word,' became flesh and dwelled among us. Through His flawless life, His impeccable character, His wondrous words I can hear God's voice. He asserted boldly and without apology, 'The words that I speak unto you, they are spirit, and they are life' (John 6:63). On another occasion He insisted. 'I am the way, the truth, and the life: no man cometh unto the Father, but by me' (John 14:6).

From the foregoing it is obvious that anyone can hear God's voice; it is possible for us to be reached. But the burning question of communication is, Do we hear? By that I mean much more than merely making contact. This was a perpetual point of pain to our Master when He was among men. Over and over His comment was, 'Ears you have, but you hear not!'

Hearing is much more involved, much more complex than it appears on the surface. It embraces more than just being spoken to by God. It involves three very definite aspects of interaction with Him.

If, in actual fact Christ the Good Shepherd has been granted entry into the little fold of my life, then I will have begun to become familiar with His voice. This then implies that I do *recognize* His voice. I learn to distinguish it from the many other voices calling to me amid a confused society and a complex world. I come to that awareness where I am alert and attuned to the special attributes of Christ's call to me personally. I am like young Samuel who, in response to the voice of God, replied, 'Speak, Lord, for thy servant heareth.'

O great Shepherd, I am listening. I am attentive. I am waiting for Your word to me. I am ready to recognize what You have to say to me.

The second aspect to hearing God's voice is that I *respond* to it. He chooses to communicate with me in order to impress upon me His intentions and desires. He has good intentions toward me. They are in my own best interests and it is incumbent upon me that I recognize this, take them seriously, and respond accordingly.

The instant sheep hear and recognize their shepherd's voice, they lift their heads, turn in the direction from which the sound comes, and cock their ears to catch every syllable. Whether resting, feeding, or fighting, everything else is forgotten for the moment because they have heard their owner's call. It commands their full and undivided attention. Something new and different is about to happen.

The same should be true of us in responding to God's voice. It should command our undivided attention. We should never allow the other interests and demands of our often busy lives to blur the gentle appeals that come to us from Christ. He does not blow mighty bugles to gain our attention. We are not hounds being called to the hunt, but sheep being led in the paths of righteousness. If we are not sensitive to the overtures of His Spirit and quickly responsive to the distinct promptings of His Word, we are not going to go anywhere with Him.

It is often frustrating to a shepherd when he calls his sheep to discover that though they may have recognized his voice and responded to it, they still refuse to move. They simply will not come running when called.

Again and again I have watched a flock of sheep in which there were a few recalcitrant ones. Standing there stupidly and stubbornly they simply shake their heads, waggle their ears, and bleat out a pathetic 'blah!' For the shepherd calling them, this is frustratng.

The same thing is too often true among God's people. We recognize His voice, we respond to it to a degree, but we will not move. We will not act. We will not run to Him. We adamantly refuse to comply with His wishes or co-operate with His intentions for us.

Our attitude and actions are as absurd as any 'Blah!' bleated by some stupid, stubborn sheep. We stand still, not moving a step toward Him who is so fond of us. We appear to be almost paralysed ... impotent to move a step ahead in the will of God.

Now the reader may well ask, 'How does a person move toward Christ? How does he, so to speak, 'run to do His will'?' It is obvious that if we are to benefit from hearing His voice we must step out to do what He calls us to do.

This involves much more than merely giving mental assent to what we may have heard. It simply is not enough just to agree with what God's Spirit may have said to us. It goes far beyond even becoming emotionally excited about what we have heard. It is possible for people to weep tears of bitterness or remorse yet never move toward God. It is equally ineffective for individuals to become merely ecstatic about some spiritual issue, for, when the emotion has passed, they are still standing precisely where they were before the call came from Christ.

What then is the step needed to move us? It is an action of our will. It is the deliberate *choice* of our disposition to *do that which we have been called to do*.

We refer to this as the *response of faith in action*. It is the compliance of our will to God's will through straightforward obedience and glad co-operation.

Truth becomes truth to me, and spiritual life becomes spiritual life to me only when I actually do the thing Christ calls me to do!

Not until this actually takes place do we move toward the Shepherd or begin to experience the benefits of His care and management. We may know all about Him in a theoretical, doctrinal way. But actually living, walking, and communing with Him in a personal encounter will be something foreign and unknown.

Unfortunately many who call themselves Christians, who consider themselves the followers of Christ, who claim to be the sheep of His flock, are really still strangers to His voice. They have yet to know the precious and special delight of actually *knowing Him*.

Our Lord referred to this in a solemn statement He made in the Sermon on the Mount. It is full of pathos and poignant pain: 'Not every one that saith unto me, Lord, Lord, shall enter into the kingdom of heaven; but *he that doeth the will of my Father which is in heaven*. Many will say unto me in that day Lord, Lord. ... And then will I profess unto them I *never knew you*' (Matthew 7:21–23).

The relationship between the shepherd and his sheep, between Christ and those whom He calls, is one of personal, profound *knowing*; for He knows me intimately, He knows me by name.

Only those who are acquainted with the pastoral life of a sheep owner in the Middle East or Africa are able to grasp how thoroughly these people know their livestock. Their livestock are their very life. Sheep, goats, cattle, camels, and donkeys are both the centre and circumference of their entire social scene.

If one goes to visit a village, the order of greeting and salutation is first to ask how the owner himself is faring. Then one inquires after the health of his sheep and cattle. Following that one asks about his children, then lastly his wife or wives. This is not intended as any slur on his family, but it does point up the enormous importance attached to livestock. They are the paramount consideration in the life of the owner.

A second remarkable aspect of the care of animals in these countries is that each one is known by name.

These names are not simple common names such as we might choose. Rather, they are complex and unique because they have some bearing upon the history of the individual beast. For example, an ewe might be called: 'The one born in the dry river bed,' or 'The beautiful lamb for which I traded two pots of honey.'

During the years when my family and I lived among the Masai people of East Africa I was deeply moved by the intense devotion and affection shown by the owners for their stock. Out in the grazing lands or beside the watering places they would call their pets by name, and it was sheer joy to watch their response as they came to the shepherd's call to be examined, handled, fondled, petted, and adored.

Some of these sheep had literally grown up as

members of the family household. From their earliest days they had been cuddled, hugged, fed, and loved like one of the owner's own children. Every minute detail of their lives was well known and fully understood.

A remarkable picture of this is portrayed for us in 2 Samuel 12:3, where the prophet of God rebuked King David for his adultery with Bathsheba, when he likened Uriah to a poor shepherd with only one little lamb.

But the poor man had nothing, save one little ewe lamb, which he had bought and nourished up: and it grew up together with him, and with his children; it did eat of his own meat, and drank of his own cup, and lay in his bosom, and was unto him as a daughter.

Is it any wonder that such ewes and lambs were called by endearing names? It is little marvel that every detail of their lives, every unusual facet of their character was known intimately.

This is the picture portrayed for us by Christ when He made the terse statement: 'He calleth his own sheep by name.'

Most of us are totally unaware of just how well God really does know us. We are oblivious to the staggering truth that every aspect of our lives is fully known to Him. If we examine the Word of God on this subject we will discover that even from our conception in our mother's womb all the hereditary factors that combined to make us each the unique individuals that we are have been known to God.

A careful reading of Psalm 139 assures us that we are known far beyond human knowledge, even in the environmental influences that have shaped us, by God who comprehends our complexities. All the multitudinous idiosyncrasies which make each of us distinct individuals are known to our Lord and Master.

The Good Shepherd may well be a stranger to me, but I am no stranger to Him!

When in the process of time an individual opens the sheepfold of his life to Christ, he may feel he is inviting a stranger to enter. Yet the truth is that He who enters is not a stranger at all but the One who has in fact known us from before birth.

This discovery is really double-pronged. It is at the same time both reassuring, yet also alarming. It is wonderful to realize that at last there is someone who does know and understand me. If I have been the type of person who has played games with others and pulled the wool over their eyes, I will find I can't do it with God.

The hypocrisy has to end. I must begin to be open and honest with Him who knows me through and through – who calls me by name.

In calling to his sheep, the shepherd desires to lead them out of the sheepfold. Sheepfolds, especially in the East, are not pretty places. Their names may sound picturesque and romantic, but the enclosure where the sheep spend the night usually is an appalling spot.

Within the enclosing walls of stone, timber, bricks, or brush there is a continual build-up of dirt, debris, and dung. Not a blade of grass survives the eternal tramping of a thousand hooves. And as the seasons come and go the sheepfold lies ever deeper in its accumulated dung. The odours can be atrocious after rain and vile in the heat of the summer sun.

The good shepherd is up early at break of day to fling

open the gate and lead his sheep out into fresh pastures and green grasslands. He will not allow his flock to linger within the corral for an hour longer than is necessary. There they can only stand still in the scorching sun or lie down to try and rest in the dirt and dung that clings to their coats and mats in their wool.

Gently the shepherd stands at the gate and calls to his own to come outside. As each animal passes him he calls it by name, examines it with his knowing eye, and, if necessary, searches with knowing hands beneath its coat, to see if all is well. It is a moving interlude at the dawn of each new day: a time of close and intimate contact between the owner and his flock.

The parallel in our own lives is not difficult to discover. It is in the little circle of our own constricted living that most of us feel most secure, most relaxed and perhaps most familiar.

But our great Good Shepherd calls us to come out of the restricted, petty round of our cramped lives. He wishes to lead us out into fresh new pastures and broad fields, perhaps to new places we have never been before.

The surprising thing is that many of us are not aware of just how drab, soiled, and dusty with accumulated debris our lives really are. We keep milling about in our same little circle. We are totally preoccupied with our self-centred interests. We go around and around, sometimes stirring up quite a dust, but never really accomplishing anything worthwhile. Our lives are cramped, selfish, and plagued with petty pursuits.

The tragedy of all this is that it can apply to every aspect of our lives. It can be true in a physical dimension where we allow ourselves to be cramped within four small walls or within the narrow confines of a city house or apartment. We can be cramped, too, in abused and neglected bodies.

We can likewise find ourselves corralled in a moral and mental dimension. We will not move out into new areas which enlarge the horizons of our minds or new experiences that stir and challenge our souls. We cringe from new vistas and fresh pursuits that will get us off the barren ground of our familiar old style.

Equally so is there a sense in our spiritual lives where God by His gracious Spirit calls us from and leads us out of our cramped experiences. He invites us to move out into the rich, nourishing pastures of His Word. He wants us to roam abroad in the wide ranges of new relationships with others of His flock. He longs to lead us beside still waters; in paths of righteousness; up into the exhilarating high country of the summer ranges where we are in close communion with Him.

The intentions He has for us are all good. His desires and aspirations for us are enormous, full of potential for unimagined benefit to us and others. Because the thoughts He thinks toward us are thoughts of peace and blessing, let us not hold back! It is the truly wise one who will allow himself to be led out into the broad fields of God's gracious blessings and benefits.

CHAPTER 4

℃

The Shepherd
Puts Forth His Sheep

And when he putteth forth his own sheep, he goeth before them.

(John 10:4a)

As was pointed out in the preceding chapter many sheepfolds are polluted places. Even the environs around the sheepfold often become barren, trampled, and eroded by the passing to and fro of the flock. So if they are to benefit from the outlying fields and meadows they must be put out to pasture.

A good shepherd simply does not permit his stock to linger long on the barren, contaminated ground around the corral. There is nothing of value there for them to feed upon. The corral is essentially a place of protection during darkness.

The diligent owner will be up at dawn to put his flock afield. This is a self-imposed discipline. He must bestir himself before the sun breaks over the eastern skyline, but this he does gladly and willingly for the sake of his sheep.

A reason for this is that because of the aridity of so much sheep country, he simply must get them out on grass early to benefit from the dew that lies on the herbage at dawn. Often this is the only moisture available for the flock. Frequently in these semi-desert countries there are no clear running streams nor placid pools of water where they can be refreshed. The total moisture intake to maintain body metabolism and vigour must come from dew-drenched vegetation.

Another point of interest is that this is the coolest time of the day. The atmosphere is moist and fragrant with the night air that has settled over the land. The heat has mostly dissipated during darkness. Mosquitoes, flies, and other insects are semidormant, less active, allowing the sheep to graze peacefully.

Turning to our lives we find that much the same principles hold true in our quiet times with the Master. It is noteworthy that most of the truly great men and women of God through the centuries are those who have met with Him early in the day. It is significant that so many of His most intimate 'saints' have been those who literally allowed themselves to be 'put out' into fresh fields of intimate association with Christ at break of day.

It is in these still hours that the quiet dews and refreshing presence of God's gracious Spirit descend upon us. It is then that the frantic world is still. It is then that the clamour and conflicts of our complex lives are quieted. It is then that we sense our own spirits can best be silent, responsive, and sensitive to the stimulus of His own strong Spirit.

Our Shepherd, our Lord, our Master Himself, when He was here among us as a man, delighted in these quiet hours in communion with His Father. The gospel record confirms how often He slipped away to be alone in private prayer and meditation. It was the time of refreshment for His soul; the time of restoration for His body and uplift for His spirit.

It is not always easy to be up and alert at an early hour. It demands a degree of self-discipline which is more than many can meet. But it is the interlude of enormous benefit to those who will allow themselves to be 'put out' to this extent. So often, especially when we are weary, the comfort of our warm beds is so appealing. The natural, normal inclination is to simply sleep on.

Yet a little sleep, a little slumber, a little folding of the hands to sleep: So shall thy poverty come as one that travelleth, and thy want as an armed man.

(Proverbs 6:10–11; 24:33–34)

The impoverishment which comes to us is often much greater than we are aware. Not only is it in a spiritual dimension, but it is equally so in mind and body. The reason for saying this is because the early hours are among the best of the day. It is then we are rested. Our minds are alert; our bodies are refreshed; our spirits are still. We are fully prepared for whatever new and fresh experience our Lord may have in mind for us. And if we deprive ourselves of this opportunity for a firsthand encounter with the living God, then our total lives are at a lower level than they could or should be.

It is the alert person who in a positive and distinct way presents himself or herself at dawn to the great Shepherd of the soul, who flourishes under God's care. In a dramatic way the course of the entire day's events are established. A strong, pervading, impelling awareness of God settles over us. We become acutely aware that we are, by a decisive action of our wills, putting ourselves at His disposal, to be put where He wishes during the day. We realize that we are going out into the turmoil of our times; into the chaos of our society; into the broken world of our generation, *not alone but with Him*.

It is because of this knowledge, this awareness, that, as God's people, we can be put out into a troubled generation with strength, serenity, and stability. It is He who puts us into the place of His appointment. It is He who will put us into the green pastures of His choosing. It is He who will make even our most desperate days of benefit to a beleaguered world. This He will do even to the refreshing of our own lives.

Why then, it may be asked, are so many of us reluctant to be put out of our little lives? Why are we so loath to have our life habits disturbed? Why are we so unwilling to be put out either for the benefit of ourselves or the welfare of others – including our Master Himself?

The answer is rather startling, yet simple. It is largely because most of us are stubborn and selfish. We find it much easier and more comfortable to confine ourselves to the familiar little round of our old self-centred lives. We are so enfolded with the comforts and conveniences that have conditioned our existence that we are reluctant to have our constricted circle of living disturbed. Our days may be drab and dry, as barren as any eastern sheepfold with its dust, dung, and debris, but we will not be put out of it.

Some dear souls are fully aware that this is so. In a way they come to almost abhor their own dry existence. But instead of allowing themselves to be put out they turn inward to indulge in endless self-pity and boredom.

Somehow they feel it is no fault of their own that they are caught in a confining little circle of hopelessly selfish living. They are so preoccupied with their own petty interests that the idea of being drawn out to new fields and fresh experiences is both unwelcome and frightening.

They have ears, yet they are deaf to the pleas of perishing people around them. They have eyes, yet they cannot see the broken humanity, homes, and hearts all about them. They have spirits, yet they are shrivelled, shrunken, and atrophied with self-interest, unable to sense the needs and heart hunger of a sick society, a world groaning in despair.

To such our Great Shepherd comes, intending to put them out where they can count for something substantial in His economy.

Let us look at this whole concept in a practical and simple way. Let us remind ourselves that because our God has been all over the ground before He knows what He is doing with us. He does not put us out into places or experiences where we are caught in a crisis. There are no crises with Christ. He has all foreknowledge. He is totally familiar with every circumstance that will or can confront us.

It follows then that wherever He chooses to put us it is for Him familiar ground. We are not going out blind. We are setting out under His guidance. Our confidence is in His faithfulness to find the places where not only we, but also He and others will benefit most from our just being there. It is not a case of relying on our wits, intelligence, or insight. Rather, it is a question of unquestioned reliance on His utter reliability to put us into the right place at the right time in the right way. Because He is all-knowing and all-understanding and totally trustworthy we can depend fully on His faithfulness to do that which is best.

Now this applies to every aspect of our lives. In no way is it or can it be confined to just our spiritual experiences. With God, every aspect of life is totally sacred the moment He touches it. There is no distinction in the mind of God, as there is in ours, between secular and sacred when He has a dynamic part in it. He desires that the total round of our little lives be lifted out of the mundane round of impoverished days, to the lofty and broad sweep of living to our fullest capacity under His control. He wants to broaden our horizons.

This is true because He declared unequivocally, 'I am come that they might have life, and that they might have it more abundantly' (John 10:10).

What does this involve in basic terms? In Christian thinking there is too often a tendency to deal in abstract values and intangible ideas. Let us get down to basic human behaviour. Perhaps we can begin with our bodies, our physical makeup.

If in truth I am God's person; if Christ has in fact entered my life, my body belongs to Him: He resides there. My right to do with it as I choose has been abdicated. It is now the residence of His gracious Spirit who is entitled to be sovereign in its conduct and care. I no longer have any right to misuse or abuse it. It is not to be overworked, overstressed, overfed, overindulged with drink, nor overcharged with sex.

As the sheep of Christ's care this body is to be under His management. It is to be put out of the confining, restricting, damaging environment of just four walls and cramped quarters. It is to be exposed fully and freely to the benefits of fresh air, sunshine, clean water, wholesome food, moderate exercise, and adequate sleep. These are provisions made for it by God. I should be willing to be put out to see they are met. This will benefit not only myself, but also my family, friends, and anyone else who encounters this healthy, wholesome, energetic, vigorous person.

Turning to my soul with its mind, emotions, and will, precisely the same principle applies. This is my person, now indwelt by the living Spirit of the living God. I shall not permit it to be cramped and contaminated by exposing it to such dusty trivia as newspaper propaganda, pornography, cheap debasing literature, hours of low calibre television programmes, or rubbish from the mass media.

Instead, God's Spirit will lead me to expose myself to the finest in art, literature, and music. He will put me into situations where my mind can be improved and my soul can be stimulated with that which is beautiful and noble and lofty. I can and will become a person of broad interests, noble aspirations, and enormous enthusiasm because I belong to Him and He wishes to put me out into wide fields of fruitful and useful endeavour to benefit my generation.

The same is true in the realm of my spirit, where I commune with Him. In the deep intuition of my innermost being where I 'know him,' Christ comes to enlarge my life and the understanding of His will.

He leads me to browse widely and ruminate richly in His Word. He puts me out to touch a hundred or a thousand other lives by His direction. He enriches my fellowship and contact with those outside the little circle of my sheepfold. In short, because He does all this it is possible to make an impact on my generation out of all proportion to my one little life – because He is in it with me.

CHAPTER 5

ꙮ

The Sheep Follow

... and the sheep follow him: for they know his voice.
(John 10:4b)

In chapter 3 we learned how the sheep come to recognize their shepherd's voice and respond by running when called. Over a prolonged period of time they become acutely aware that it is always in their best interests to do this. They have learned to trust it, to rely on it, but even more significant, to actually enjoy hearing it.

This is simply because the voice and the shepherd are as one. His voice denotes his presence. His voice indicates he is there in person. His voice represents his power, authority, and ability to protect them in danger while also providing for their every need.

In essence the sheep become so acquainted with that voice that they know it intimately. They come to expect it. That voice of that owner speaks peace and plenty to them. To hear and know that voice is to be constantly reassured of the shepherd's care for them. It is evidence of his affection and faithfulness to them.

Precisely the same can apply to the Christian under Christ's control. His voice is not something we shrink

from. It does not disturb or dismay us. We do not find it
troubles us when He speaks.

We also learn to delight in hearing Him. We look
forward to having Him speak to us. We enjoy the
increasing awareness of His presence; we relish the individual interest He shows in us; we revel in the close intimacy of communion with Him. We delight in knowing
assuredly that He has come to be with us and we can be
with Him, ready and eager to follow Him.

Nowhere is there stress or strain in this relationship
with the Shepherd of my soul. Its keeping has been
deliberately entrusted to Him. A calm, strong, quiet
assurance pervades me that in His care all is well.
Absent from this commitment of myself to Him is any
fear or foreboding. *I know Him. I know His voice. I know
all is well.*

And this knowing applies to all of my life. It embraces
not only the past and the present but applies equally to
the unknown tomorrows. My days need not be charged
with anxiety. There is no need to inject unnecessary
stress into my sojourn of this day. He is here. His voice
speaks strength, serenity, and stability to my soul.

So where He leads me I will follow!

Etched indelibly upon the walls of my memory is one
tropical night when all alone, with no one near but God
Himself, I went out to walk softly beneath the rustling
palms beside the Pacific Ocean. My life, it seemed, had
reached an absolute impasse. There seemed no point to
pushing on. Everything had ground to a deadly stand-
still. The future looked forbidding; in fact, it appeared
positively hopeless.

From the depth of my being I cried out to Christ. Like
a lost sheep bleating in desperation from the thicket in

which it was stuck fast, I longed to hear my Shepherd's voice. He did not disappoint me!

He heard. He came. He called. He spoke. And in His voice that night, speaking to me clearly, distinctly through His Word, by His Spirit, my soul was reassured. I could hear Him say, 'Entrust the keeping of your soul and life to Me. Let Me lead you gently in the paths of righteousness and peace. My part is to show the way. Your part is to walk in it. All will be well!'

It was so. And it has been to this day.

The question in all of this is, 'Do I really *want* to follow Him? Do I really *want* to do His will? Do I *want* to be led?'

Some of us say we do without really meaning it. More than anything else it is like a sentimental wish. It is a half-hearted hope. It is a pleasant idea we indulge in during our better moments. Yet, too often deep down in our wills we still determine to do our own thing and go our own wayward ways.

It is precisely at this point where we come to grief in our walk with God. It is presumption of the worst sort to claim His commitments to us, made so freely and in such generosity, while at the same time refusing to comply with His commands or wishes because of our own inherent selfish desires.

Whatever else happens there remains this one, basic fundamental fact that only the person *who wants to follow* Christ will ever do so. All the rest will become strays.

This word 'follow' as used by our Lord implies much more than just the thought of sheep tagging along blindly behind their owner. It has within it the connotation of one who deliberately decides to comply with specific instructions.

For example, if one purchases a complicated clock or other piece of equipment that is to be assembled, along with it will come a sheet of instructions. At the top will be printed in large bold letters, 'THESE DIRECTIONS MUST BE FOLLOWED.' In other words, there can be no guarantee that it will work unless the directions are complied with and carried out to the minutest detail.

It is the same in carrying out God's commands. His clear instructions for our conduct and character have been laid out for us in His Word and in the life of our Lord, the Word enfleshed. There rests with us then the obligation to comply. As we co-operate and follow through we will find ourselves progressing. New areas of life, exciting experiences of adventure with Him will emerge as we move onto fresh ground. I quote here from *A Shepherd Looks at Psalm 23*: 'As mentioned earlier it is no mere whim on God's part to call us sheep. Our behaviour patterns and life habits are so much like that of sheep it is well nigh embarrassing.'

First of all, Scripture points out the fact that most of us are a haughty and stubborn lot. We prefer to follow our own fancies and turn to our own ways. 'All we like sheep have gone astray; we have turned every one to his own way' (Isaiah 53:6). And this we do deliberately, repeatedly, even to our own disadvantage. There is something almost terrifying about the destructive self-determination of a human being. It is inexorably inter-locked with personal pride and self-assertion. We insist we know what is best for us even though the disastrous results may be self-evident.

Just as sheep will blindly, habitually, stupidly follow one another along the same little trails until they become ruts that erode into gigantic gullies, so we humans cling to the same habits that we have seen ruin other lives.

Turning to 'my own way' simply means doing what I want. It implies that I feel free to assert my own wishes and carry out my own ideas. And this I do in spite of every warning.

We read in Proverbs 14:12 and 16:25, 'There is a way which seemeth right unto a man, *but* the end thereof are the ways of death.'

In contrast to this, Christ the Good Shepherd comes gently and says, 'I am the way, the truth, and the life: no man cometh unto the Father, but by me' (John 14:6). 'I am come that they might have life, and that they might have it more abundantly' (John 10:10).

The difficult point is that most of us don't want to come. We don't want to follow. We don't want to be led in the paths of righteousness. Somehow it goes against our grain. We actually prefer to turn to our own way even though it may take us into trouble.

The stubborn, proud, self-sufficient sheep that persists in pursuing its old paths and grazing on its old polluted ground will end up a bag of bones on ruined land. The world we live in is full of such people. Broken homes, broken hearts, derelict lives, and twisted personalities remind us everywhere of men and women who have gone their own way. We have a sick society struggling to survive on beleaguered land. The greed and selfishness of mankind leaves behind a legacy of ruin and remorse.

Amid all this chaos and confusion Christ the Good Shepherd comes and says, 'If any man will follow me, let him deny himself, and take up his cross, and follow me' (Matthew 16:24). But most of us, even as Christians, simply don't want to do this. We don't want to deny ourselves, give up our right to make our own decisions. We don't want to follow; we don't want to be led.

Of course, most of us, if confronted with this charge, would deny it. We would assert vehemently that we are 'led of the Lord.' We would insist that we follow wherever He leads. We sing hymns to this effect and give mental assent to the idea. But as far as actually being led in paths of righteousness is concerned, precious few of us follow that path.

Actually this is the pivot point on which a Christian either 'goes on' with God or at which point he 'goes back' from following on.

There are many wilful, wayward, indifferent Christians who cannot really be classified as followers of Christ. There are relatively few diligent disciples who forsake all to follow the Master.

Jesus never made light of the cost involved in following Him. In fact, He made it painfully clear that it was a rugged life of rigid self-denial. It entailed a whole new set of attitudes. It was not the natural, normal way a person would ordinarily live, and this is what made the price so prohibitive to most people.

In brief, seven fresh attitudes have to be acquired. They are the equivalent of progressive forward movements onto new ground with God. If one follows them he will discover fresh pasturage, new, abundant life, and increased health, wholesomeness, and holiness, in his walk with God. Nothing will please Him more, and certainly no other activity on our part can or will result in as great benefit to lives around us.

1) Instead of loving myself most I am willing to love Christ best and others more than myself.

Now love in a scriptural sense is not a soft, sentimental emotion. It is a deliberate act of my will. It means that I am willing to lay down my life, put myself out on behalf of another. This is precisely what God did for us in Christ. 'Hereby perceive (understand) we the love of God, because he laid down his life for us' (1 John 3:16).

The moment I deliberately do something definite either for God or others that costs me something, I am expressing love. Love is 'selflessness' or 'self-sacrifice' in contradistinction to 'selfishness.' Most of us know little of living like this, or being 'led' in this right way. But once a person discovers the delight of doing something for others, he has started through the gate which leads into one of God's green pastures.

2) Instead of being one of the crowd I am willing to be singled out, set apart from the gang.

Most of us, like sheep, are pretty gregarious. We want to belong. We don't want to be different in a big way, though we may wish to be different in minor details that appeal to our selfish egos.

But Christ pointed out that only a few would find His way acceptable, and to be marked as one of His would mean a certain amount of criticism and sarcasm from a cynical society. Many of us don't want this. Just as He was a man of sorrows and acquainted with grief, so we may be. Instead of adding to the sorrows and sadness of society we may be called on to help bear some of the burdens of others, to enter into the suffering of others. Are we ready to do this?

3) Instead of insisting on my rights I am willing to forgo them in favour of others.

Basically this is what the Master meant by denying one's self. It is not easy nor natural to do this. Even in the loving atmosphere of the home, self-assertion is evident and the powerful exercise of individual rights is always apparent.

But the person who is willing to pocket his pride, to take a back seat, to play second fiddle without a feeling of being abused or put upon, has gone a long way onto new ground with God.

There is a tremendous emancipation from 'self' in this attitude. One is set free from the shackles of personal pride. It's pretty hard to hurt such a person. He who has no sense of self-importance cannot be offended or deflated. Somehow such people enjoy a wholesome outlook of carefree abandon that makes their Christian lives contagious with contentment and gaiety.

4) Instead of being 'boss' I am willing to be at the bottom of the heap. Or to use sheep terminology, instead of being 'Top Ram' I'm willing to be a 'tailender.'

When the desire for self-assertion and self-aggrandizement gives way to the desire for simply pleasing God and others, much of the fret and strain is drained away from daily living.

A hallmark of the serene soul is the absence of 'drive,' at least drive for self-determination. The person who is prepared to put his personal life and affairs in the Master's hands for His management and direction has found the place of rest in fresh fields each day. These are the ones who find time and energy to please others.

5) Instead of finding fault with life and always asking: Why? I am willing to accept every circumstance of life in an attitude of gratitude.

Humans, being what they are, somehow feel entitled to question the reasons for everything that happens to them. In many instances life itself becomes a continuous criticism and dissection of one's circumstances and acquaintances. We look for someone or something on which to pin the blame for our misfortunes. We are often quick to forget our blessings, slow to forget our misfortunes.

But if one really believes his affairs are in God's hands, every event, no matter whether joyous or tragic, will be taken as part of God's plan. To know beyond doubt that He does all for our welfare is to be led into a wide area of peace and quietness and strength for every situation.

6) Instead of exercising and asserting my will, I learn to co-operate with His wishes and comply with His will.

It must be noted that all the steps outlined here involve the will. The saints from earliest times have repeatedly pointed out that nine-tenths of being a Christian, of becoming a true follower, a dedicated disciple, lies in the will.

When a man allows his will to be crossed out, cancelling the great 'I' in his decision, then indeed the Cross has been applied to that life. This is the meaning of taking up one's cross daily – to go to one's death – no longer my will in the matter but His will be done.

7) Instead of choosing my own way I am willing to choose to follow in Christ's way, simply to do what He asks me to do.

The Sheep Follow

This basically is simple, straightforward obedience. It means I do what He asks me to do. I go where He invites me to go. I say what He instructs me to say. I act and react in the manner He maintains is in my best interest as well as for His reputation.

Most of us possess a formidable amount of factual information on what the Master expects of us. Precious few have either the will, intention, or determination to act on it and comply with His instructions. But the person who decides to do what God asks him has moved onto fresh ground which will do both him and others a world of good. Besides, it will please the Good Shepherd.

God wants us all to move on with Him. He wants us to walk with Him. He wants it not only for our welfare but for the benefit of others as well as His own reputation.

Perhaps there are those who think He expects too much of us. Maybe they feel the demands are too drastic. Some may consider His call impossible to carry out.

It would be if we had to depend on self-determination or self-discipline to succeed. But if we are in earnest about wanting to do His will, and to be led, He *makes this possible* by His own gracious Spirit who is given to those who obey (Acts 5:32). For it is He who works in us 'both to will and to do of his good pleasure' (Philippians 2:13).

CHAPTER 6

❦

A Stranger
They Will Not Follow

*And a stranger will they not follow, but will flee from him:
for they know not the voice of strangers.*

(John 10:5)

After long and intimate association sheep become
beautifully adjusted to their owner. They develop a
touching and implicit trust in him and only in him.
Wherever he takes them they simply 'tag along' without
hesitation. In quiet and uncomplaining reliance upon
him they accompany him anywhere he goes. In his
company they are contented and at rest.

This can be equally true in our Christian experience.
Unfortunately for many of us it is not always so. Despite
the tendency not to trust ourselves completely to
Christ, there are those occasional times when we have.
Almost all of us have known what a stimulating delight
it has been to respond to the Master's voice, to run to do
His will, and thus discover His remarkable provision
for us. We call this living or walking by faith.

Because the world is so much with us and we are so
much in the world, our responses to Christ are not always
as acute as they could be. Because from early childhood

we have been conditioned to materialistic or humanistic or scientific concepts, it is not always easy to distinguish God's voice from the many other voices calling to us from the contemporary world. Because we have been taught and trained to be busy, active, energetic individuals, the main thrust of our times is to be people 'on the go.' This is true even if we really don't have any clear idea where we are going or what our ultimate destination may be.

Modern man is often a frustrated, frantic, fearful person racing madly on his own man-made treadmill.

This is not just true of the twentieth-century western world. It has ever been thus in the history of our race. It matters not whether an individual's life is spent in the feverish, high-pressure atmosphere of a modern executive office in Manhattan or in the feverish, humid, swamplands of the Amazon basin where a primitive hunter struggles to survive. All men know something of the unremitting, unrelenting fever of living.

And to all of us Christ comes with His incredible call, 'Come unto me, all ye that labour and are heavy laden, and I will give you rest' (Matthew 11:28).

This invitation is not one to lethargy or indolence. It is not a formula for opting out of life. It is rather the delightful way of walking through the tangled turmoil of our times in quiet company with Christ.

To put this down on paper is fairly simple. To put it into daily practice is much more demanding and difficult. The reason I say this is simply because it is not just Christ who calls us to Himself. It is not just the Good Shepherd who invites us to walk with Him in the paths of right living and right relationships. It is not just the One who loves us deeply and desires our companionship who would have us follow Him.

There are scores of foreign influences appealing to us. On every side there are false pretenders to our ownership. We are sometimes surrounded by counterfeit 'shepherds' who would have us believe they have our best interests at heart. When, in reality, they are predators disguised in various cloaks of respectability bent on our destruction. In some cases they are already among us, parading themselves as one of our own, while at the same time plotting our ruin.

In the Scriptures they have been given various names. In the Old Testament they are referred to frequently as 'the shepherds which feed themselves and not the flock.' Our Lord called them 'false prophets' or 'wolves in sheep's clothing.' Elsewhere they are called 'dogs' who devour the sheep.

In some cases these 'strangers' have occupied places of prominence in our society. They may be preachers, teachers, writers, lecturers, broadcasters, or people of great influence posing as our protectors. Some may well go beyond even this and parade themselves as 'saviours' to their fellowmen. They invite their contemporaries to come along with them and follow in their footsteps.

To a much lesser degree, but just as dangerous, are those common people who in their own quiet, subtle way insinuate themselves into our intimate circle of companions. They may be members of our family, among our friends, in the societies we join, in our business world, amid professional people, or even in the church.

It requires constant alertness on our part not to be victimized by imposters. We simply cannot afford to follow strangers if we are to survive as contented Christians who are attuned only to the call of our Master.

It may seem to the reader that this point is being unduly laboured here. But the simple fact is that it is literally impossible to live in serenity of soul if we are torn between trying to follow conflicting calls at the same time. Our Lord was blunt about this. He stated emphatically, 'No man can serve two masters: for either he will hate the one, and love the other; or else he will hold to the one, and despise (ignore) the other' (Matthew 6:24).

Too many of us have tried too long to make the best of both worlds. We have tried to live with one foot following Christ and the other following the false ideas and teachings of our times.

And the plain position which the Good Shepherd takes is a simple one: 'My sheep – those who *know* Me – simply will not follow strangers.' How easy it sounds; how difficult to do!

It is, of course, outside the scope of this book to list or even enumerate the false ideologies, misleading concepts, damaging philosophies, and strange teachings which are so much a part of the contemporary scene. They proliferate on every side. They are spewed out in floods of printed matter, in radio broadcasts and television shows that now engulf the entire planet – to say nothing of the person to person contacts.

But broadly all of these strange and false concepts are based on the following themes.

1. Humanism. Man is master of his own destiny. He is the supreme being in the universe. There is no superior power or intelligence to which he need appeal.
2. Materialism. The chief end of life is the attainment and acquisition of tangible values. The measure of a

man's success is not the quality of his character but the quantity of things he has accumulated, or knowledge (human) he has acquired.

3. Scientism. Only that which can be subjected to the scientific method of examination is real. It must be evaluated empirically on the basis of our five fallible finite senses. Any dimension of divinity or deity is ruled out as invalid.

4. Atheism. Insists that there cannot be such a Being as God. All that exists does so by pure chance. Existence which is evolutionary has neither purpose nor meaning nor direction.

5. Religionism. Man's blind, unguided groping after God. The wild guessing at what God may be like. An abortive attempt to interpret the character and conduct of God from the distorted viewpoint of a man still in the darkness of his own sin and despair.

6. Spiritism. All of the occult, including demonism and satanic emulation. This includes all aspects of contact with the realm of evil spirits in opposition to God our Father, God the Son, Jesus Christ, and God the Holy Spirit.

7. Higher Criticism. In Christian circles it denies: the authenticity of God's Word, the deity of Christ, the necessity for the redemption and reconciliation of sinful men to a loving God.

If and when we detect these notes sounding in the voices which call to us as Christians we should be on guard at once. Paul, with his brilliant intellect, broad background of education, and enormous spiritual perception warned the church at Colossae: 'Beware lest any man spoil you through philosophy and vain deceit, after the tradition of men, after the rudiments of the world, and *not after Christ*' (Colossians 2:8).

Apart from the falsity of strange and unfamiliar teaching there is a second way in which God's people can reassure themselves that these imposters are in fact false shepherds. That is by the actual character and conduct of their lives.

Invariably a man or woman lives what he or she truly believes. Our life style is an unconscious reflection of our inner convictions, and inevitably it will be found that the behaviour pattern of the so-called 'false shepherds' – 'false prophets' – 'wolves in sheep's clothing' will be a dead giveaway as to who they really are.

Put in the language of Scripture we say, 'By their fruits ye shall know them.' No matter how smooth, subtle, or reassuring their words or manner may be, ultimately it is the quality of their lives which will declare their true identity.

As Christians we are wise to not only examine carefully the content of the voice we are called by, but also the character of the one who calls to us. A person's words may drip with honey but be potent poison coming from a corrupt conscience.

It is true we may be likened to sheep because of our mob instincts. But we need not be always ignorant, dumb sheep. If we have heard and known the delight in our Shepherd's voice; if we revel and rejoice in His companionship, we are worse than fools if we do not flee from strangers to Him.

Sheep are among the most timid and helpless of all livestock. Though they will often hammer and batter each other, both rams and ewes, they will run in panic from the least threat of unknown danger. I have seen an entire flock rush away in blind fear simply because one of them was startled by a rabbit bursting out from beneath a bush.

Yet, in a peculiar manner they will sometimes stand still and stare blankly when a powerful predator comes among them. They will huddle up in tight, frightened little knots, watching dumbly while one after another of the flock is torn to pieces by the wolf, bear, leopard, cougar, or dog that may be ravaging them, or similarly they may be stolen by rustlers.

The only sheep that have any chance to escape are those that flee for their lives. They must get out of danger. There is simply no other hope of survival. Somehow they must separate themselves from the attacker who would destroy them.

Our Lord knew all this. He was thoroughly familiar with the hazards of sheep management. No doubt many of the shepherds who had come to His carpenter's shop in Nazareth to have Him build tables and benches for their humble homes had regaled Him with tales about the terrible losses they suffered from predators and rustlers.

This is one of the favourite topics of conversation for sheepmen. And always, in the end, they know that the only place of safe protection for the sheep is close to the shepherd himself, within earshot of his voice.

The voice that is such an assurance to them is at the same time a terror to their enemies. That voice, which speaks of safety and well-being in the Master's care, instils fear and respect in the raiders.

To thrive and flourish, the sheep have to be ever under the sound of that familiar, friendly voice. To be lured away or distracted by any other is to face utter destruction or complete loss.

When I was an impressionable young man, one of the jobs given to me was to paint a huge building. At that time, because of a tempestuous boyhood and great adversity in my late teens, I was bitter and hostile toward society. My early life had been a tough struggle to survive amid severe hardships. So my mind was fertile ground for subversive ideas.

Working with me on the big barn, teaching me the tricks and skills of painting, was an old master craftsman. He was a Swede and an excellent painter. But he was also an ardent and avowed revolutionary. Day after day, sitting side by side high on the swing stage, he poured his subversive propaganda into my malleable mind.

It remains a miracle that my entire life was not destroyed by that invidious, crafty campaign. But some twelve thousand miles away, half-way around the world, my dear mother, widowed and lonely, poured out her soul in tears that her wayward son would be spared from the snares and attacks of the enemy.

And one day, unable to endure the perverse propaganda poured into my ears by the old painter, I went to my boss and demanded another job where I could work alone. I wanted to be free. I wanted to flee from my foe. Something about that smooth, subtle voice of destruction alerted me to my mortal danger.

I give God thanks that other work was provided for me. It was possible to separate myself from the one who would have ruined me. To flee from a strange voice that brought foreign and damaging ideas was my only salvation.

Later in life, when my own children were teenagers, soon to leave home, I counselled them to do the same.

Whenever they found themselves in the company of those who were not God's people, who were endeavouring to destroy them, there was one simple solution: 'Just get out of there.'

'The sheep will flee from strangers for they do not know their voice.'

It is not weakness to do this. It is wisdom. Most of us, sad to say, simply are not skilled enough nor astute enough to match wits with our opponents. We are not sufficiently familiar, nor can we be, to fully understand or master all the devious and destructive devices of false philosophies, cults, religions, and ideologies of our modern world.

But what we can do is to become so grounded in God's Word, so familiar with our Master's voice, so attuned to His will and wishes, so accustomed to His presence, that any other voice alerts us to danger. It is a question of having our souls and spirits in harmony with His. It is a matter of living in close communion with the Shepherd of our lives. Then, and only then, will the threat of strange voices be recognized.

This does not mean that if I live in an environment or culture where one or two false philosophies predominate I am to remain ignorant of them. No, I will learn all about their insidious tactics to take God's people unawares. And in my alertness to their depredations I may well save both myself and others from their ravages.

Engaging the enemy in endless disputes and arguments seldom achieves anything. Paul was aware of this when he wrote to his young protégé, Timothy. Over and over he advised him against becoming embroiled in unprofitable debates with those who posed pointless and false issues.

What Christ asks us to do as His followers is to concentrate on keeping close to Him. Our major distinctive as His disciples should be the unique life we have because of our intimate association with Him. He resides with us and in us. We likewise live with Him and in Him. Therein lies our strength, our serenity, our stability, and our safety. There is simply no substitute for this wondrous relationship with Him in a warped world.

His audience of that day, except for the young man born blind, and the young adulteress, whose lives He had entered, just could not understand what He said. Nor can most of our contemporaries.

Me in Christ

CHAPTER 7

ౌ

The Doorway for the Sheep

Then said Jesus unto them again, Verily, verily, I say unto you, I am the door of the sheep. All that ever came before me are thieves and robbers: but the sheep did not hear them.

(John 10:7–8)

In the first parable of this discourse, our Lord made clear what He meant when He spoke of entering into the fold of one's life. Now, in the second parable, He proceeds to elaborate in great detail on what it means for a man or woman to enter into His life. By that is implied the way whereby we come into His care, enjoy His management, and revel in the abundance of His life shared with us in gracious generosity.

Again it must be emphasized that His audience did not really understand Him. When He completed His teaching they charged Him with being insane ... possessed of an evil spirit, and unworthy of a hearing. And since that time millions of others have been bewildered by His teaching.

But the man born blind and the young woman taken in adultery, as well as a few others whose lives He had touched and transformed, understood Him. They knew it was God who had entered their lives. Also they had been introduced into a new life in Christ which was a dimension of living unknown to them before. These few grasped what it was He said.

Perhaps as we proceed to study His statements we, too, can enter into a fuller comprehension of the spiritual truths He shared with His audience. To do so is to have the horizons of our spiritual understanding widened by His words.

'I am the door of the sheep.' Put into our modern idiom we would say: 'I am the doorway, the entrance, for the sheep.' Too often people have the wrong idea that our Lord referred to Himself only as the actual door or gate used to close a passageway into a sheepfold. This is not the picture.

The whole process of sheep management, of folding sheep, is combined with the control of doorways and gateways. It is by means of opening and shutting these passageways that the flock is moved methodically in and out, from place to place. They pass in through it to the protection of the fold within.

A flock has both an interior life within the shelter of the sheepfold and an exterior life outside. It is by means of the doorway, through the opening of the gate, that they enjoy both ingress and egress to a fully rounded and beneficial mode of life.

In the experience of every Christian whose life Christ has entered by His gracious Spirit, there are really two distinct areas of living. There is that inner life which the Quakers sometimes refer to as 'the interior life.' It is a personal, private, precious communion which a person enjoys within the inner sanctum of his own soul and spirit.

Then there is that outer life in which one is in contact with fellow Christians. It does not just end there, however, for it reaches out to touch all the world around us. This we refer to as our 'exterior life,' where thousands of contacts are made in a lifetime of interaction with our contemporaries.

The person under Christ's control will sense and know the hand of the Good Shepherd directing him in both areas. He will be acutely aware that it is through Him he passes in and out peacefully wherever He leads us.

Whether it is within the stillness of our own spirits or without in the noisy world around us, He is there. This acute awareness of His presence opening or closing the way before me is a magnificent reassurance to my soul that all is well.

The doorway was of tremendous import in Hebrew tradition and thought; much more so than in our culture. It was against the background of the Hebrew respect for 'the door' that Christ made this assertion repeatedly – 'I am the door.' We do well to examine this briefly in order to fully comprehend what He meant.

Early in her history as a nation, Israel had been enslaved by the Egyptians. For nearly two hundred years her people had been driven by their taskmasters to toil in the dreadful slime pits. There under the broiling sun they made mud bricks with which to build the great, elaborate cities of their enemies.

Though this subservient people lived in their own little peasant hovels by the Nile, they were still prisoners of their Egyptian lords. In desperation they cried out for deliverance. God responded to their cry and sent Moses to wrest them from the land of their bondage.

The final great act of their emancipation had to do with the door of each man's home. A spotless Passover Lamb was to be slaughtered for each household. Its blood was to be liberally sprinkled on the lintel over the door, and on both doorposts. Any person passing through this door to the shelter of the house within was assured of perfect protection and absolute safety from the awesome judgement of the great destroying angel who swept through Egypt in the darkness.

But also by the same door anyone going out entered into the magnificent exodus which was able to deliver the enslaved from their bondage. A person went out through that door to liberty, freedom, and a new dimension of life under God's direction (Exodus 1–15).

It was the blood of the innocent Passover Lamb, applied to the owner's doorway, that guaranteed him peace within and protection without. He had come directly under God's care and control within a new life of freedom.

And so it is in the experience of any man or woman who complies with the provisions of Christ. As we come to rely implicitly upon the efficacy of His laid-down life and spilled blood on our behalf, He, God's own Passover Lamb, in very fact becomes the doorway for us. It is through Him that we enjoy a magnificent inner security and through Him that we go out to engage in an adventurous life of new-found freedom under His direction.

Later in the history of the nation Israel, clear and specific instructions were given regarding the doorway to a man's home. The great laws and commandments of God to His people were to be inscribed on long, thin strips of parchment. These were to be carefully

wrapped around each of the doorposts through which a
person passed in and out of his home. Thus the resident
was continually reminded, as were any strangers or visitors who came to call on him, that he and his family
lived and moved under the command and control of
God. Their going out and their coming in from that
time forth were under the guidance of God's Word
(Deuteronomy 11:18–21).

Again this was a beautiful concept clearly portraying
to God's own people the fact that they were under His
care. It was under His hand and under His gracious
guidance that in truth they could live securely. As they
passed their days going in and out of their humble
homes it was to find sweet serenity within and strong
safety without. Jehovah God was with them to guide.
The Shepherd of their souls was their salvation in every
situation.

We see this same remarkable theme and emphasis
reiterated throughout the teachings of our Lord. He
stated emphatically in His great Sermon on the Mount
that the gateway or doorway through which anyone
entered into an abundant life of new-found freedom
was in truth a restricted one. One could not think that
he could pursue any course he chose and still come out
right. If he did this he would end up in disaster – a
wayward, wilful, lost sheep.

No, the way to safety within and security without was
only through the gateway of the Good Shepherd's care.
Not many would either find or follow that route. Most
preferred to go their own proud, perverse path to perdition.

Jesus the Christ was even more specific about this
matter when, just before His crucifixion, He stated

simply: 'I am the way, the truth, and the life: no man cometh unto the Father, but by me' (John 14:6).

Putting this into plain language He is saying: 'I am the way in and through which anyone can enter into a splendid new life with God. It is through Me that a man or woman comes to discover truth, reality, purpose, and meaning. It is through Me that one comes into the intimacy of the family of God our Father.'

This is the main thrust of the entire New Testament. It is remarkable to see stated over and over the assertion that it is in and through Christ we live.

Through Jesus Christ I have peace with God.

Through Jesus Christ I am justified.

Through Jesus Christ I am forgiven my failures and sins.

Through Jesus Christ I am accepted into God's family.

Through Jesus Christ I am set free from slavery to sin and self.

Through Jesus Christ I am resurrected.

Through Jesus Christ I have immediate access to God in prayer.

And so the list could go on as a paean of praise to Him who has loved us and redeemed us and reconciled us to Himself by His own generous laid-down life.

In a word, it may be said that He, and only He, is the doorway into abundant living.

As in the previous parable, here again the Lord reiterates that anyone who ever preceded Him in our experience was a thief or robber. He was a thief in that if he induced us to do our own thing and go our own way he robbed us of our rightful inheritance.

The reason for this escapes most people. We are

conditioned by the culture of our society to believe that we are in the world merely to gratify our own selfish desires and drives. We are taught that to a great degree everything is relative. If my impulse is to push my way to the top of the totem pole, I should do so, even if it means trampling on others along the way. It's just too bad if others are injured. After all, it's a tough world we live in, and life is really a struggle to survive.

So, little by little as time goes on, many of us do not believe that the standards established by God are relative to our age. We discard His directions for living. We ignore His instructions for our conduct. We turn each to his own way only to find that our difficulties deepen. We see ourselves caught up in a worldly way of existence. Life becomes a meaningless mockery. God's absolute values of integrity, loyalty, justice, honour, love, and fine nobility are cast aside. And in their place we find ourselves an impoverished people left only with discouragement and despair. We are robbed blind and left destitute with broken lives, broken hearts, broken minds, broken homes, broken bodies, and a broken society.

Jesus was speaking a truth we should pay attention to when He said that it was possible for us to be pillaged and plundered by the false philosophies and crass materialism of our times. Unhappily most people simply won't believe Him. They know better, or so they think. But they end up broken and beaten.

There is a second, and even more subtle way in which we ignore Him as the 'way' and put others 'before Him'. It has to do with our basic priorities in life.

Again it is helpful to go back into the early Hebrew teachings and traditions. The first of the Ten Commandments given by God to Moses in Exodus 20 states

explicitly, 'Thou shalt have no other gods before me!'
God knew that to do so would spell certain disaster.
No one, no thing, no human ideology could begin to
compare with God Himself in wisdom, might, love, or
integrity. In Him resided all that was selfless, noble, and
glorious.

For us to give ourselves or our allegiance to any other
is to impoverish and demean ourselves: it is never to
know *the best*.

Yet, in our blindness, ignorance, and folly all through
the long and tragic tale of human history, men have
sold themselves short to all sorts of strange and stupid
gods. We have bartered away our birthright for a
meagre mess of unsatisfying substitutes.

God made us for Himself. In love and concern He
intended us to be the children of His family, the sheep
of His flock, the bride for His bridegroom.

Instead of seeing, longing, and devoting ourselves to
Him, we have turned away and have put all sorts of
other gods before Him. Other interests, ideas, people,
and pursuits have been given prior place in our lives
and affections. They have all 'come before' Him.

Whatever it is to which I give most of my attention,
time, thought, strength, and interest, becomes my God.
It may be my home, my health, my family, career,
hobby, entertainment, money, or person.

But our Lord says that if they come before Him, we
are robbed. We have been stolen blind. We are poorer
than we think. Our plight is pathetic, and we have
settled for second best.

Our Lord points out in our text that those who are
truly His people, the sheep of His pasture, will not allow
themselves to be subverted by false gods. In the history

of the people of Israel this had always been one of their greatest difficulties. Often they had been warned not to follow after the pagan gods of the races around them. Whenever they gave an ear to their subtle attractions they were drawn into dreadful practices that led them to utter ruin.

It did not matter whether they did this collectively as a nation or privately as individual citizens. The end result always was retrogression and remorse. But in spite of the repeated warnings there always seemed to be those who were oblivious to the dangers of thieves and robbers. In stubborn, sometimes blind folly they would fall prey to the predators among them or around them. And the same is still true today.

It reminds me of the behaviour of a band of sheep under attack from dogs, cougars, bears, or even wolves. Often in blind fear or stupid unawareness they will stand rooted to the spot watching their companions being cut to shreds. The predator will pounce upon one then another of the flock raking and tearing them with tooth and claw. Meanwhile, the other sheep may act as if they did not even hear or recognize the carnage going on around them. It is as though they were totally oblivious to the obvious peril of their own precarious position.

We see this principle at work even among Christians. We as God's people are continually coming under attack, either from without or within. Yet many are unable to detect danger among our number. It is as though we cannot hear or see or sense our peril. Often the predation is so crafty and cunning that fellow Christians are cut down before our eyes by the enemy of our souls.

Sometimes those who do the most damage are

already among us. They insinuate themselves into our little folds. They may be in our family, among our friends, in our neighbourhood, in some small Bible class, in the community, or even in the church itself. They come bringing discord, divisions, and dissension. They rob us of the enrichment we might have from our Master by redirecting our attention to lesser issues. We get caught up in conflict and confusion that can lead to chaos. Instead of our focus being centred in Christ they get us embroiled with false and destructive ideas that may eventually lead to our downfall.

Almost invariably those who come as thieves and robbers divert our attention from the loveliness and grandeur of our Good Shepherd. They manage to redirect our interests to peripheral issues of minor importance. They will get us to expend our time and energy and thought on trivia. And while we are so preoccupied with following their 'will-o'-the-wisp' suggestions we fall prey to their deceptive and destructive tactics. We see this in such things as over-emphasis of questionable doctrines, humanistic philosophies, undue desire for feelings rather than faith in the Christian experience, disputes over biblical interpretations, excesses in legalism, worldly ways of living or doing God's work, pandering to certain popular personalities or programmes.

Throughout the teachings of our Lord, and later in the writings of the New Testament apostles (see 2 Timothy), we are warned 'not to hear' such false teachers. We are urged to turn a deaf ear to them. We are told to flee from them. If we are to survive we must dissociate ourselves from them. We do not respond to those who treacherously try to tickle our ears while cutting our throats.

This is not always easy to do, but if we are following Christ in an intimate communion, we will be aware of our danger. We will turn from those who would maim and mutilate us. We will be acutely sensitive only to the gentle voice of the Good Shepherd.

CHAPTER 8

𝒞

Entering Into a New Life

I am the door: by me if any man enter in, he shall be saved, and shall, go in and out, and find pasture. The thief cometh not, but for to steal, and to kill, and to destroy.

(John 10:9–10a)

Our Lord makes it clear that He is the door, the way, the entrance into a new life. This life in which He controls both my interior and exterior life is totally different from any life style I may have known before.

It implies a new two-way interpersonal relationship. He has come into the little fold of my life there to exercise His management of my affairs. He leads me out in due course to wider fields of contact and adventure with others in new dimensions of spiritual growth.

Yet, at the same time I find myself entering into an exciting and stimulating life style within the *enfolding control* of His presence. He has become the paramount and pre-eminent person in my daily experience. He occupies a place of greater priority in my thoughts, emotions, and decisions than any earthly companion. This applies to my family, friends, or other intimate associates.

This process of gradually allowing God to govern my life, permitting Christ to control my conduct, coming gently under the absolute sovereignty of His gracious Spirit is to enter into the remarkable and restful salvation He provides for His people.

It is a case where I am no longer enslaved to my own small, self-centred wishes. I am set free from the tyranny of my own destructive emotions. I am liberated from the bondage of my own bungling decisions. It is a case of being set free from the terrible tyranny of my own selfish self-centredness. He, the Good Shepherd of my soul, takes over the welfare of my affairs. He delivers me from the dilemma of my own self-destructive drives. I am free at last to enter into the joyous delight of just doing His will.

Sad as it may seem, many Christians do not enter into the rest and repose of this life in Christ. They may have heard about it. They may have read about it. They may even have seen it in the experience of one or two of their contemporaries, but for themselves it is as elusive as a passing daydream.

Perhaps if a parallel is drawn from the relationships between a shepherd and his sheep we can understand how one enters into this wondrous life.

Any sheep, if treated with kindness and affection, soon attaches itself to its new owner. Sheep are remarkably responsive, for the most part, to the attention and care given to them by a good shepherd. This is especially true in small flocks where the owner has opportunity to bestow his personal affection on individual animals. They quickly become his friends. A select few are actually pets. They follow him as faithfully as his own shadow. Wherever he goes they are there. It is in his company, and because of his presence, that they are ever secure and at rest.

The same truth applies in our relationship to Christ. We can in truth enter into a new life with Him whereby we enjoy the safety, surety, and security of His presence. This is not some superspiritual, once-for-all, ecstatic experience. Rather it is the quiet, gentle hour-to-hour awareness of 'O Lord, You are here!' It is the keen knowledge, 'O God, You are guiding me!' It is the calm, serene assurance, 'O gracious Spirit, in Your presence there is peace!'

There is nothing mystical or magical about this. It is the winsome, wondrous knowledge of realizing the person, presence, and power of Christ in every detail of my day. This is the meaning of salvation in its full-orbed splendour.

The entering into this life in Christ lifts me above the low level of trying to struggle with the down-drag of sin that leads so many into the deep ditch of despair. It frees me from the fret of fighting with the old selfish impulses that generally govern my life. It delivers me from the dominion of the enemy of my soul who wishes to ensnare me.

The focus of my attention has been shifted away from myself to my Shepherd. The movement of my soul has been brought to Him for direction rather than left in the dilemma of my own decision making. The responsibility for my activities has been placed squarely in His care and taken out of my hands. This means subjecting my will to His wishes, but therein lies my rest and relief from my own stressful way of life.

Such people, our Lord said, would go in and out freely and find pasture.

Many people assume that to become a Christian and follow Christ calls only for self-denial, privation, poverty, and hardships. It is a distorted picture, for in fact, though we may relinquish our old selfish life style, we discover to our delight an entrance into a much greater and broader dimension of living.

Who is the person rich in friends, loved ones, and affection? The one willing to give himself away to others. Who is the individual who finds life full, rewarding, and deeply satisfying? The person who loses himself in a cause much greater than himself, who gives himself away for the greater good of all.

And it is to this calibre of life that Christ invites us. He calls us to enter into great commitments and noble causes. He leads us into a broken world there to expend ourselves on behalf of suffering, struggling, lost humanity.

Life is too magnificent, our capacities too noble, our days too few and precious to be squandered on just our own selfish little selves. God has made us in His own great image for great purposes. Only in coming into harmony with His will and wishes can we ever begin to realize or attain the tremendous aspirations He has for us. It is in complete and implicit co-operation with His ongoing purposes for the planet that any of us ever attain even a fraction of our potential for eternal service and salvation.

Too many of us are too provincial, too petty in our outlook. We see only our own little problems. We are obsessed with only our own little objectives. We go through life cramped and constricted by our own small circle of contacts.

Christ the Good Shepherd calls us to go in and out

and find wide, broad pastures of practical and abundant service; not only for our own sakes but also for the sake of others who are as lost as we once were.

He gave us this broad view in graphic terms Himself when He sent out His twelve disciples as missionaries to the lost sheep of Israel.

A careful and intelligent reading of Matthew 9:35–10:16 discloses a delightful scene of an eastern shepherd gathering up stray sheep. Jesus had been moving from village to village, town to town, teaching, preaching, healing, and ministering to men's needs in every area of life. Seeing the innumerable multitudes of struggling souls He was moved with enormous concern and compassion for them. They were as sheep without a shepherd. They were weary, apprehensive, distraught, and scattered afield in every direction.

Turning to His twelve companions He made the comment, so often misunderstood and misinterpreted by missionaries. 'The harvest truly is plenteous, but the labourers are few.' He was not speaking of a harvest of wheat or corn or other grain, but rather a crop of lambs, a crop of lost sheep scattered by the millions, milling aimlessly across the surface of the earth.

Who and where were the workers, the labourers who could gather in the lost? There were so few able to do this difficult and delicate task.

How does an eastern sheepman gather up his stray sheep? How does He bring home the wanderers and stragglers?

He does not use dogs the way western sheepmen do. He does not resort to horses or donkeys to herd them home or round them up. Nor does he employ helicopters or Hondas as some western ranchers do.

No, the eastern shepherd uses his own pet lambs and bellwethers to gather in lost sheep. Because these pets are so fond of being near him and with him, he has to literally go out into the hills and rough country himself taking them along, scattering them abroad. There they graze and feed alongside the wild and wayward sheep.

As evening approaches the shepherd gently winds his way home. His favourite pet lambs and bellwethers quietly follow him. As they move along in his footsteps, they bring with them the lost and scattered sheep. It is a winsome picture full of pathos.

In Matthew 10 Christ actually took His twelve men and scattered them out among the lost sheep of Israel (v. 6). He warned them that He was sending them out as sheep in the midst of predators who might try to prevent them from bringing home the lost (v. 16). But they were to go anyway, because the presence of His Spirit would be with them to preserve them in every danger.

This is a precise picture drawn for us in bold colours of what our Good Shepherd requires of us. He does not demand that we embark on some grandiose schemes of our own design to do His work in the world. He does not suggest that we become embroiled in some complex organization of human ingenuity to achieve His goal of gathering in lost souls.

He simply asks me to be one who will be so attached to Him, so fond of Him, so true to Him, that in truth I shall be like His pet lamb or bellwether. No matter where He takes me; no matter where He places me; no matter whom I am alongside of in my daily living, that person will be induced to eventually follow the Shepherd because I follow Him.

Put in another way it may be said that any Christian's effectiveness in winning others is directly proportional to his own devotion to the Master. Show me a person to whom Christ is absolutely paramount and I will show you one who gently but surely is gathering in others from the pastures of the world.

This is the individual who has entered into an exciting, adventuresome, fresh mode of life in God. Day after day, under the guidance of the Good Shepherd, he goes in and out to find fresh pastures of new experience. His life touches other lives, and all the time here and there he sees others gently gathered in, because he was willing to be sent forth wherever the Shepherd best saw fit to place him.

It all sounds fairly simple. It is, if we faithfully follow Christ. It is He who assures us of effective success in helping to save the lost and scattered sheep in a shattered world. We are His co-workers, co-labourers in His great ongoing plans for rescuing the lost.

Nor is such labour without its rewards. Our God is the God of all consolation and compensation. He is no man's debtor. Those who honour Him, He will honour. If we put Him and His interests first, there will ever be ample provision for all of our needs. This is not theory. This is the truth testified to by uncounted millions of men and women who, having entered into this new life with God, have found Him to be ever faithful to them.

Any life He enters is always enriched, never impoverished. Any of our days He touches are transformed with the light and joy of His presence. To sense and know Him is to have tasted life at its sublime best.

Yet amid such living our Lord warns us that there can

still be thieves and robbers present. There are always predators prowling around the periphery of our lives, waiting and watching for opportunity to plunder and impoverish us.

In previous chapters these have been dealt with in some detail. Emphasis has been placed especially upon those aspects of our Christian lives where we can be seriously endangered by false teaching, philosophies, or ideologies.

Here, very briefly, I would like to mention just two of the more practical aspects of our times which literally come into our lives and impoverish us. Not only are we poorer because of them, but God's work is hindered from being carried out as well as it might be.

The first is idleness. We live in a culture given to greater leisure. The shorter work week means more leisure time. Indolence is an outgrowth of this. The discipline of diligent duty is disappearing. Consequently the character of our people becomes increasingly casual, careless, and irresponsible.

For young people especially, excess ease is debilitating. The sense of challenge and achievement is lacking. They are impoverished because there is so little attained to satisfy them with a sense of worthwhile accomplishment. Too often the young toss away their days while the older loaf away their lives.

As God's people we should give ourselves completely, gladly, and wholeheartedly to His enterprises upon the earth. There is much to achieve!

Then there is affluence and luxury. The world is so much with us. We have been conditioned by our culture to believe that an individual's worth is measured by his material assets. Yet Christ declared, 'A man's life does not consist of the abundance of things he owns' (Luke 12:15).

Still, there is a tendency for us to allow our attention to be centred on the acquisition of material wealth, or even academic attainments, or personal power and prestige in one form or another.

This is not to say that as Christians we are not entitled to pursue excellence in any of the fields into which God may guide us. We should strive to excel for His sake, not our personal pride. But at no time should these become a prior claim upon our thought or time or strength. If we allow this to happen we will soon discover that in truth we are being robbed of the best. We are being deprived of His presence, power, and peace in our lives. We will have settled for second best. We will be poorer than we know. This will constrict our effectiveness for Christ and will cramp our personal relationship to Him.

The Spirit of God speaking to the church of Laodicea in Revelation 3:16–20 put it this way:

So then because thou art lukewarm, and neither cold nor hot, I will spue thee out of my mouth. Because thou sayest, I am rich, and increased with goods, and have need of nothing; and knowest not that thou art wretched, and miserable, and poor, and blind, and naked: I counsel thee to buy of me gold tried in the fire, that thou mayest be rich; and white raiment, that thou mayest be clothed, and that the shame of thy nakedness do not appear; and anoint thine eyes with eye-salve, mayest see. As many as I love, I rebuke and chasten: be zealous therefore, and repent. Behold, I stand at the door, and knock: if any man hear my voice, and open the door, I will come in to him, and will sup with him, and he with me.

What the Good Shepherd desires above all else is that He might have the wondrous delight of entering *fully* into my life, there to share it with me. And I in turn can enter wholeheartedly into His great life, there to experience the remarkable fulfilment which He intended for me as His person. All of this is the purpose of His love for me.

CHAPTER 9

The Abundant Life

I am come that they might have life, and that they might have it more abundantly. I am the good shepherd: the good shepherd giveth his life for the sheep.

(John 10:10b–11)

Any shepherd who is a good manager always bears in mind one great objective. It is that his flock may flourish. The continuous well-being of his sheep is his constant preoccupation. All of his time, thought, skill, strength, and resources are directed to this end.

Nothing delights the good shepherd more than to know his livestock are in excellent condition. He will stand in his pastures amongst his sheep casting a knowing eye over them, rejoicing in their contentment and fitness. A good stock man actually revels in the joy of seeing his animals flourishing.

There are several reasons for this. First, and perhaps foremost, is the simple fact that sheep that are in good health are free from all the trying and annoying ailments of parasitism and disease that so frequently decimate sheep. He does not have to worry about sick or crippled animals. They are thriving under his care.

Second, it means that most of his time and attention

can be devoted to the development and care of the
entire ranch. This will assure his stock of an ideal
environment in which they can prosper. He can supply
abundant pasturage, clean water supplies, proper
shelter, protection from predators, ample range, and
ideal management in every area of the ranch operation.

This is the best guarantee that the flock in his ownership will derive maximum benefit from his expertise.

Third, his own reputation and name as an esteemed
sheepman is reflected in the performance of his flock.
All of his expertise and affection for the sheep is shown
by how they prosper under his watchful eye. When they
are thriving he also benefits. Not only does he prosper
but he feels richly rewarded in soul for all his strength
and life actually poured into them.

Put another way it may be said that the outpouring of
his own being is to be seen in the excellence of his stock.
It is very much a demonstration of the eternal principle
that what a man gets out of life is what he puts into it.

Reflecting back over my own years as a sheepman I
recall clearly those happy, contented times when I literally revelled in the well-being of my sheep. Visitors
would often remark how contented and flourishing my
flock appeared. But only I knew how much work, effort,
tireless attention, and never-ending diligence had been
expended on my part for this to be possible.

My sheep had literally been the recipients of my life.
It had been shared with them abundantly and unstint-
ingly. Nothing was ever held back. All that I possessed
was in truth poured out unremittingly in order that
together we should prosper. The strength of my young
body, the keen enthusiasm of my spirit, the energy of
my mind, the alertness of my emotions, the thrust and

drive of my disposition were all directed to the well-being of my flock. And it showed in abundant measure.

This is the graphic picture our Lord had in His mind when He stated simply, 'I am come that they might have life, and that they might have it more abundantly. I am the good shepherd: the good shepherd giveth his life for the sheep.'

If we pause to reflect here a moment we must see that any person is 'good' in whatever he undertakes to the degree in which he devotes and dedicates himself to it. A 'good violinist' becomes a good violinist only by putting his time, talents, and attention into his art and instrument. Likewise a 'good runner' becomes a top athlete only to the extent that he will invest his strength and energy and interest in his sport. And the degree to which anyone becomes 'good' is the length to which he will go in giving himself unhesitatingly to his chosen vocation.

Thus, in speaking of our Good Shepherd we are compelled to consider the enormous generosity with which He gives Himself to us without stint. The very nature and character of God, exemplified in Christ, convinces us beyond any doubt that He literally pours Himself out on our behalf. All of the eternal, ongoing activities and energetic enterprises of God have been designed that we might share His abundant life.

We are not, as the people of His pasture, merely the recipients of good gifts which He dispenses to us in random fashion from afar. To think this way is to be terribly impoverished in our lives.

For much of my early Christian life I laboured under this delusion. To me God was a distant deity. If perchance I needed extra strength or wisdom or patience to face some perplexing problem He who resided off in the immensity of space somewhere could be appealed to for help and support in my dilemma. If my conduct was commendable He would probably, hopefully, cooperate. He would condescend to comply with my requests. If all went well He might just drop down a bit of wisdom or strength or patience to meet my need for the moment.

To imagine or assume that this is abundant life, or abundant living, is a caricature of the true Christian life. Yet multitudes of God's people struggle along this way. Their lives are impotent and impoverished because of it.

The simple truth is that the abundant, dynamic life of God can be ours continuously. It is not something handed out in neat little packages as we pray for it sporadically.

A man or woman has the life of God to the extent that he or she has God. We have the peace of God to the extent that we experience the presence of Christ. We enjoy the joy of the Lord to the degree we are indwelt by the very Spirit of God. We express the love of God to the measure we allow ourselves to be indwelt by God Himself.

God is not 'way out there somewhere.' He is here! He not only resides within anyone who will receive Him, but equally important is the fact that He completely enfolds and surrounds us with His presence. He is the essence of both our inner life and outer life. 'O God, You are here! O Christ, You have come that I might have abundant life. O gracious Spirit, You are as invisible as the wind yet as real as the air that surrounds me, which I inhale to energize my body! You are within and without.

'It is in You, O my God, that I live and move and have

my being. You are the environment from which my total life is derived. You are the energy and dynamic of my whole being. Every good and every perfect bestowal is derived from You. The vitality of my spirit, the energy of my emotions, the drive of my disposition, the powerful potential of my mind, the vigour of my body; in fact, every facet of my total, abundant life is a reflection of Your life, O Lord, being lived out in me and through me.'

To become aware of this is to become charged mightily with the abundant life of God, in Christ, by His Spirit. This is to experience being 'in Christ,' and 'Christ in me.' This is to *know* God. This is to enjoy eternal life, the life of the eternal One being expressed through my person. This is, as Paul put it, 'knowing Christ and the power of his resurrection.'

This life of God, given so freely to us in an undiminished supply from an inexhaustible source, is not intended to end in us. We are not an end in ourselves. The abundant outpouring of God's life to His people is intended to be an overflowing, out-giving, ongoing disposal of His benefits to others around us. More than this, it is designed to bring pleasure, delight, and blessing back to our Lord Himself. It is not just a case of His blessings being bestowed on us, but also our abundant lives in return being a blessing to Him.

Bless the Lord, O my soul: and all that is within me, bless his holy name. Bless the Lord, O my soul, and forget not all his benefits

(Psalm 103:1–2).

The full and complete awareness of this concept of abundant Christian living can come to us only as we grasp the nature and character of God, our Father. The Scriptures reveal Him to be love. By that is meant not a selfish, self-indulgent, sentimental love, but its opposite.

The love of God spoken of so extensively is total selflessness. It is God, in Christ, sharing Himself with us unhesitatingly. It is He giving Himself in glad, wholehearted abandonment to us. It is God pouring Himself out for His people. It is God losing Himself in our little lives that we might know the abundance of His life. It is God giving Himself to us without measure in overflowing abundance so that in turn His life spills out from ours to go running over our weary old world in streams of refreshing.

The life of God comes to us in many ways. So majestic and marvellous are they that this little book cannot begin to list or catalogue them all. The life of God given to men is the same life that energizes the entire cosmos. It sustains the universe. It is the essence of being.

The best a mere mortal can do is to go quietly to some place, still, alone, there to meditate before the splendour of our God.

I sense something of His glory in the wonders of the world He made: the flaming sunrises and sunsets that still the soul; the awesome grandeur of mighty mountain ranges and sweeping plains; the restless roar of ocean waves and winds and tides; the fragrance of forests or the green glory of rich grasslands; the austere stillness and rugged solitude of gaunt deserts; the delicate beauty of flowers, trees, and shrubs; the incredible diversity of insects, birds, and mammals; the beauty of sun and cloud, snow and rain.

All of these contribute something to the total environment which supports and sustains me. Each in its own way contributes to the well-being of my person. They energize and feed my body. They stimulate and quicken my soul. They enrich my spirit. They make me what I am ... a man sensitive, receptive, and alive to the world around me – my Father's world – His provision for my well-being, joy, and abundant life. He has come. He has made it all possible. He has put it at my disposal for full and enriched living.

All that is sublime, beautiful, dignified, noble, and grand has this as its source. The finest in our literature, music, arts, science, and social intercourse has its base in the generous giving of our Lord. All that contributes to our physical health, energy, and acumen as individuals is grounded in the good gifts and undiminished life of God poured out to us upon the planet.

And yet in His magnanimous and magnificent generosity He does not just leave it at that. God has deliberately chosen to articulate Himself in terms I can comprehend. He has spoken. His Word has been received, recorded, and reproduced in human writing. He has not withheld His will or wishes from us earthlings in mystical obscurity. It is possible to know precisely what He is like. He has articulated Himself in meticulous terms understandable to man. He has given us clear and concise self-revelations as to His gracious character, impeccable conduct, and friendly conversation. We know who it is with whom we have to do. He does not deal with us according to our foibles and failings, but in amazing mercy and gracious kindness, as our Father.

As though all of this is not enough, He has gone even

further in coming to us as God in man. He, the living God in Christ, has come among us, wholly identified with us in our human condition and human dilemma. He has not spared Himself. He was born among us, lived among us, worked among us, served among us, taught among us, died among us, rose among us, and ascended among us to reclaim and repossess His place of prominence.

All of this He did willingly and gladly to deliver us from the plight of our own peril upon the planet. He came to set us free from the folly and foibles of our own perverseness and pride. He gave His life to redeem us from our slavery to sin and selfish self-interests and Satan. He gave Himself to seek and to save us who were lost. He came to call us to Himself. He came to gather us into His family to enfold us in His flock. He gave Himself to make us His own, the recipients of His own abundant, abounding life.

To those few, and they are relatively few, who have responded to His overtures, He still comes, even today, and gives Himself to us by His gracious Spirit. He is with us. He is our counsellor. He is our companion. He is our 'alongside one.' He is our comforter. He is our closest friend. He is here in rich and wondrous intimacy.

'I am come that you might have life, My life, and that you might have it in overflowing abundance.' These are still His words to us today.

CHAPTER 10

ℭ

The Hireling

But he that is an hireling, and not the shepherd, whose
own the sheep are not, seeth the wolf coming, and leaveth
the sheep, and fleeth: and the wolf catcheth them, and
scattereth the sheep.
The hireling fleeth, because he is an hireling, and careth
not for the sheep.

(John 10:12–13)

Our Lord used contrast for dynamic effect. It was one of
the secrets of His remarkable, arresting teaching. He used
contrast to display in bold, bright strokes the great truths
we human beings have such difficulty in comprehending.

He told about the rich man and the poor beggar
Lazarus who lay at his doorstep. He recounted the incident of the haughty, proud Pharisee praying while the
contrite publican struck his breast begging for mercy.
He contrasted the prodigal with his very 'proper' elder
brother. And now, in this parable, Christ brings before
us the behaviour of a hireling as it is contrasted with the
Good Shepherd in caring for sheep.

Our Lord previously pointed out how the people of
God's pasture could, under His control, enjoy an abundant, rich life with Him.

He made clear how God's life, poured out in rich measure on my behalf, enables me to enjoy abundant living in every area: physical, mental, moral, emotional, and spiritual. He told how life in Him contributes to a wholesomeness and holiness of unique quality; that it is entirely possible for a man or woman to be so intimately associated with God as to reflect His character to a sceptical society.

Yet, in bold contrast to all of the foregoing, Jesus made it clear that not all sheep were under a good shepherd. Some suffered because of the bad behaviour of hireling shepherds.

During the time of our Lord's sojourn in Palestine, servants were of two sorts. They were either bond or free. They were either slaves owned outright by their masters or free people who worked temporarily for meagre wages. In fact, because of slavery, the worth and dignity of a human being was much less esteemed than it was in a free society. After all, if people could be bought and sold at random in a slave market they were really not of much more value than cattle or furniture.

It will be recalled that when Judas bartered with the high priests for the betrayal of his Master, the price of thirty pieces of silver was agreed upon. This was the going price, then, of a slave in the slave market.

If a slave served his owner well and the two became attached to each other, the master often offered to set him free. The slave could then choose either to go free or become a bond slave or bond servant. Of his own free will he could choose to remain, for the rest of his life, as a servant who, because of his love for the master, chose to remain in his family.

To confirm this the owner would take his slave to the

doorpost of his home. Placing the slave's ear against it, he would pierce the lobe with an awl, pinning it momentarily to the post. This drew blood. This indicated that a bond was sealed for life, and that this slave had in fact become a love servant for the remainder of his days. He would never leave that family. He would be ever faithful to his owner. He was a part of that household. Their life was his. His life was theirs.

There was none of this devotion about a hireling. A hireling had no permanence. He was a casual labourer who came and went at will in a rather haphazard way. He would be here today and gone tomorrow. He was essentially a transient worker. He took no special interest in his job. As soon as a few shekels jingled in the deep folds of his loin cloth he was gone. He would seldom settle down or take any responsibility seriously. His average wage in Jesus' day was a penny a day. The less work he could do to earn this the better it suited him. Like a dandelion seed drifting on the wind he floated about the country looking for the softest spot to land. And if the place did not please him he would soon take off for another.

Sometimes, but not often, one of these drifters would be employed to tend sheep in the owner's absence. It was seldom a satisfactory arrangement. For that reason our Lord used the hireling to represent those who were entrusted with the sheep, but had no real love or concern for them. The secret to successful livestock husbandry is an essential love for the animals under one's care. And this the hireling lacked. He had no stake in the flock. They were not his. He could care less what became of them. They were but the means whereby he could make his 'fast buck,' and then get out.

The Hireling

As a young man of twenty-five I was entrusted with the management and development of a large livestock ranching operation in central British Columbia. There were thirty-six men on the various crews hired to run the ranch. We were in a rather remote, though choice, area, where the glamour and glitter of cities seemed far away.

Among us there was a common joke that we really had three crews: one was coming; the second was working temporarily; and the third was leaving. These were all hired men, passing through, who stayed in this remote and lonely location only until they had gathered up enough to move on to a more desirable job.

In bold contrast I recall vividly the love, loyalty, and undivided devotion of the Masai in East Africa to their animals. For the years we lived among them I never ceased to marvel at the incredible fortitude of these people in providing the best care they could for their livestock. No price was too high to pay to protect their stock from predators. Why? Because they owned them. They had a stake in them. They loved them. They were not hirelings.

Just a few days after we moved into the Masai country, a small, slim boy about ten years old was carried up to our house. He had, single-handed, tackled a young lioness that tried to kill one of his flock. In total self-abandonment and utter bravery he had managed to spear the lion. The mauling he took almost cost him his life. We rushed him to the nearest hospital twenty-seven miles away where his young life was spared, as by a thread. But why did he do this? Because the sheep were his. His love and honour and loyalty were at stake. He would not spare himself. He was not a hireling.

God has, all through history, entrusted the care of

His sheep to so-called undershepherds. And not all of them have proven to be as loyal as the Masai lad, nor as brave as young David, later Israel's great king, who slew the lion and the bear that came to raid his father's flock.

Inevitably in the nature of human affairs there appear those who pretend to be genuine but are not. The ancient prophets of Israel cried out again and again against those who posed as shepherds to God's people, but who instead only plundered them for their own selfish ends.

And the word of the Lord came unto me, saying, Son of man, prophesy against the shepherds of Israel, prophesy, and say unto them, Thus saith the Lord God unto the shepherds; Woe be to the shepherds of Israel that do feed themselves! Should not the Shepherds feed the flocks?
Ye eat the fat, and ye clothe you with the wool, ye kill them that are fed: but ye feed not the flock. The diseased have ye not strengthened, neither have ye healed that which was sick, neither have ye bound up that which was broken, neither have ye brought again that which was driven away, neither have ye sought that which was lost;
But with force and with cruelty have ye ruled them.
And they were scattered, because there is no shepherd: and they became meat to all the beasts of the field, when they were scattered.
My sheep wandered through all the mountains, and upon every high hill: Yea, my flock was scattered upon all the face of the earth, and none did search or seek after them.

(Ezekiel 34:1–6)

The same situation prevailed in Jesus' time. Those who posed as the protectors and leaders of the people, the priests, Pharisees, scribes and Sadducees, were but rank opportunists who plundered and abused the people. The rake-off in the temple trade alone in Jerusalem exceeded $35,000,000 a year. Most of it went to line the pockets and oil the palms of the oppressors. Little wonder Christ went storming through the temple to clear it of its counterfeit activities shouting, 'You will not make my Father's house, a place of plunder ... a den of thieves!'

His confrontation was always with the ecclesiastical hierarchy of His times. They were not true shepherds. They did not love their charges. They did not care deeply for those in their care. They never wept over the plight of their people who were sheep gone astray. They were hirelings. They were there to grab what they could get for themselves.

Is it any wonder our Lord thundered out His great imprecations against them? Here, He the great Good Shepherd, saw His people abused and betrayed by those who had no interest in them whatever.

And the same applies to all church history since His day. God's people have always been parasitized by imposters. Men have worked with the flock only for what they could get out of it; not for what they could contribute to the well-being of their people.

It was this sort of thing that nearly ruined me as a young man. There was within my spirit a strange, powerful, deep desire to *know* God. I literally thirsted and hungered for spiritual sustenance. I longed to be fed truth that would satisfy my innermost craving.

Sunday after Sunday my wife and I would attend whatever churches we could. Some of them were small and struggling. Others were large and pretentious.

Some of the preachers were proper and orthodox but seldom shepherds. Again and again I came hoping to be fed, but there was nothing.

Frustrated and angry I would storm home, and vow never to enter a church again. 'I'm like a sheep going to the feed trough hoping to find hay or grain, and there is only dust and chaff!' I would storm to my gentle wife. In her wisdom, kindness, and patience she would prevail on me to keep going, for sooner or later she was sure a few straws would be found here and there.

Why was this? Because many of the men who were supposed to be shepherding God's people were only hirelings. They were in the job for what they could get out of it. It was obvious they spent no time communing with Christ. It was clear the Scriptures were not a *living* Word to them. They had no great love either for God or for His people. What happened to their charges really did not seem to matter.

Eventually some of these men came to know me personally, but even after they had entered into our lives, their casual indifference and lack of genuine concern astonished me.

In one community I attended services diligently for nearly four years. At the end of that time I had been taught virtually nothing. I was a stranger in a far country, away from my home land, but no shepherd seemed to care for my soul.

At that period in my life I was under tremendous attack from the enemy of my soul. Almost daily I was exposed to onslaughts against the great truths of God's revelation in His Word. Subtle suggestions and crafty cynicism were working havoc in my convictions. The wolves were at work on me but there was no shepherd around who really seemed to be concerned about this wandering sheep.

Alone and unattended I fled for safety. I knew not really where to run. Like a sheep blinded with fear and seized with panic I simply turned to run in my own stupid way. And the result was that I went far astray. I ended up far from my Good Shepherd. The hirelings had literally let me fend for myself.

The net result can be expressed in the words of the grand old prophet Ezekiel:

For thus saith the Lord God; Behold, I, even I, will both search my sheep, and seek them out.
As a shepherd seeketh out his flock in the day that he is among his sheep that are scattered; so will I seek out my sheep, and will deliver them out of all places where they have been scattered in the cloudy and dark day.

(Ezekiel 34:11–12)

Only the tender compassion of Christ, only the understanding of the true Shepherd of my soul, only the gentle overtures of the gracious Spirit of God could ever retrieve this wild and wayward one from the cloudy and dark days of his despair. Because in His patience and perseverance He pursued me along my wayward path, because He gathered me up again and drew me back once more in selfless love, was I saved. And for this I shall be eternally grateful to my God.

But what desperate despair I could have been spared if only someone had cared for my soul at that stage of my life. Those to whom I looked for help were only hirelings. They would not stand up to the enemy. They would not engage the wolves that were raiding my life and the lives of others. They would not risk a confrontation. They simply turned tail and left us to be torn and scattered.

The same is still true. There are ministers, teachers, scholars, writers, and leaders who pose as champions of Christianity. But when the enemy comes in they are shown in their true colours. They back away rather than risk a confrontation. They settle for withdrawal rather than beard the lion or bear, or assail the wolf.

They turn and flee in the face of violent attack. Others remain silent while their people are deceived, harried, and driven to despair. Only the Good Shepherd cares enough for His own to lay down His life for them.

It must be He who, living His life through and in His true undershepherds, enables them also to lay down their lives for the sheep. They must be prepared and willing to be expendable for the sake of others. They are not hirelings, they are His slaves of love. Paul calls himself 'a bondservant of Jesus Christ.'

Men or women who enter God's service should regard this as an enormous responsibility not only before God but also to those whom they serve. It is something which is not undertaken lightly or casually for personal gain, but with an eye to eternal consequences.

In any enterprise where we are co-workers with Christ there is incumbent upon us the obligation to realize that this is not a hit-or-miss affair. His view of His work in the world is a sincere and serious one. And He expects that those who enter His enterprises will take a similar attitude.

When we give ourselves to serve the Lord, the

primary motivation should not be one of personal gain or advantage. Rather, the predominant desire ought to be one of serving the Master out of love and gratitude for His goodness to us. We are freely, willingly choosing to be a benefit to others, not just for their sakes or our own self-gratification, but for His sake.

It is only the undershepherd, whose first and foremost devotion and consecration is to Christ, who can stand up to the strains and stresses of shepherding. If one's devotion is only to people, deep, disappointing disillusionments are bound to come. But for the one whose service is centred in Christ there comes the strength and serenity to meet all the storms.

We love Him because He first loved us.

We love others because He first loved us.

We love at all because He first loved us.

This is what it means to be a love slave and not a hireling.

CHAPTER 11

The Shepherd Knows His Sheep and They Know Him

I am the good shepherd, and know my sheep, and am known of mine.

(John 10:14)

In all of Scripture this must surely be one of the most reassuring statements made by our Lord to His people. Oh, the wonder and joy of being known by God! The strength and consolation of being in the care of Christ who fully and completely understands us!

Such awareness and such knowing stills our spirits, soothes our souls, and fills us with quiet awe. 'O God, You do know me through and through.'

The ultimate measure of a good shepherd is how well he knows his sheep. Just as we might say that the measure of a good artist or a good gardener or a good mechanic is the extent to which he 'knows' the materials with which he works.

This 'knowing' implies much more than just mere acquaintance or contact with sheep. It means the shepherd is so familiar with his sheep, has handled them so much, that he knows their every trait, habit, and characteristic. He can predict their behaviour under any given set of circumstances. He understands all their peculiarities. He is never surprised or taken aback by their unusual idiosyncrasies. He is at ease with them, comfortable in their company, delighting in their management.

The full impact of this unique relationship between livestock and their owners came home to me with enormous impact during the years my family and I lived among the Masai people of East Africa. These nomadic livestock owners believed implicitly that to them, and only them, had God given the original responsibility for husbanding livestock.

The Masai were tremendously proud of their supposed management skills with sheep and cattle. They entertained a haughty superiority toward anyone else who tended stock. And much of their claim to fame in this field was based on their knowing individual animals intimately.

In part their pride was justified. The animals under their care were their very life. They gave themselves to them with unstinted devotion. No demand was too tough nor any risk too hazardous to insure their well-being. They would go to any lengths, day or night, to protect them and care for them.

But over and beyond all this lay the incredible intimacy and personal awareness each owner had for his own charges. Many of the lambs, kids, and calves had been hand-reared within the affection of the family circle. They were fondled, hugged, caressed, and called by cute pet names. Bonds of enduring affection were forged from birth that the ensuing years could never break.

Again and again I would watch, awe-struck, as one of

the Masai would go up to one of his favourite beasts in the field and spend time caressing it. He would speak to it in endearing terms. He would examine and scrutinize it carefully, checking to see that all was well. This was not something done only on rare occasions. It was a normal part of the appealing relationship between shepherd and sheep.

Some of the fondest memories that came back to me from those years on Africa's sun-drenched plains are wrapped up in small boys shepherding sheep. I can still see them holding lambs gently in their arms. I can see them calling to their pets who came running at the sound of their voices. I can see the obvious pleasure and delight with which the sheep revelled in this attention. They sensed and knew all was well when they were in their owner's embrace. Here was safety and assurance. They were known.

When we turn our attention to our own lives in the care of the Good Shepherd we discover some powerful parallels. If we can grasp them they may well revolutionize our whole relationship to God.

It is essential for us to face the fact that God has known us from our earliest beginnings. By that I do not mean just collectively as a race of people upon the planet, but in a much more private and personal way as an individual human being from the hour of my conception in my mother's womb.

Such knowledge alone startles some of us.

In fact some find it alarming.

Amid a society where, especially in large urban centres, it is possible to live almost anonymously, this is shattering.

We in the western world have become extremely

skilled at living behind a false facade. We wear masks. Seldom do we disclose our true identity. We try to present a brave front to the world, even though within we may be shattered, broken people. We proceed on the assumption that most people really don't know us and don't care. We often run a bluff on others, based on the premise that they will not or cannot be bothered to really find us out.

The net result is that for many, life becomes a sham. It is almost playacting. It is played by people playing little games with each other. Much of it is really make-believe. It lacks depth, honesty, or sincerity. People become phonies, they are riddled with scepticism and cynicism. They really don't know where they are at.

Against this background of confused and bewildered life God steps onto the stage and states dramatically, surely, and without apology, 'I know you! I understand you! I have known all about you all the time!'

Just the thought of such 'knowing,' of such insights terrifies most people. In their phony pretence they want to run, to flee, to escape, to hide behind their masks.

But for others of us, this knowing comes at long last as a great relief, a great release from our restless roaming. 'O Lord,' our spirit cries out, 'at last I have been found. Now I am found out. I am known! I can step out of the shadows of my own stumbling steps into the full splendour of Your knowledge. Take me. Search me. Examine me carefully. Put me right. Let me be Yours. And please, You be mine!'

It is only when a person sees himself as known before God that he will get serious with Him. Until this happens we go on playing our pathetic little games with Him. We behave as though we were indeed doing Him a great favour to allow Him to draw near. What colossal conceit! What incredible stupidity. How long will we delude ourselves?

In contrast David, himself a shepherd, cried out exultingly in Psalm 139:

O Lord, thou hast searched me and known me. Thou knowest my downsitting and mine uprising, thou understandest my thought afar off. Thou compassest my path and my lying down, and art acquainted with all my ways. For there is not a word in my tongue, but, Lo, O Lord, thou knowest it altogether. Thou hast beset me behind and before, and laid thine hand upon me. Such knowledge is too wonderful for me; it is high, I cannot attain unto it. Whither shall I go from thy spirit? Or whither shall I flee from thy presence? If I ascend up into heaven, thou art there: If I make my bed in hell, behold, thou art there. If I take the wings of the morning, and dwell in the uttermost parts of the sea; Even there shall thy hand lead me, and thy right hand shall hold me. If I say, Surely the darkness shall cover me; even the night shall be light about me. Yea, the darkness hideth not from thee; but the night shineth as the day: The darkness and the light are both alike to thee. For thou hast possessed my reins: Thou hast covered me in my mother's womb. I will praise thee; for I am fearfully and wonderfully made: marvellous are thy works; and that my soul knoweth right well.

(vv. 1–14)

Before such affirmations we are stilled. In wonder and joy we are awed. 'O Great, Good Shepherd of my soul, how wondrous to know that You know me!'

For the Christian this awareness can become a potent

power in his walk with God. An enormous desire to be open and honest with his Master will descend upon him. The mask will be removed from him by the Spirit of God as He works in his life. A sense of earnestness and simple sincerity will replace the superficiality of his former life style.

He will take God seriously. He will begin to obey His Word. He will be sensitive to the voice of His gracious Spirit. He will allow no petty pride or other obstacle of self-will to obstruct the movement of God's Spirit in his life. He will allow himself to come under Christ's control.

In contrast to the world's way of working, God, by His Spirit, begins to do His work at the centre of our beings. The world's view is that if an ideal environment of better housing, hygiene, health, and nutrition is supplied, along with improved education, man will become better and better. History has repeatedly demonstrated the fallacy of this idea.

God's approach is the opposite. His gracious Spirit touches and enlivens man's spirit. If allowed to, He will illuminate the whole inner life. He will permeate the total personality transforming the disposition, emotions, and mind. The net result will be that the remade man will alter his whole environment.

A good environment does not guarantee good men.

But noble men do generate an improved environment.

So God's Spirit begins His re-creative work within us by touching our spirits. He makes us alive to what is right and what is wrong. He impresses upon us what we 'ought to do' and what we 'ought not do.' We become acutely God-conscious. We are aware of what He wants. We know His wishes. We are alerted to His aims and ambitions for us.

This is what it means to have a Christian conscience. We wish to cooperate with Christ. He knows us. We know Him. We have common interests.

Likewise in the area of our communion with Him, we begin to discover that there can be an ongoing discourse between us. He speaks to me. I speak to Him. This intercourse finds full expression in prayer, praise, petitions, and personal awareness that He is ever present.

It takes time to do this. It is profound. It cannot be hurried or rushed. The man who would know God must be prepared to give time to Him.

It is tremendously helpful to speak privately but audibly to the Lord. Let Him know you love Him, that you are fond of Him, that you are deeply grateful for all His kindness.

Not long ago I visited an elderly lady who claimed she had known Christ for more than thirty years. I asked her if she enjoyed conversing with Him quietly in the privacy of her own elegant home. I inquired if she ever told Him how much she loved Him.

Her response was an outburst of embarrassed laughter. 'Oh,' she blurted out blushingly, 'only you would ever suggest such a thing, Phillip.' But I left her home wondering just how well she really knew the Good Shepherd.

In his first epistle the apostle Peter put it this way: 'Unto you therefore which believe he is precious' (1 Peter 2:7).

Why? Because I am His and He knows me through and through. And even though He knows the worst, He still loves me with an everlasting love.

This knowing is the great central theme that runs like

a chord of gold all through John's first epistle. To know the love of God. To know that we have His life. To know that He hears us. To know that we belong to Him, etc.

Such knowledge is strength. It is stability. It is serenity. It is the solid assurance upon which my relationship to the Good Shepherd stands secure.

There is nothing ambiguous or vague about it. There are no ifs, maybes, perhaps, supposes, or assuming it may be so. I know!

As the Spirit of Christ expands His influence within my life He will begin to penetrate my personality. If allowed to do so He can pervade my mind, emotions, and disposition.

No doubt the ultimate, acid test of Christianity is the dramatic and beneficial changes wrought in the personality and character of people. Weak become strong. Deceivers become honest. Vile become noble. Vicious become gentle. Selfish become selfless.

Perhaps the area in which there is the most cover-up is that of our minds. Most people live very private thought lives. Even within the intimate family circle it is possible to retire and withdraw into the inner sanctum of our minds and imaginations.

Were some of the scenes there enacted, to be exposed, it would shock and startle our family and friends to find what sort of world we moved in mentally.

It is sobering to realize, 'O God, you know all my thoughts.' It is equally solemnizing to remind ourselves always, 'And, O God, I know You know!'

This is a purifying discipline. In the presence of His impeccable person it humbles, cleanses, and converts me, turning me from the wickedness of my ways to walk softly in His sight.

As He is allowed to move into my emotions the same process is at work. The same eternal promise holds true. There can be no pretext, no pretence, no playing around, pretending to be so pleasant or pious while within we seethe and boil with pent-up perverseness. 'O Lord, You know me!'

With other human beings ill will, hatred, bitterness, envy, old grudges, jealousy, and numerous other heinous attitudes may be masked with a casual shrug of the shoulder or forced half smile. But we simply cannot pull the wool over God's all-seeing eyes. We may kid ourselves that we are getting away with the cover-up, but we don't kid God.

Over and over, when our Lord moved among us as a man, He emphasized the importance in His estimation of our inner attitudes. They were the ultimate criteria to a man's character. He simply could not tolerate false pretenders, who, though appearing to shine like mausoleums in the sun, were filled with dead men's bones.

'O God, You know my anger, resentment, impatience, hostility, and many other evil emotions; I know You know.'

What is the solution? Somehow my soul must be cleansed. The debris and dung of a thousand terrible thoughts and imaginations must be swept from my life. It is my sins and iniquities which have come between me and my God. Where is the solution?

I am ever reminded of Hercules who was given the impossible assignment of cleansing the gigantic Aegaen stables. Thousands of horses had deposited their dung within its walls until a literal mountain of manure engulfed the place.

Hercules knew full well, even in his own great strength, that he could never remove the accumulated filth. Instead, he went high into the hills and there found a rushing mountain stream. He diverted it from its course and directed its clear flowing waters through the huge stables. In a short time the surging stream had flushed away all the dung. The stables stood clean because of the sparkling water from the high country.

It is a sublime picture of the wondrous work God's gracious Spirit can effect in a Christian's life. Only as He is allowed to surge freely through the rooms and galleries of my inner life can they ever be cleansed from the dark thoughts, the evil imaginations, the angry emotions, and evil decisions of my disposition.

If in open honesty and genuine earnestness I come to Christ and open my person to Him, He will come in. He will penetrate every part of me. He will purify. He will fill with His presence. His peace will permeate me. His power will be mine in inner strength.

This power will enable me to make proper decisions. His presence at work within me will empower me to both will and do His good pleasure. I shall find harmony and unity between Him and myself. There will be common purposes, common aims, common joys we share. Why? Because He knows me and I know Him.

These titanic changes which can be effected within my spirit and soul by God, can likewise be accomplished in my body. It is He who designed and fashioned men and women in all of their complexities. He knows and fully understands all the instincts, desires, and appetites of our physical make-up.

As we allow ourselves to come gently and increasingly

under His control, we will find it affects how we handle our bodies. They will be nurtured and treated with respect. They will not be abused or misused. We will find it possible to so discipline ourselves and direct our activities that even in our bodies there will be a blessing, and that not only a benefit to us but also a benediction to others.

It is possible for God's people to live in moderation, wisdom, and exuberant joy. We can so conduct ourselves amid a corrupt society and sick culture that we are a credit to our Master.

We can practice moderation in our daily habits. It is as much God's good will for me to eat wholesome food, drink pure drinks, enjoy regular rest, revel in regular exercise, and relish the beauty of His creation as it is to go to church. All is sacred and sublime when touched by the delight of His presence with me.

I do not know Him only within the confines of a cathedral. I do not meet Him only within the pages of a Bible or in the still moments of meditation. I can encounter and commune with Christ my Shepherd anywhere along the long winding trails of life that we walk together.

My walk with God need not in any sense be a spectacular display of special dedication. It need not have any carnival atmosphere about it to be convincing. I don't have to indulge in theatrics to impress either Him or other human beings.

What He desires most is that I walk with Him humbly, quietly, and obediently. The communion between shepherd and sheep is sweet and secure because *He knows me* and *I know Him!*

CHAPTER 12

C

One Flock of One Shepherd

As the Father knoweth me, even so know I the Father: and I lay down my life for the sheep. And other sheep I have, which are not of this fold: them also I must bring, and they shall hear my voice; and there shall be one fold (flock), and one shepherd.

(John 10:15–16)

This is an appropriate point at which to pause for a moment in studying this parable. Always it is important to keep in mind a clear picture of the setting in which our Lord made His statements.

A young man was born blind. His eyesight was restored by Christ and then he discovered who his benefactor was. In his incredible gratitude the healed man rejoiced not only in new-found physical sight, but also in new-found spiritual sight. He actually *saw* Jesus as his great deliverer, his Saviour, his Redeemer. Though he had been excommunicated and cut off from any further association with the religious leaders, this was only a small loss – for he had found the Christ. He had come to know Him who could give great meaning and direction to his previously derelict life. In humble awe he believed. And with touching appreciation he worshipped Jesus, bowing down before Him in glad submission.

This act of obeisance scandalized and horrified the Jews. They were infuriated even further when the Master made it clear that it was in fact they, who thought they saw and knew and understood spiritual realities, who were blind. The accusation enraged them. Like a pack of bloodhounds closing in on their prey, they encircled Him, bent on His destruction. Their blood boiled. Their eyes blazed with hate.

This next statement Jesus makes – 'As the Father knoweth me, even so know I the Father' – was outrageous enough that they charged Him with being utterly insane, if not possessed of a demon.

Of course, it was proof positive of their own self-delusion. They stood confronted by the One who was the light of the world but whose presence only accentuated their own dreadful darkness. They were encountering heaven's royalty in disguise. Yet they rejected God's anointed Prince of Peace with impassioned pride. He who stood encircled by them came from God, knew God, was very God, but they were totally blind to His being.

In just a few more moments they would pick up rocks from the ground ready to break His bones and dash out His brains. If they could not still Him with spiritual arguments, they could slay Him with stones. Men forever try to silence God, but He does not go away that easily. He always has the last word.

It was not within man's power, nor will it ever be, to do away with God. If His life was to be put on the line, it would be at the time of His own choosing and in the manner of His own choice. No man would deprive Him of this honour or privilege. Jesus later made this clear to His would-be assassins.

What so enraged them was His claim to divinity. 'I know the Father. The Father knows me.' There was nothing vague or tenuous about this intimate relationship. It was not a knowing of hearsay or secondhand acquaintance. It was in truth a knowing of the most profound, personal sort. It implied the interaction of co-equals, the unequivocal unity of total oneness. Jesus, in His final statement to His foes on this important occasion, said, 'I and my Father are one!'

This straightforward claim to deity completely undid His audience. And it has been the stone over which uncounted millions have stumbled since.

Unless we grasp the profound and enormous implications of this claim of Christ to being known and knowing God, all the other remarks made later will have no relevance. I say this in sincerity to remind the reader that our Lord was not just a good man; He was also the great God in human guise. His claims to a special knowledge and relationship with His Father were recognized by the Jews as outright insistence on His personal deity.

Not only were they unwilling to accept Him as such, but the same has been true for most men during the past twenty centuries.

If we are to 'see,' if we are to 'understand,' we must face the formidable fact that this One was none other than God. He was the God of the Godhead who knew from before the creation of planet earth what plans were made to preserve and restore human beings to a proper relationship with Himself.

He was the God who would have to identify Himself

with men in their darkness and dilemma of despair and deception. He would have to interpose His own pure and impeccable life on their behalf, as a substitute for their grievous sins that incurred the judgment of a righteous God. He who knew no sin, of necessity had to be made sin with our wrongdoings, in order that we might be made right with His amazing righteousness.

Only as He Himself, in His own person, exhausted and absorbed the penalty for our wrongs in His death, could we be acquitted and set free. This freedom to be His, to follow Him, to become the people He intended, must of necessity be bought for us at an appalling price.

The price paid was His own life. It was His righteous, sublime life poured out as a supreme propitiation for our pride, perverseness, and pollution. This satisfied the awful abhorrence of a selfless God for our selfish sins, but also delivered us from death, alienation, and the despair of our dreadful dilemma.

Like the young man born blind, only a tiny handful of human beings have ever seen or grasped this truth .

In his simplicity and sincerity he had allowed the great Shepherd of his soul to enter the fold of his young life. He had allowed Him to take control. He had allowed the Good Shepherd to claim him as His own.

The cost to him, too, had been great to come into the care of Christ. His contemporaries had cut him off from the synagogue. They had ostracized him from their company. They had heaped scorn and abuse upon him. He had done no wrong. His only misconduct was to come into Christ's care, to become one of His flock.

The flock of God has never been very large.

Our Lord made it clear few would come into His care.

Most of us are sheep who turn to our own way and go astray.

Yet scattered across the world are those who are His.

Down the long avenues of human history the Good Shepherd has been out among us, gathering up those who would come.

With enormous compassion and great tenderness He looked at the young man whose sight had just been restored. 'Other sheep I have, which are not of this fold.' All over the earth there are other lives, individual sheepfolds, scattered like so many sheep astray, whose intimate folds He is eager to enter. This young man's life was but one tiny fold out of uncounted thousands which in their sum total would make up His final flock.

It is important to recognize the difference between a flock and a fold. The shepherd is said to have only one flock. This flock is the sum total of all the sheep which belong to him. But almost always his flock is distributed widely, especially if he is a wealthy owner, among many folds across the country. Put another way, we can say that one sheepman's flock is made up of many different folds. The modern rendering of John 10:16 is much more accurate than the King James version which confuses the reader by stating 'There shall be one *fold*,' rather than, 'There shall be one *flock*,' which is correct and clear.

When we lived among the Masai people of East Africa it impressed me how one livestock owner would have his animals scattered in small groups all across the countryside. One very wealthy man whom I came to know quite well actually owned more than 10,000 head of stock. But these were not all cared for in one place. They were distributed in little clusters here and there, scattered widely among many kraals.

Yet, the sum total of them all comprised his one unit, one herd, one flock under one owner.

It will help the reader to understand this concept if we look at modern farming practices on the prairies. During pioneer days it was common for each individual family to own and operate its own homestead. These small holdings of land comprised either a quarter (160 acres) or half (320 acres) section of land, a full section being one square mile or 640 acres.

With the advent of power equipment and expensive machinery most farmers found they needed more land to justify the investment made in expensive tractors, ploughs, drills, and combines. The upshot was that the more prosperous and efficient farmers began to buy up random quarter or half sections their neighbours might sell them.

The final result has been that today one man's farm may well include numerous pieces of land scattered all across the country at random. Yet he refers to them in total as 'my farm.'

I knew of one wealthy grain grower who owned seventeen different quarter sections. Separately, each was a unit of its own. Collectively they comprised his one farm. The same is true with sheepmen. All their folds together become their one flock under one owner.

Looking now at Christ's flock, we see clearly that it is composed of many different lives (little folds) scattered at random all across the earth. He is ever active and at work bringing men and women into His care and under His control. He gathers them up from the far-flung corners of the world. He has been energetically engaged in this enterprise since the beginning of human history.

A magnificent and splendid overview of Christ's achievements through the centuries is painted for us by John in the Book of Revelation. Under the unction and inspiration of God's own gracious Spirit he writes glowingly this great song.

You are worthy to take the scroll and to open its seals, because you were slain, and with your blood you purchased men for God from every tribe and language and people and nation.
You have made them to be a kingdom and priests to serve our God, and they will reign on the earth.

(Revelation 5:9–10, NIV)

And so the eyes of our spiritual understanding are opened to see our Good Shepherd, relentlessly, tirelessly, eagerly calling to Himself those chosen ones who will respond to His voice and come to His call. He brings them in from every tribe, every language, every race, every nation.

His majestic voice has rung out over all the earth. In unmistakable sounds He calls out to any who will come. With enormous compassion He cries out to men 'Come unto me, all ye that labour and are heavy laden, and I will give you rest.'

None other has ever extended to wayward wanderers such a winsome, warm invitation. But most men spurn it. They turn instead each to their own perverse path that leads into peril and ultimately to perdition.

Yet from out of earth's milling masses a small flock is being faithfully formed. We find members of that flock scattered here and there. By no means are they confined to any one church, denomination, or sect. Rather, they are distributed widely, and spread rather thinly through a multitude of groups and gatherings of diverse doctrines.

It has been my great privilege through the years of my long life to have rich fellowship with other Christians all over the world. My travels have taken me to some forty different countries. The places where I met other people who knew Christ as their Good Shepherd would take a whole book to describe fully. I have stood solemnized in some of the most impressive cathedrals ever erected by man and there sensed and known that others of His flock were with me in the care of Christ. By the same measure I have sat in tiny mud huts in Africa and grass thatch houses in southeast Asia where the Good Shepherd had also gathered up some of His sheep.

You see, the ultimate criteria is not the church, the creed, the form of communion, or even the cherished and contested claims to special spiritual insight which determine a person's position. It is simply this: 'Do they or do they not hear Christ's voice?'

He Himself said emphatically, 'Other sheep I have. Them also I must bring. They shall hear My voice.'

To hear Christ's voice, as was pointed out in a previous chapter, means three essential things.

1. I recognize it is God who calls me to Himself. He graciously invites me to come under His care, to benefit from His management of my life, to accept His provision for me.
2. I respond to His overtures by taking Him seriously. I alert myself to act. I open my life to Him so He may in truth and reality enter to share it with me.
3. I then run to do whatever He wishes. I co-operate

with His desires. I regularly do His will. Thus I enter fully into the greatness of His life, grateful for His care.

This is to 'hear' Christ's call and to respond.

Any man or woman who does this belongs to Him, is a member of His flock, a sheep of His pasture. Our Lord has them here and there in ten thousand times ten thousand tiny folds, each flourishing under His infinite love.

ℭ

Christ Lays Down and Takes Up His Own Life

Therefore doth my father love me, because I lay down my life, that I might take it again. No man taketh it from me, but I lay it down of myself. I have power to lay it down, and I have power to take it again. This commandment have I received of my Father.

(John 10:17–18)

Over and over in this book the point has been made that the hallmark of the Good Shepherd is His willingness to lay down His life for His sheep. It cannot be otherwise. The essential nature of Christ demands it. Because He is love, selfless love, this must be so.

This love of God is the most potent force extant in the universe. It is the primal energy that powers the entire cosmos. It is the basic driving initiative that lies behind every good and noble action. Without it all men of all time would languish in despair. They would grope in darkness. Ultimately they would know only separation from the goodness of God **which is** death.

But – and it is a remarkable 'but' – Christ was willing to leave His glory; to come among us expressing that love, giving tangible form to it in a sacrificial life. I have written of this love at great length in *Rabboni*. Here I quote from its pages without apology: 'With our finite minds we cannot probe but a short distance into the vastness of Christ's pre-earth existence. But with the enlightenment that comes to our spirits by His Spirit we sense and feel the magnitude of His enterprises in arranging and governing the universe.

'Such enlightenment comes from His Spirit. He the Eternal Spirit of the Infinite God; the same Spirit of the Eternal Christ; was simultaneously in everlasting existence with both the Father and The Son, Our Christ. He like them was engaged in the enormous activities that long preceded even the appearance of the planet earth.

'In all the enterprises which engaged this tremendous triumvirate, there was perfect coordination of concept and ultimate unity of purpose in their planning. Unlike human endeavours there was never any discord. Friction was unknown simply because there was no selfish self-interest present. Between God The Father, God The Son (Jesus Christ) and God The Spirit, there flowed love in its most sublime form. in fact this love was of such purity that it constituted the very basis of their beings.

'We earth men can barely conceive of a relationship so sublime that it contains no trace of self-assertion, no ulterior motives for self-gratification. But that is the secret to the strength of God. Here was demonstrated the irresistible force of utter self-lessness. In the total giving of each to the other in profound "caring" for each other lay the love of all eternity. This was love at its loftiest level. This was love at its highest source. This was love, the primal source of all energy.

'Just as there is stored within an atom enormous power because of the inter-action between neutrons, protons and electrons, likewise there was inherent unlimited energy in the Godhead because of the inter-relationship between Father, Son and Spirit. And the essence of this energy was love.

'In that outer world love was the moving force behind every action. Love was the energizing influence at work in every enterprise. It was the very fabric woven into every aspect of Christ's life. It was in fact the basic raw material used ultimately to fashion and form all subsequent matter.

'To the reader this may seem a bit obscure, a bit beyond belief. But if we pause to find parallels upon our planet, earth, we may soon see the picture in practical terms. What is the most irresistible force upon the earth? Love? What pulverizes strong prejudice and builds enduring allegiance? Love? What binds men together in indestructible devotion? Love? What under-lies all generous and magnanimous actions? Love? What is the source of strength for men and women who gladly serve and die for one another? Love? What ener-gizes the loftiest and most noble enterprise of human hearts and minds? Love? If this be true of selfish mortal men, then how much more is it the very life of God – And this is the life of Christ.

'It was in the setting of a realm permeated by love that the generous thought of sharing it with others came into being. Of course it could scarcely be other-wise. For if heaven was such a happy home it would scarcely have been consistent for God to want to keep it to Himself. Love insists on sharing.

'So the concept was born of love that other sons and daughters should be brought into being who could participate in the delights of paradise. That such a remarkably generous endeavour was even considered is in keeping with the character of God. He chose to do this in love and out of love simply because of who He is.'

Praise be to God and Father of our Lord Jesus Christ for giving us through Christ every possible spiritual benefit as citizens of Heaven! For consider what he has done – before the foundation of the world he chose us to become, in Christ, his holy and blameless children living within His constant care. He planned, in his purpose of love, that we should be adopted as his own children through Jesus Christ – that we might learn to praise that glorious generosity of his which has made us welcome in the everlasting love he bears toward his Beloved.

(Ephesians 1:3–6, *Phillips*)

'Like all other divine enterprises it undoubtedly first found expression in the mind of God The Father. Yet it was agreed to completely by God The Son and fully endorsed by God The Holy Spirit.'

All of this Christ did deliberately, freely, gladly out of His own generous good will toward us. It was not that we deserved or merited such magnificent mercy, but it was because of His own inherent character. He really could not do otherwise. There was nothing in us to earn His gracious attention. *The only compulsion upon Him was the compulsion of His own wondrous love.*

Are we surprised then that it is for this reason He stated He was loved so dearly by God the Father? This love was not and never can be anything soft or sentimental or insipid. Rather, it is strong as steel, tough as tungsten, yet glittering with the incandescent brilliance of a diamond.

It had to be for Him to endure the abuse and calumny of His earth days at the hands of wicked, selfish men. His entire interlude upon the planet represented the utmost in ignominy. Born into a peasant home, surrounded by the appalling filth of an eastern sheepfold, His birth could not have been more debasing. The long years of His youth and early manhood were spent in the most wicked town in Palestine. Nazareth was notorious for its wicked ways. Yet there He toiled, sweated, and hewed out a meagre living working in wood to support his widowed mother and siblings .

He lived in abject poverty without a home to call His own. He literally laid Himself out for others. His strength and stamina flowed out to those who followed Him. His great vitality restored the sick, raised the dead, fed the masses, ministered to those in sorrow, and propelled Him from one end of the country to the other with incredible energy. Everywhere He went, men and women sensed the touch of His strength, the impact of God's love upon them.

Inherent in Christ in perfect poise were the divine life of undiminished deity and the delightful life of untarnished humanity. Though He was the suffering servant, He was also the magnificent Lord of glory – God, very God.

At His death this became supremely evident. In that terrible agony of the garden, in the ignoble lynching by the mob under cover of darkness, in the atrocious trials and beastly behaviour of men determined to destroy Him, in the crucible of His cruel crucifixion, He emerges ever as the One in control. He chose to die this way. He chose deliberately to lay down His life in this manner. It was all His doing and His dying for dreadful men.

No matter what the scoffers and sceptics may say, He stands at the central crossroads of human history as its supreme character. No other individual, with so little ostentation, so shaped the eternal destiny of men.

But His death was not His end. It was but the conclusion of a magnificent chapter in the story of God's plan for man.

Death could not hold Him. Decay and decomposition could not deteriorate Him. The spices and wrappings and grave clothes that enfolded Him were for naught. They were powerless to prevent His resurrection. With majesty and growing grandeur He took His place of power. His position of omnipotence was reinstated. His coronation as King of Kings and Lord of Lords was celebrated in the throne room of eternity.

All of this Jesus foreknew and declared fearlessly to the young man born blind. He stated these facts with calm assurance to any who would listen – the Pharisees, Scribes, and others who now encircled Him .

They knew full well what it was that He implied. He was in truth telling them that He was none other than God. He was declaring unashamedly that He, their Messiah, the anointed One of God, their Promised One, was now among them. He had chosen to come to His people. It would be but a brief sojourn, and then He would return to the splendours from whence He came.

But why had He come? Why suffer? Why lay down His life? Why endure such agony for sinners?

Because men were lost. And His commission from His Father was that He should come to seek and to save those who were lost. He knew this to be His unique responsibility in the redemptive enterprises of God. He recognized it was His responsibility to carry out and execute in precise detail this executive order of the Godhead.

His audience then, and most men ever since, refused to believe they were lost. In truth it is exceedingly difficult to convince human beings that they are in peril. Like the Scribes and Pharisees of Jesus' day, we are prone to pride ourselves upon our religiosity, our cultural achievements, our educational attainments, our material possessions, or any other attributes which we naively suppose are indicators of our success in living.

We who are in the family of God, who have been found by the Good Shepherd, often seem to forget just how 'lost' we really were. As we look out upon a confused society and bewildered world we allow its trappings and trumpetings to blind us to the lostness of our families, friends, or acquaintances. We are dazzled by the glittering exteriors and flashing facades put on by people in desperate peril away from God. Fine language, impressive homes, beautiful cars, elaborate furnishings, glamorous holidays, affluent incomes, sharp clothes, and clever minds are no criteria for having either succeeded or found the reason for our being. We can have all these and still be far from God.

This explains why God, in Christ, by His Spirit, continues to pursue men. His approach to them polarizes people. He is willing to lay down His life for them in order that He might also take it up again in them. Some are delighted to discover He has drawn near, ready to pick them up in His own strong arms. Others turn away, go their own way, and refuse adamantly to have anything to do with Him. To those who respond He gives Himself in wondrous ways.

Behold, the Lord God will come with strong hand, and his arm shall rule for him: Behold, his reward is with him, and his work before him.
He shall feed his flock like a shepherd: he shall gather the lambs with his arm, and carry them in his bosom, and shall gently lead those that are with young.

(Isaiah 40:10–11)

What a remarkable portrait this is of our Lord, laying down His life for His sheep. He feeds them; He leads them gently; He gathers them up in His strong arms; He carries them close to His heart.

It is in this way that He also takes up His life again in us. Caught up into His care, encircled by His strong arms, enfolded within His love, we find ourselves *in Him*. This is part of the great secret to sharing in His life.

Much more than this, however, is the fact that it is to Him an endless source of satisfaction. He looks upon the outpouring of His life, the travail of His soul, the generous giving of Himself repaid and returned in sons and daughters brought to glory. Men and women, retrieved from their utter lostness and dereliction, are restored to the grandeur of wholesome godliness and new life in Him.

Often as I let my mind wander back to the great storms and blizzards that we went through on my ranches I recall scenes full of pathos and power. Again and again I would come home to our humble cottage with two or three tiny forlorn, cold lambs bundled up against my chest. They would be wrapped up within the generous folds of my big, rough wool jacket. Outside hail, sleet, snow, and chilling rain would be lashing my face and body. But within my arms the lambs were safe and sure of survival.

Part of the great compensation for enduring the blizzards, fighting the elements, and braving the storms was to pick up lost lambs. And as I picked them up I realized in truth I was taking up my own life again in them; my life that had been expended freely, gladly on their behalf.

It is as I am found in Him that He, too, revels and rejoices in my being found. No wonder there is such rejoicing in heaven over one lost soul who is brought home.

Sad to say, many of Jesus' hearers did not and could not understand. In fact, they went so far as to say He was insane.

🜩

Christ in Me
and Me in Christ

℃

To Believe in Christ is to Belong to Christ

Jesus answered them, I told you, and ye believed not: the works that I do in my Father's name, they bear witness of me.

But ye believe not, because ye are not of my sheep, as I said unto you.

My sheep hear my voice, and I know them, and they follow me.

(John 10:25–27)

This is an appropriate point at which to reflect on the polarization produced by Christ. This aspect of His life has ever proven to be an enigma to human beings. The unchangeable, irrefutable truth manifest in this One inevitably polarizes people. There is no middle ground. There can be no straddling the fence of neutrality. Either we believe in Him or we don't.

Perhaps polarization should be explained briefly. Whenever truth, that is to say absolutes, or eternal verities are presented to a person they produce one of two reactions. The first reaction is that the soul and spirit in search of God responds positively and promptly. There is an immediate move toward the truth. The spirit lays hold of, and takes to itself, the verities presented. They become a veritable part of one's life. They are the vitalizing, energizing, invigorating life of God moving into human character, human conduct, human conversation. They change, colour, and condition a person until he is conformed to Christ.

The alternative is the opposite; it is a negative reaction. The end result is a rejection of truth, which of course implies ultimately the rejection of Christ.

This was eminently true in His days upon earth, and it is the same today. And on this occasion his attackers went so far as to declare Him either a raving maniac or one possessed of a devil. Eventually their animosity and reaction to Him became so violent they schemed to destroy Him. Several times He slipped through their clutching fingers, but eventually, like bloodhounds, they brought Him to bay. Nor were they satisfied that He was stilled until they saw Him suspended on a cruel Roman gibbet. There, hanging midway between earth and sky, writhing in agony, they were sure His disquieting and disturbing declarations would terminate in His death.

But truth simply does not die that way.

Truth does not disappear in the face of evil.

Truth is indestructible just as God is indestructible.

Truth endures forever.

Truth remains eternal.

So down the long avenues of time men have turned angrily amid the darkness and despair of their dreadful deeds to attack truth. They have derided it, despised it, and tried to demolish it. Or better, we should say that in their blindness and ignorance they have so desired. Why?

The clearest and most concise answer to that enormous, unending question is given by Christ Himself:

For God so loved the world, that he gave his only begotten Son, that whosoever believeth in him should not perish, but have everlasting life. For God sent not his Son into the world to condemn the world; but that the world through him might be saved. He that believeth on him is not condemned: but he that believeth not is condemned already, because he hath not believed in the name of the only begotten Son of God. And this is the condemnation, that light is come into the world, and men loved darkness rather than light, because their deeds were evil. For every one that doeth evil hateth the light, neither cometh to the light, lest his deeds should be reproved. But he that doeth truth cometh to the light, that his deeds may be made manifest, that they are wrought in God.

(John 3:16–21)

On this particular occasion our Lord's adversaries ranted and raged at Him. 'How long are You going to keep us in doubt?' 'If you really are the Christ tell us plainly!'

The pathetic aspect of the whole scene really was their own positive refusal to accept what He had said as truth.

Repeatedly He had declared His identity. They knew from their familiarity with the Old Testament Scriptures that this One who now stood before them was none other than the promised Messiah. He was God's Anointed. He was the Great, Good Shepherd foretold by the prophets and seers of their people. David, Isaiah, Ezekiel and others had predicted that the true Shepherd would come to gather up and restore the lost sheep of Israel.

Over and over Christ had asserted that He was in fact

that One. He was here. The Good Shepherd was among them. He was calling to His own. He was gathering them up ... those who would come.

But they adamantly refused to believe Him.

They simply would not accept Him.

They rejected and repudiated all He said.

Yet, over and beyond all of this He endeavoured to convince them of His credentials by repeated demonstrations of His deity.

He performed all sorts of remarkable miracles that were positive proof and incontestable confirmation of His divinity. They had heard Him preach good tidings to the meek and poor. They had watched Him bind up the broken-hearted. They had seen Him liberate those who were captive to evil spirits, disease, or their own deranged minds and emotions. They had been there when He spoke comfort to those who mourned. They had seen sorrow turned to gladness.

They had been witnesses to the full and total fulfilment of all that Isaiah predicted in 61:1–3

The spirit of the Lord God is upon me; because the Lord hath anointed me to preach good tidings unto the meek; he hath sent me to bind up the broken-hearted, to proclaim liberty to the captives, and the opening of the prison to them that are bound; To proclaim the acceptable year of the Lord, and the day of vengeance of our God; to comfort all that mourn; To appoint unto them that mourn in Zion, to give unto them beauty for ashes, the oil of joy for mourning, the garment of praise for the spirit of heaviness; that they might be called trees of righteousness, the planting of the Lord, that he might be glorified.

And still they would not believe. Still they would not receive Him.

Accordingly it is absolutely essential for us, as it was for them, to grasp fully what it really means 'to believe,' 'to receive,' for by Christ's own simple statement He insisted that only those who do believe belong to Him.

'To believe' implies much more than merely giving my mental assent to truth. It is much more than merely agreeing to what God has to say.

There are literally hundreds of thousands of people who profess to be believers who do this much. They agree in a formal manner to the truth as it is revealed in the Scriptures. They subscribe in a rather ambiguous way to the teachings of Christ. They believe that in some rather obscure way He was a historical character who came to earth to reveal truth to us. He was really no more than another of the great prophets or teachers who claimed divine attributes and abilities.

But this simply is not enough!

Even the evil spirits believe this much and tremble.

Without a doubt the greatest single weakness in Christendom the world around is so called 'believism.' It is an anachronism that millions who claim to believe are in reality a repudiation of the living Christ. Their characters, conduct, and conversation are a living travesty of the truth they claim to exemplify.

This is why Christianity and the church is eternally being charged with hypocrisy. It is why so many who are outside claim that those inside the church are charlatans. It is why to be a true believer is difficult, simply because so often the behaviour of our so-called brethren betrays them and us. We are all lumped together and labelled as imposters. And our dilemma only deepens when all around us, amid the confusion and criticism, men and women insist they are all believers, when in truth their behaviour may well be a reproach to Christ.

In our Lord's discourses He equated believing with drinking. To believe truth, to believe Him, was in fact to imbibe truth, to imbibe Him.

> *... He that believeth on me shall never thirst.*
> (John 6:35)
> *If any man thirst, let him come unto me, and drink. He that believeth on me, as the scripture hath said, out of his belly (innermost being) shall flow rivers of living water.*
> (John 7:37–38)

To believe in Christ is not just to give endorsement in an objective manner to what He has done and said on my behalf.

To believe in Christ is to fully accept both Him and His truth so that I actually take Him into my life in deliberate, volitional action, that goes on continuously.

Put another way it means this: He, the living Christ, is actually allowed to so enter the whole of my life that He shares it with me, lives it with me, becomes an integral, vitalizing part of it. In other words, He is in me and I am in Him.

The closest parallel to this is marriage.

It is possible to read about marriage, talk about it, discuss it, and debate it. But until you find another whom you implicitly trust and love enough to invite into your life to share it with you, you know virtually nothing about the truth of all that marriage implies. It must be experienced to be known. It must be tried to be understood. It must be undertaken to be enjoyed. It must be engaged in to be believed.

It is the same with Christ. He is referred to in Scripture as the Bridegroom and we His bride.

The second closest parallel to this is the intimate interrelationship between a shepherd and his sheep.

We can discuss shepherding, read about it, study it, observe it, and even enjoy watching it. Yet until we actually participate, we really know nothing about it except in a very remote, detached, and impersonal way.

And this is precisely the point Jesus made when He said: 'You don't believe, simply because you don't actually belong to Me. You aren't My sheep.'

All through this book and also in *A Shepherd Looks at the 23rd Psalm*, I have endeavoured to point out in unmistakable language what it really means to 'belong' to Christ. I have tried to show what is involved in 'coming under Christ's control.' I have indicated the great joys and benefits and advantages of allowing our lives to actually be managed by Him who made us, who bought us, and who is legitimately entitled to own us.

Yet, the point must be made again here that the decision as to whether or not this will happen rests with us. Christ comes to us. He calls to us. He invites us to turn to Him. He offers to take us under His care. He longs to lead us in His ways. He desires to share life with us. He wants us to enter fully into the joys of His ownership. He delights to give us all the advantages and benefits of His life.

In short, He wants to be in our lives and for us to be in His.

Are we or are we not prepared to have this happen? It is an intimate association from which most of us shy away. We really are afraid of this involvement. To speak of 'believing' in this way makes most of us uneasy. We are not at all sure we wish to be so completely committed. There is so much at stake! Yes! all of this life; all of eternity; all of myself is at stake.

It is only the person prepared to become open and available to God, who positively responds to truth as it is revealed in Christ, the Great, Good Shepherd, who will 'hear' His voice.

To hear Him is to 'recognize' that this One is in truth none other than God, very God.

This being so, what He says and what He does will be taken seriously. We will respond to Him in powerful ways of acceptance and total personal commitment.

Evidence of this will be apparent in a deliberate and eager willingness to do whatever He requires. This 'running' to do His bidding demonstrates faith and confidence in Christ of a potent sort. This is to believe in Christ – to know God!

It is this intimate interchange and private interrelationship between Christ and me that becomes such a unique relationship. It is in truth the 'knowing,' of which Christ as the Good Shepherd speaks with such affection. He is in my life; I am in His. He knows me; I know Him. He is mine; I am His.

This is a precious relationship. The acute awareness that He knows me and I know God in Christ is the most profound and potent influence I am privileged to know as a man. In its awareness lies great rest.

There is about this knowing an element of elevation that induces me to attain lofty living and noble conduct far beyond anything I might otherwise have thought possible. This knowing is the powerful, potent presence of the very person of Christ made real in my everyday experience by His gracious Spirit.

Finally, there is the inescapable reality that this knowing has a profound purifying effect upon my life in all its activities. I live and move and have my being in company with Him who is altogether noble. He is royalty. He is my Lord, my Owner, my Master, and in His close company I scorn that which is corrupt.

Only those who know Him in this manner, who believe on Him to this extent, who receive Him without reservation in this way find it appropriate to follow Him.

I have used the word appropriate deliberately here. It implies that to follow Christ, as following Him has been explained previously in this book, is not something absurd or unrealistic or unreasonable. Rather, to follow Him becomes the proper, reasonable, and appropriate thing to do.

To follow Christ means I become intimately identified with His plans and purposes for the planet and for me as a person. His wishes become my wishes. His work becomes my work. His words become my words. His standards, values, and priorities become mine. His interests become my interests. His life becomes my life.

In a word: He is in me; I am in Him. There is the place of peace. Here lies serenity, strength, and stability amid earth's troublous times.

CHAPTER 15

Eternal Life in the Hand of the Shepherd

My sheep hear my voice, and I know them, and they follow me.
And I give unto them eternal life; and they shall never perish, neither shall any man pluck them out of my hand.
(John 10:27–28)

At the head of this chapter, John 10:27,28 have been deliberately set down together. They cannot be separated. These verses constitute one continuous concept.

The incredibly beautiful relationship between the Shepherd and His sheep can be and only is possible provided the sheep hear His voice, are known of Him in intimate oneness, and so follow Him in quiet, implicit confidence.

The eternal life inherent in Him, whereby they shall never perish, within which they can enjoy endless security under His hand, are benefits made possible only in constant communion with Him.

If for a moment we turn our attention to a human shepherd and his sheep we will see this to be self-evident.

Those sheep which remain in the shepherd's

personal care are the ones which derive and draw their very life from his provision and possession of them. They have at their disposal all the resources of his ranch. They thrive under the expertise of his skilled management. They enjoy the eternal vigilance and loving protection of his care. Under his hand they flourish because they are 'handled' with affection by one who is tremendously fond of them. In fact, they are his very life. In turn he becomes to them their very life.

Looking back in gentle reminiscence across the distant years of my own life as a sheepman this remains its most memorable aspect. There was a profound and deeply moving sense in which all my life, all my strength, all my energy, all my vitality was poured into my flock. It simply had to be so if they were to enjoy an optimum life under my management.

The 'life' which they had in such rich measure and overflowing abundance was but an expression of my own life continuously given to them day after day. The lush green pastures, the lovely wooded parkland where they could shelter from summer sun and winter winds, the clear cool water to slake their thirst, the freedom from predators or rustlers, the protection against disease and parasites of all sorts, the loving attention and intimate care of one who delighted in their on-going well-being all reflected my own life lived out through them.

They came to be known and recognized uniquely as being 'Keller's sheep.' They had upon them the indelible, unmistakable mark of belonging to me. Their health, quality, and excellence were a declaration of whose they were.

Yet, it must be emphasized that this life, this special

care, this exquisite sense of security and well-being was theirs only as long as they remained on my ranch and under my hand.

In my book on Psalm 23 I told in detail of certain sheep which were never really satisfied to stay in my care. They were always looking for a chance to slip out through a hole in the fence. Or they would creep around the end of the enclosure that ran down to the seashore at extreme low tide. Once they had gotten out, they were exposed to enormous perils. Some wandered far off to become lost up the road or into the woods. And there they fell prey to all sorts of disasters.

With all of this in mind our Lord made it clear that our own relationship to Him is the same. The remarkable eternal life which He gives to us is His own life transmitted to us continuously as we remain in close contact with Him. His vitality, His vigour, His view of things are mine as long as the communion between us is constant.

It is a mistake to imagine that eternal life, the very life of the risen Christ, is some gift package dropped into the pocket of my life at some specific point in time; that once it has been bestowed I automatically have it forever.

Life, any kind of life, physical, moral, or spiritual, simply is not of that sort.

Life is correspondence between an organism and its environment. Life goes on only so long as the organism is deriving its sustenance from its surroundings. The instant it no longer draws its support from its environment, life ceases. At that point the organism is declared to be dead.

This principle applies in the realm of my body – physical. It holds true in the region of my soul – moral. It is so in my spirit – spiritual.

All of life originates with God irrespective of whether it be physical, moral, or spiritual. To assume that He bestows only spiritual life to human beings is a distortion of truth.

The whole of the biota, the total physical, chemical, and biological environment which supports my physical body comes from Him. He designed it. He programmed it. He set it in motion. He sustains it. He maintains its meticulous functions. He enables me thus to derive my physical life and well-being from His wondrous world around me. The moment I can no longer do this I am said to be physically dead.

Precisely the same principle operates in my soul. My mind, emotions, and will are stimulated and sustained by correspondence with the moral environment that surrounds me. This is the realm of human relationships and ideologies. It is the world of ideas, concepts, and culture expressed in literature, science, the arts, music, and accumulated experience of the human race.

A person can be acutely, vividly alive to all of this. Or he can be likewise virtually dead to it. For some it is well nigh life itself. Yet even here every capacity anyone has to correspond or communicate with this total soulish environment comes from God. It is He who has arranged, ordered, and programmed all that is excellent, beautiful, and noble in the arts, sciences, and humanities. Man has only just gradually uncovered all that formerly lay hidden from his restricted vision.

So in truth, all moral, all soul life is derived from our Lord, for without the capacities of mind, emotion, and will bestowed upon us by Him, we would have no way of enjoying even this life.

Again, it may be legitimately stated that the moment

I can no longer derive moral stimulation and uplift from this realm I am said to be dead to it. What is more, it is perfectly possible to be physically alive yet morally dead to one or more or all of God's life in this region.

I am said to be morally alive only so long as I draw life from those generous and godly gifts bestowed upon me by a benevolent and loving Master. He so designed me as to live on this noble lofty plane as His person.

What has been said of physical and moral life also applies in the region of my spirit. There, deep within my inner life, lies my conscience, my intuition, and my capacity to commune with God by His Spirit.

I am said to have spiritual life only so long as there is being derived directly from God a measure of His life. It is He who in the realm of my conscience alerts me to absolute verities, ultimate truth. It is in this way I know what I ought to do, what I ought not to do. I am alive to what is appropriate and proper behaviour before Him and what is not.

It is in the realm of my intuition that I enjoy that ultimate dimension of living, in knowing God. It is in the unique awareness of being alive to Him that I enjoy life at its loftiest level. There steals over my stilled spirit the sure knowledge that it is in Christ I live and move and have my being. This is to know also that I am known of Him, intimately, personally, and with profound affection.

So there flows between His gracious Spirit and my spirit an interchange of life – His life. I am in Him; He is in me. There is an ongoing, continuing interrelationship whereby He imparts His life to me and takes up my little life into His.

To know, experience, and enjoy this communion

with Christ is to have eternal life. This is what Christ meant when He said unashamedly, 'I give unto them eternal life.'

He went on to add emphatically, 'They shall never perish.'

As long as my communion with Him continues, His life is imparted as a clear flowing stream from the fountain source of His own magnificent, inexhaustible self. He comes to me continuously in never-ending life to energize and invigorate me. I am His, to be the recipient of an ever-renewed life. He is mine to be the bestower of every good and perfect gift needed to sustain me through all eternity.

He has no other intention than that this relationship should be one of eternal endurance.

My part is to remain ever open, responsive, and receptive to the inflow of His life to mine. It is His life that surrounds and enfolds me on every side. In any situation, at any time, in any place I can breathe quietly, 'O Christ, You are here. You are the ever-present one – the great "I Am." Live Your life in me, through me, in this moment, for I, too, am in Your presence ready to receive You in all Your splendour.' The person who so lives in Christ's presence shall never perish. He it is out of whose innermost being cascades clear streams of life-giving refreshment to those around him. This is the individual who is an inspiration and blessing to his generation, and to his God.

Those who live this joyous and serene communion with Christ are the men and women who know they are in God's hand. Nor will they ever make a move or entertain a thought that would take them out of His hand.

To know that God's hand is upon me for good is

perhaps the most precious awareness a human being can savour in his earthly sojourn. To be acutely aware – 'O my Shepherd, You are enfolding me in Your great strong hand!' – is to sense a sweet serenity that nothing can disturb. To realize the intimacy of the Master's touch upon every minutiae of my affairs, to experience His hand guiding, leading, directing in every detail of each day, is to enter a delight words cannot describe.

My part is to be sensitive to His gentle Spirit. My part is to obey instantly His smallest wish. My part is to wait quietly for the unfolding of His best purposes and plans. In harmony, unity, and mutual pleasure we commune together along the trails of life. He becomes my fondest friend and most intimate companion. More than that, He becomes my life.

This is the life of serene security. This is the relationship of quiet relaxation. This is the life of rest and repose; for the person willing to be led of the Lord there is endless enjoyment in His company.

The ancient prophet Isaiah portrays this for us in an exquisite word picture of the Great Shepherd of our souls.

O Zion, that bringest good tidings, get thee up into the high mountain; O Jerusalem, that bringest good tidings, lift up thy voice with strength; Lift it up, be not afraid; Say unto the cities of Judah, Behold your God! Behold, the Lord God will come with strong hand, and his arm shall rule for him: behold, his reward is with him, and his work before him.
He shall feed his flock like a shepherd: he shall gather the lambs with his arm, and carry them in his bosom, and shall gently lead those that are with young.

(Isaiah 40:9–11)

It has always been our Lord's intention to hold His people in His own strong hand. It is the most profound longing of His Spirit to lead us gently in the paths of right living. He is eager and happy to gather us up into His powerful arms where no harm can molest us.

The intentions of God toward His own are always good. He ever has their own best interests at heart. His desires are only for their well-being. He is a Shepherd of enormous good will and deep compassion for the people of His pasture.

It is ever He who holds us in His hand, if we will allow ourselves to be so owned and loved. We do not have to 'hold on to Him' as so many wrongly imagine. How much better to rest in the quiet assurance of knowing His hand is upon me rather than doubting my feeble efforts to hold onto Him.

This is one of the great secrets to a serene life in Christ. It does not come instantly, overnight so to speak. It is the gradual outgrowth of a life lived quietly in gentle communion with Him.

Imperceptibly there steals over my spirit the assurance that with Him, all is well. He makes no mistakes. He is ever here. And so long as I remain acutely aware of His presence, nothing can separate me from His love and care.

Who shall separate us from the love of Christ? Shall tribulation, or distress, or persecution, or famine, or nakedness, or peril, or sword? As it is written, For thy sake we are killed all the day long; we are accounted as sheep for the slaughter. Nay, in all these things we are more than conquerors through him that loved us. For I am persuaded, that neither death, nor life, nor angels, nor principalities, nor powers, nor things present, nor things to come, Nor height, nor depth, nor any other creature, shall be able to separate us from the love of God, which is in Christ Jesus our Lord.

(Romans 8:35–39)

❦

CHAPTER 16

The Good Shepherd is God!

My Father, which gave them me, is greater than all; and no man is able to pluck them out of my Father's hand. I and my Father are one.

(John 10:29–30)

There are occasions on which it is imperative that an author share his own inner struggle in search of spiritual truth. For all of us there are sections of the Scriptures where we have found difficulty in arriving at veracity. All of us are pilgrims on the path, and no matter how sincerely we endeavour to follow our Good Shepherd, there are times when we stumble .

For me the two verses above, taken together, 'seemed' to pose an insurmountable problem. In verse 29 our Lord states that His Father 'is greater than all.' In almost the next breath He asserts He and His Father are one.

The false cults who eternally deny the deity of Christ have capitalized on this 'apparent' contradiction. In fact, it is a passage they exploit to the maximum in order to undermine the faith of those who have placed their simple confidence in Christ as God, very God.

It was not until I undertook a deep study on this section that at last the clear light of its meaning began to break through. What previously was puzzling has now become exceedingly precious. And it is with distinct joy and a sense of triumph that the closing chapter of this book can be written.

Once more light has replaced darkness, love has taken the place of despair. The result is that I am much richer for it, and I trust you the reader will be as well.

In Dr Weymouth's remarkable translation this reads, 'What my Father has given me is greater than all, and no one is able to wrest anything from my Father's hand. I and the Father are one.'

In the translation by Knox the meaning is made even more clear. 'This trust which my Father has committed to me is more precious than all else; no one can tear them away from the hand of my Father. My father and I are one.'

What is this trust of such supreme importance?

What is this enormous responsibility?

What is greater than all else in God's estimation?

Wonder of wonders, and marvel of marvels, it is His own keeping of His own sheep!

This disclosure humbles my spirit and draws me to Him with bonds of love stronger than steel, tougher than tungsten.

To realize that from God's standpoint the most precious thing is the preservation of His people, those who have come to put their confidence in Him, who have come under His control, overwhelms our hearts. In response to such compassion and caring for me there springs up within my soul an overflowing stream of gratitude. 'O my God, how great You are! O my Shepherd, how wondrous are Your ways!'

I really know of no other declaration by our Lord that so stills my spirit in quiet adoration and gentle awe. To know that though I am weak and wayward and often downright difficult to handle, to Him who loves me I am very precious. This pulverizes my pride and draws me to Him.

There is something tremendously touching in this truth. It strips away all the misgivings I may have about belonging to the Shepherd of my soul. It overwhelms me with confidence and joyous assurance. 'O Christ, to You I am precious!' 'O great Shepherd, to You I am special! O Father, to You I am the supreme object of Your care and affection! I have been accepted, beloved, and wanted above all else.'

Is it any wonder that He will do everything possible within His power to preserve and keep me in His hand? Am I surprised to see that the supreme price paid for my reconciliation to Him, was paid gladly and freely with His own life? It was His precious blood shed so willingly for us that now makes us so valuable. It is His touch upon my life and its transforming power to take a sinner and change him into a joyous son that makes me so precious to Him.

It is not who I am that makes me special to God.

Rather, now, it is *whose* I am that makes me precious.

There is no intrinsic merit in my makeup that He should esteem me as someone significant. In fact, the opposite is the case, for by His revelation He declares me to be undone before Him.

But bless His dear name, it is the impact of His life upon mine that makes all the difference. It is the immense emancipation of His salvation that sets me free to follow Him. It is the joyous sharing of Himself with me by His Spirit that empowers me to do His will. It is the strong touch of His mighty hand upon my life that changes my character, alters my conduct, and conforms my life style to His.

This is to become His person. This is to become the sheep of His pasture. This is to become a member of His family. This is to enjoy an exquisite, intimate relationship in which I am His and He is mine. No wonder then that to Him I am exceedingly precious.

Of course, to our contemporaries we may not seem to be very special. In fact, some may even look upon us with a jaundiced eye, calling us 'odd,' 'religious fanatics,' or even 'square.' But let us never forget that they do not see us as God does. They can, at best, observe only our outward appearance and behaviour, whereas our Shepherd knows us through and through. And though knowing even the worst about us still loves us with an enduring love – because we are His.

This truth came home to me with tremendous impact as a young man when I started to build up my first sheep ranch.

Because all my life previously I had worked with cattle, sheep seemed strange and unfamiliar. So I sought expert advice and help from anyone who would give it to me. I was determined that I would keep only the finest stock and breed the best animals it was possible to produce. There would be no half-way measures. My sheep were special and would become increasingly precious.

I went to see an elderly, white-haired, highly esteemed sheep breeder who lived about thirty miles away. He was a Scot, who, like so many livestock men from Scotland, stand tall among the world's finest breeders of quality animals. Gently and graciously he led me out to his fields where his flock was grazing. In a small pasture about a dozen superb, big, strong rams were resting in the shade.

An endearing look of comingled love, affection, pride, and delight filled his soft brown eyes as he leaned on the fence rail letting his gaze run over his rams.

'Well,' he said softly, 'pick out whichever ram you wish, son.' He smiled at me warmly, 'You are just a young man starting out with sheep. I want you to have the best!'

I replied that only he knew which was the finest ram. It was he who had poured the long years of his life and skill and expertise into these sheep. It was he, who, with infinite care, patience, and perseverance had selected those which ultimately would become the finest stock on the whole continent. Only he knew which was the most valuable ram in his possession. Only he knew how great and precious it was to him.

Not hesitating a moment he swung open the gate with his big gnarled hands and strode in among the rams. Quickly he caught hold of a fine, handsome ram with a bold, magnificent head and strong conformation.

'This is Arrowsmith II,' he said, running his hands gently over the ram. 'He is the supreme Grand Champion Suffolk Ram and has won all the top awards across the country!' He rubbed the ram's ears softly in an affectionate caress. 'No one else has ever handled him but me. He's my top prize ram ... tremendously valuable ... more than that ... very precious to me in a very personal way!'

I could understand exactly what he meant. I was not

surprised to see a misty look steal across his eyes. And I considered it one of the greatest honours of my life that he would permit me to take the ram home to become the top sire for my flock.

That day it came home to me with great clarity that what made the difference between one sheep and another was the owner. In whose hand had they been? Who was responsible for breeding, raising, and shepherding them? Was it a grand flockmaster? Was it a superb sheepman?

And so it is with us. Are we in God's hands? Who is handling us, shaping us? Whose are we? Whose life is molding mine?

Jesus said, 'I and the Father are One!' It matters not whether we speak of being in the hands of God our Father, or under the control of Christ our Good Shepherd, or guided gently by the gracious Holy Spirit; we are inevitably in the hands of God.

To us today this is fairly understandable. We accept this concept without question. To us who believe He is precious (1 Peter 2:7).

But in speaking to the Pharisees, His straightforward declaration that He was one with His Father immediately alienated His audience. His simple, honest, legitimate claim to deity antagonized His hearers. He was declaring Himself to be God, very God, and they determined to destroy Him for it.

On that dark day when the mob grabbed up rocks from the ground to stone Him, they recognized that He had answered their query: 'If Thou be Christ – tell us plainly!'

He had, and they rejected His claim.

He said He was One with God the Father, and they were furious.

He had come to them as the Good Shepherd, prepared to lay down His life for His sheep, but they would not have Him.

Only two young people from among this angry, hostile crowd had responded to His invitation: the young woman taken in adultery and the young man born blind. Both had felt the touch of His hand on their lives. Both had turned to Him for restoration. Both went on from there exulting in a new dimension of life. They were remade in the Shepherd's care.

The same choice still confronts mankind.

The majority still spurn the Good Shepherd.

Yet to those who hear His voice, respond to His call, come under His care, follow Him, His commitments come true. They find life, overflowing life, fulfilling life, and they find it in rich measure. It is *life in Christ and Christ in them.*

A Shepherd Looks at
the Lamb of God

Ɛ

Contents

Introduction   307

PART I   THE LAMB OF GOD IN SYMBOLS

1 *Our Need for the Lamb*   313
   Adam and Eve's Necessary Covering
2 *No Substitute for the Lamb*   321
   Cain and Abel's Offerings
3 *The Son is the Lamb*   326
   Abraham's Test of Obedience
4 *The Passover Lamb*   332
   The Saving of the Firstborn
5 *The Sin-Bearing Lamb*   342
   The Scapegoat in the Wilderness
6 *The Suffering Lamb*   351
   Isaiah's Word Pictures of the Lamb of God

PART II   THE LAMB OF GOD IN PERSON

7 *The Lamb of God Incarnate*   375
   The Redeemer Comes

Reflections   410

Introduction

'*THE LAMB OF GOD ...*'

What an unusual title! Among the countless varieties of animals, why was this particular species chosen most often to portray God's Son? What special significance does it bear?

Is it merely a picturesque pet name, or does it denote some profound truths about this person of divine origin?

Who *is* the One who bears this title? Why? From where does it come? To where does it lead?

These and a score of similar questions are generated by a study of this unique name, '*Lamb of God.*'

Strangely, yet significantly, He who alone wears this title entered into human history as The Lamb of God. Even the circumstances of His birth set the tone for this special name. He was born in a crude, contaminated, mideastern sheepfold outside Bethlehem.

This fact was driven home to me with intense and terrible force one day deep in the desert of Pakistan. I was in a remote village, alone, when suddenly a fierce, unexpected cloudburst and electrical storm drove me to seek shelter in a tiny mud-walled hovel. A very aged, white-bearded old man had beckoned me to come in out of the lashing fury of the storm.

Bending over deeply to crawl through the low doorway, I fumbled my way into a dark and gloomy one-roomed abode. It took my eyes several minutes to adjust to the darkness within. The place was full of acrid smoke from a small dung fire burning between three cooking stones on the earthen floor. The air was fetid with the vile odours of livestock and sheep dung, for several of these animals shared the same tiny space.

In one corner, close by the fire, crouched the frail little form of a tiny, teenage girl, possibly the old man's daughter. Her large, luminous dark eyes were filled with a certain foreboding as she clutched a tender, newborn infant to her breasts. The baby whimpered slightly as the girl, wrapped about only with a soiled, threadbare, cotton cloak, rocked it gently in her thin arms.

Not knowing Pakistani, all I could do was huddle quietly, close to the smoky dung fire, while the storm beat upon the mud walls. Tiny rivulets of water ran down the dark walls where the rain leaked through the shabby roof

Amid the gloom; amid the awful pungency of sheep, goat and other animal manure; amid the appalling poverty of this poor peasant's surroundings, God's Spirit spoke to me in unmistakable, unforgettable terms: '*This is how I came amongst men!*'

The revelation came to my spirit with a force equal to the most ferocious thunder clap of the storm sweeping over this remote desert village. 'O God, to what utter and absolute depths of privation and unspeakable pollution You descended to deliver us from our despair!'

All our fancy Christmas concerts; our pretty Christmas cards; our glowing lights; our glamorous paintings of the Nativity; our ornate gift packages; our tinsel and treats and trees – all these are but a travesty of the true conditions under which Christ came into the world.

Since that interlude, nearly twenty years ago, when I huddled in that desert shepherd's hut with a teenage mother and her suckling, newborn child, Christmas has never been the same again for me.

Those who first came to pay homage to that other newborn Babe in the Bethlehem stable were ordinary shepherds. In awe, wonder and simple faith they looked upon God's Lamb and were jubilant.

But wise men came, too, across the distant desert wastes of the then-known world. They came to honour and revere the Christ Child, the Prince of Peace, Heaven's Potentate, the Mighty God – yet also 'The Lamb of God' in very truth (Isaiah 9:6).

Beyond the simple shepherds, beyond the wealthy wise men, beyond the patriarchal priest Simeon and the aged Anna, who prayed so fervently for God's people, were His young mother, Mary, and her husband, Joseph. They also bowed low before this God-child. In this Lamb af God they glimpsed the salvation of God. In Him they recognized a Light which would give light to the entire Hebrew and Gentile world.

Some thirty years later the sturdy carpenter of Nazareth laid down His hammer and chisel for the last time. Crossing the countryside, He came to meet 'the greatest man ever born of woman' – the fiery desert prophet, John the Baptist. As Jesus approached the blazing firebrand, whom one would have expected to point out qualities of strength and power, John exulted triumphantly, '*Behold, The Lamb of God, who taketh away the sin of the world!*'

This one, born in Bethlehem of Judea as foretold so accurately by the ancient prophets of His people, stood quietly before John and requested to be baptized in the Jordan. Not that He needed cleansing or absolution, but here He was distinctly identified with men in their human dilemma.

Later, looking upon this Christ, God's anointed One, there was torn again from The Baptist's innermost spirit the irrepressible declaration that *this man Jesus, is the Christ, The Lamb of God!* We will discover what it was in John's announcement which caused two of his own disciples to begin at that time to follow Jesus.

John the Baptist is one of many witnesses who answers our question, 'Who is this One who bears the title, *The Lamb of God?*' Further on we will be considering others in Scripture who point eloquently and dramatically to Jesus, The Lamb of God.

There are six major word pictures, profound illustrations, in the Old Testament concerning The Lamb of God. We will look at each of these and at the unfolding picture of Christ himself provided in these passages.

❦

PART I

The Lamb of God
in Symbols

CHAPTER 1

🙢

Our Need for the Lamb

Adam and Eve's Necessary Covering

Unto Adam also and to his wife did the Lord God make coats of skins, and clothed them.

(Genesis 2:31)

Mankind's need for The Lamb of God did not begin in a Bethlehem stable 2,000 years ago. Neither did The Lamb of God himself have His beginning there. The shepherd's stall was not His introduction into human history. The account of His initial entry into the world is but the narrative of that point in time when God, very God, chose to part the stage curtains of history behind which He had moved in majesty undetected by most to step out on centre stage.

There in full view, The King of Glory, God in mufti, God disguised in human form, clothed and masked by our flesh and form, moved amongst men. Here was The *Lamb of God*. God's Son – in fact, God in person – had come to the lost sheep of men. He was unknown, unrecognized, but for a handful of men, humble in heart, receptive in spirit.

Indeed, this Lamb of God was none other than the very person of the eternal God! He was the visible expression of the invisible God. He was the One who had been in company with the Father before ever the worlds were formed or the planet earth was shaped and fitted for human habitation.

He was The Lamb of God who, 'from before the foundation of the world' (Revelation 13:8) was slain and suffered that men and women lost and perishing in the slime-pits of sin might be redeemed, reconciled and restored to walk with Him in paths of righteousness.

This concept of Christ as the ever self-sacrificing, ever self-giving One, yet very God himself is one of the most difficult for us mortals to grasp. First, simply because we are finite. We are locked into and conditioned by our time/space limitations. As human beings we are born, live our little lives upon the planet, then perish. The few brief years of our short life span speed past us. The entire performance is like a swift dream that passes quickly from cradle to grave, as Shakespeare stated, 'each man in his turn playing many parts.' The idea of an eternal God – or even beyond that, an eternal *redeeming* God – is as elusive to our human understanding as the northern lights.

During these few years on earth, we are totally preoccupied with the pressing events of the immediate moment which touch upon our lives. We are naturally and inevitably preoccupied with survival amid the restless masses. We are driven inexorably to become self-centred, self-preoccupied in the scramble to succeed. And this is the second reason why it is so terribly difficult for us to envision, to grasp the love of God expressed so poignantly and profoundly in the person of His Son – the self-giving, self-sharing, self-sacrificing Lamb.

In fact, if anything, we recoil against such a concept. We see it as utter folly and foolishness. This sort of self-less love, of laying down one's life for another in need, of giving in order that others may gain, seems to us silly and absurd. In our hopeless cynicism and dark despair, we can scarcely conceive of a God who is gracious enough, good enough, generous enough, let alone great enough to go out of His way to give *himself* to save us from our sin.

But that is precisely what He does. It is what He always has done. It is what He always will do. He is the same eternal, unchanging, constant, compassionate Christ who from everlasting to everlasting lays himself out that man might live. And the few bright but painful years of His human sojourn are but a glimpse of His eternal performance in the unseen realm.

The remarkable revelation given to us mortal men by His own sublime Spirit is that of God, very God, dwelling and acting in the eternal dimension of the ever-present *now*. With Him there are no time/space limitations. With Him there is no restriction of space, no duration of days. With Him there is only the ever-present, ever-enduring I AM.

A thousand years with Christ is as one day and one day is as a thousand years. Even beyond this, a million milleniums are as one moment and one moment as a million milleniums. Because of this timeless quality, the unrestricted giving of God; the sharing of God; the sacrifice of God displayed for us in the central climax of Calvary is portrayed in the divine dynamic that meets the needs of uncounted millions upon millions of men and women for all time everywhere.

When in His own self-revelation, by His own Holy

Spirit, God reveals to our recoiling spirits that He himself has been, is, and ever will be *The Lamb slain, The Lamb given, The Lamb shared, The Lamb who sacrifices himself in our stead*, we turn away from Him. It is more than our darkened souls and stony spirits can assimilate. Such a disclosure of the divine dimension cannot penetrate our sin-calloused souls. This is why the prophet cried out, 'Who hath believed our report, and to whom is the arm of the Lord revealed?' (Isaiah 53:1).

Yet the Scriptures from Genesis to Revelation are a record of God dealing with men in love and patience. From the first couple who communed with Him in the garden of Eden to the glorious city of eternal beauty revealed to the aged Apostle John, it is The Eternal Lamb who is portrayed for us. We poor, struggling, sinning mortals can scarcely comprehend this.

The recorded events depicted in the Bible speak eloquently and profoundly of this ever-suffering One. Long before earth was formed, God was gripped with grief and sorrow. This is the reason that Jesus is 'The Lamb slain from before the foundation af the world.' For with His eternal foresight He acutely anticipated the agony and sorrow that would be His because of wayward man, 'like sheep gone astray,' turning to their own way, selling out completely to their strong-willed selfishness.

That such behaviour would not only lead them to utter self-destruction but also would break in upon His own great love with enormous suffering of spirit would seldom occur to men. Blinded by the deception of the archenemy of their own souls, misled by the evil one and their own overwhelming preoccupation with sensuality, it would not dawn on them, or any of us, that it is our sin which has brought His suffering; it is our stupendous self-will which has caused His sorrow.

God made man for himself. He ordained, before ever earth was formed, that He should have sons and daughters with whom He could commune in pure delight. In the councils of eternity He determined that there should be those who would walk and talk and live with Him in intimate harmony.

Because of sin and evil, all this glorious plan was thrown into chaos and confusion. Every step God took to bring sons and daughters to glory was strewn with the sharp stones of His own suffering, the cutting wounds of His own great grief. We simply must see somehow, sometime, that God has suffered, *suffered*, SUFFERED, for us sinning people. This suffering has never diminished, either before or after Calvary.

Every significant illustration in the Old Testament involving an earthly sacrifice is but a portrayal of the self-sacrifice borne by God himself.

When Adam and Eve deliberately, flagrantly asserted their own selfish desires to oppose God's best wish, His best will for them, He was pierced through with a thousand pains. These were but a foretaste of the iron spikes that would just as surely pierce His hands and feet, pinning Him to a cruel cross.

Men always do this to God. God has not changed; men do not change. Sinful men are still nailing God to the cross of their own conceit and indifference. They don't 'give a dime' about what happens to Diety just as long as they can live as they like. It doesn't matter a whit to them if Christ does die a thousand deaths for their misdeeds.

For one who has spent countless hours enthralled with the beauty of God's creation, it stretches my imagination beyond its limits when I attempt to visualize the beautiful garden in which God placed the first man and woman. The Garden of Eden was both home and vocation for this pair. And even beyond the beautiful, soul-stirring environment and challenging, fulfilling occupation was their daily, unrestricted fellowship with God himself!

When Adam and Eve laid bare their own strong wills, and did such despite to the loving care of their loving God, they stood stripped, naked and exposed in the gross ignominy of their shame. They were alienated from their Father. They were tasting the bitter fruit of their folly. Their end was death – spiritual, moral, physical death. They had brought it upon themselves. The personal loss to them is symbolized by the theological phraseology, the Fall of Man!

In amazing compassion and concern, God did not destroy them. He did not turn away from these two whom He himself had designed and created in selfless love. Instead, He suffered for their sakes. As a substitute for their punishment, God slew two innocent animals, most probably lambs, skinned them and clothed His earth children in their pelts.

Oh, how Adam and Eve *needed* that covering! They had to have it for their bodies, which had immediately begun to die and needed protection from the elements; for their minds, which were now handicapped by selfishness and were vulnerable to attacks from the enemy of their souls; and for their spirits, which were already dead from the moment of their sin, that could be made alive only through the redemption those two lambs represented.

With their wilful, selfish choice, Adam and Eve laid the groundwork for that same choice by the myriads of their descendents all down through history. But it is not only Adam's sin that hurts God now; it is our own sinful thoughts, words, and deeds which 'crucify the Lord afresh.' This first sublime, significant sacrifice on earth to portray the suffering of the Lamb before the foundation of the world was a portrayal to Adam and Eve, *and to their offspring*, of the cost to God for their wilful wrongdoing. Two innocent lambs had to die. Their blood had to be spilled. Their lives had to be laid down in order to provide a covering for the man and woman standing exposed in sin before a loving, caring, suffering God. The covering for Adam and Eve was a symbol of the covering necessary for the whole human race.

There was no inherent, intrinsic merit in the death of the lambs themselves. There was no spiritual efficacy in the warm, red blood that drained from their veins. There was no divine defence against the Justice of God in the two skins now covering Adam and Eve. All the subsequent sacrifices that would ever be made upon earth, all the millions upon uncounted millions of lambs that ultimately would be slain upon thousands of altars in ages yet to come, were but a dim reflection of the unutterable remorse, sorrow, pain, and grief of a suffering Saviour.

Not all of these sacrifices combined could ever properly compensate for the sinfulness of man. The blood of lambs could never in itself make adequate reparation for the wretched attitudes and actions of the human race. What folly to ever feel it could! No indeed, a thousand times no – nothing that man could do would ever be able to make amends for his misdeeds against God. It was only, always, and ever will be *what God has done* that can suffice to pay the price. Only the laid-down life of God, the poured-out love of God, the pure and holy righteousness of God wrapped around our mortal souls could ever, ever atone for our dreadful behaviour.

CHAPTER 2

ℰ

No Substitute for the Lamb

Cain and Abel's Offerings

... Abel was a keeper of sheep, but Cain was a tiller of the ground.

(Genesis 4:2)

I have been both a 'keeper of sheep' and a 'tiller of the ground.' Born and raised in Kenya, East Africa, to a Swiss family on a large country estate, I have always loved wildlife and the out-of-doors.

At the age of 18, I left home to attend the University of Toronto in Canada for training as an agrologist. My keen interest in all growing things was there nurtured and developed in preparation for the many years I later spent in agricultural research, land management and ranch development. So, in the area of crop production, and in the broader realm of the science of agriculture, I have been 'a tiller of the ground.' On the other hand, many aspects of my life as a sheep man, the time when I was a 'keeper of sheep,' have been shared with readers of *A Shepherd Looks at the 23rd Psalm* and *A Shepherd Looks at the Good Shepherd*.

There is no sense in which these two occupations of field husbandry and animal husbandry are not perfectly acceptable, satisfying and pleasing to God. The conjunction 'but' used in the introductory Scripture passage is only for the purpose of contrast.

Both the sons of Adam and Eve had grown up with the knowledge and understanding of animal sacrifice. In their early years, this had been explained by their parents in very simple terms. But as they grew older, they received a clear, strong presentation concerning sin, its subsequent guilt, and the need for redemption from sin and guilt through the sacrifice of a lamb. At the time covered in this Scripture portion, they had been instructed in the appropriate propitiation for their human wrongdoing and arrogant pride against God. Because of this spiritual training from their parents, both Cain and Abel now sensed that sacrifice of some sort must be made for their own misdeeds.

Though the true meaning of the sacrifice, the ultimate realization in Christ himself was no doubt only a hazy picture far off in the future, Abel, the younger of the two boys, took this teaching very seriously. In careful solemnity he selected the choicest ram from his crop of lambs. With contrition, repentance, and in submission of his will, he killed the innocent creature, offering it as a substitute for himself for his sin.

This is the first record of a human being's deliberate choice of God's appointed way for making appropriate atonement between himself and his God. It was not the slaying of the lamb which somehow earned God's favour, but it was the *One* whom that slain lamb represented which made this an action of implicit faith. Abel was saying, 'O God, just as I have seen this little lamb's life laid down on my behalf, so I realize it represents Your life laid down in my stead.' This simple shepherd offered the lamb to his loving God, confident it would be accepted because it portrayed in flesh and blood the divine life of The Eternal Lamb himself.

God looked on in love. He accepted the sacrifice. He was satisfied. Abel depended on God's generosity, not on his own good conduct. Here was the pattern for proper reparation for all men for all time. Their total dependence must be upon divine intervention, not on their own human effort.

Forgiveness, acceptance, acquittal, reconciliation between God and man could never be achieved by man's strivings, by man's manipulation. How could sinful, fallen man ever erase the wounds, dissipate the remorse, or undo the dreadful damage to God's gracious, generous nature? Even if it were possible for a person to 'turn over a new leaf', to change his selfish direction by his own willpower, how could he erase the former years of sin and selfishness, the years of grieving a loving Heavenly Father? No, there is no way for the wrongdoer to redeem himself. The sin, the injury against God, needs the propitiation found only through the great Mediator himself.

This Abel realized. This Abel understood. This Abel acted upon in faith. This Abel saw as his only salvation. And thereby he was declared by God himself to be righteous, delivered from condemnation, cleansed from sin, and acquitted of the verdict against him. He was now accepted of God as a son.

Cain had received the same instruction, the same training from his parents as his brother Abel. He too should have understood the significance, the symbolism inherent in the death of a lamb for his sins.

It would seem from the Genesis account of this story

that Cain surveyed his shepherd brother's sacrifice and arrogantly concluded, 'Shepherd Abel has brought a lamb for sacrifice; I, Farmer Cain, will bring an offering representative of *my* vocation.'

Everything about Cain's offering spoke of self-effort, self-interest, self-reliance. Nothing there even remotely portrayed the sacrifice of love poured out by God in His own self-giving for lost men as *The Lamb slain*. The fruit and grain came from the ground already cursed by God because of the intrusion of evil in the earth.

This concept of self-assertion was repeated in a tragic incident later on in biblical history when Moses broke the typology of Christ as the Living Water and '*smote the rock*' rather then speaking to it. Though the water did flow forth from the rock for the thirsty children of Israel, God had to deal severely with Moses for this breach of trust. He was not allowed to enter Canaan nor lead the Israelites on the final leg of their journey into the Promised Land.

To God, Cain's offering was an insult and injury. It was an affront. It was a destructive element in the second portrayal of Christ as The Lamb of God.

Cain's offering could not be accepted. It was an attempt at self-merit and was of no value. Our human reasoning would cry out, 'But Cain was *attempting* to please God; it was not as if he did not bring an offering at all!' From God's point of view, Cain's circumvention of His clear instructions concerning the sacrifice represented again the Fall of Man – man's pride, selfishness, independence, the turning 'to his own way' to which Isaiah referred centuries later. In the very act of the offering, Cain was saying, 'I will not bow to my Creator and Redeemer; I do not need the efficacy of the blood spilled.' And, beyond this, Cain's arrogance had tarnished this eloquent picture of The Lamb slain in our stead.

Even so, the Scripture indicates that Cain could have even then brought a lamb offering to God, been forgiven and propitiated for his sin. But he hardened his heart against God and against his brother Abel; anger and jealousy mastered him; in the end, Cain became a murderer.

Now, thousands of years later, the implicit teaching in the story of Cain is that the cross of Christ cannot be circumvented. As the need for redemption is clearly seen in the story of Cain's parents, so the fact that *there is no substitute for Christ's redemption* is seen clearly in Cain's story.

CHAPTER 3

𝒞

The Son is the Lamb

Abraham's Test of Obedience

*Take now thy son, thine only son Isaac, whom thou lovest,
and get thee into the land of Moriah ...*

(Genesis 22:2)

Perhaps only a father can truly understand the drama
and pathos found in the story of Abraham and Isaac on
Mount Moriah. My earliest memories of my own
father, an American-Swiss layman whom God called as
a missionary to East Africa, are shadowed by impres-
sions of a tough, demanding man, though I had no
doubt of his love for me. But later on, by the time I was
in my teens, the Holy Spirit had worked in Dad's life,
changing him into a truly caring, gentle, kindly person.
He became a model, a pattern for my own responsibilities as a father.

I can only shake my head in awe and wonderment as I
attempt to picture either Dad or myself in Abraham's
position at the time of this Scripture passage. What an
incredible test of love and faith!

A thousand years of time had passed since the symbolic offerings which were considered in the previous
two chapters. Now God, again calling to Abraham with

whom He had an intimate friendship and with whom He had previously spoken in direct and unmistakable ways, was clearly and categorically commanding the great desert nomad to take his son, the child of his old age, up to Mt Moriah, 'and *offer him there for a burnt offering*'!

Often God's people read His Word with questions or doubts about His true meaning, His real intent. 'The Lord cannot *really* be saying anything quite so severe or stern.' We hope that there is some other meaning, some 'spiritual' interpretation which will 'get us off the hook' and out from under responsibility for obedience.

It was almost as if the Lord was overstating His word to Abraham so that there would be no room for a shadow of doubt in his mind concerning God's instructions: '… thine only son Isaac, whom thou lovest …' The relationship between Abraham and Isaac was very special, different than a usual father-son relationship. Isaac was the child of promise, son of Sarah's old age.

Perhaps thoughts of Ishmael, his firstborn, flashed through Abraham's mind. Though Abraham's love for Ishmael is in no doubt, would the test have been as profound, as poignant, if God had asked that Abraham's first son, the one he had had with Hagar, be sacrificed?

We can only imagine the kind of night Abraham spent after hearing God's word to him. Abraham could have been forgiven if he had waited a few days to be sure he had understood correctly, that this was not some dreadful mistake. But he 'rose up early' the next morning, after having gotten little or no sleep, and without delay began his sorrowful mission. The dear old man must have died a thousand deaths as he and his son approached the mountain.

We have no indication that this special son Isaac had questions or was concerned that anything was amiss until the third day of travel. Abraham had seen the summit in the distance and instructed their two travelling companions to stay behind with the ass while 'I and the lad go yonder and worship, and *come again to you.*' There is no inkling here of a father's heavy heart or that there was any doubt concerning their return. But when Abraham laid the wood for the fire on Isaac, took a knife in one hand and fire for the altar in the other, and they had begun that long climb up Mt Moriah, then Isaac said, 'Father, we have the knife, the fire and the wood; *but where is the lamb?*'

Isaac had received the same spiritual training that Cain and Abel received; he knew that the appropriate sacrifice for this time of worship and communion with God was a lamb. Was this question he now addressed to his father purely academic, or did he sense something different about this offering? We can only guess at the thoughts going through Isaac's mind; but if he had fears, they were put to rest by Abraham's calm, simple rejoinder: 'My son, *God will provide himself a lamb* for a burnt offering.'

These words thunder down to us across the ages since that time, another thrilling reminder that the lamb sacrifice was not an invention of man's imagination to appease an angry God; rather, *God himself provides The Lamb!*

The faith of Abraham! His faith did not isolate him from asking God, 'Why?' His mind was no doubt full of questions, and a band of anguish probably constricted his chest at times. But at rock bottom, Abraham's confidence in God's was steady and unwavering. We know from Hebrews 11:17 that Abraham believed that, if necessary, God would raise Isaac from the dead in order to carry out His covenant.

Abraham and Isaac arrived at the very same spot where later King Solomon was to build his marvellous temple to God. But the 'point of no return' was fast approaching as father and son began laying up a rough altar of uncut stones. The physical exertion muted for a moment the pounding of this ancient patriarch's heart.

Then the altar was finished. Abraham laid on it the wood that would fuel the sacrificial fire. God could truly be relied upon to provide a substitute sacrifice for His son. The great Jehovah had done so for Adam and Eve. He likewise had accepted the lamb slain in simple trust by Abel. God would, now, again, intervene on behalf of him and his son Isaac.

No other sacrifice was in sight. Abraham took his beloved son, with burning, tear-filled eyes and trembling lips; bound him with rope and laid him upon the altar; he was ready to offer the dearest thing he owned in all the world to God.

His heart cried out, 'I love my son, my son Isaac, whom you have given to me; but I love you more, Lord!' Abraham stretched forth his grizzled, sunburned hand to seize the knife that would slay his son, then a voice from heaven thundered: 'Abraham! Abraham!' The patriarch's immediate answer was: 'Here am I.' His obedience to God was complete; whatever God's command, Abraham's response was that of a humble, obedient servant to the Lord.

'Do not lay your hand upon the lad,' the voice

commanded. 'I know now that your faith and love for the Lord of glory, *The Lamb of God*, is unshakeable since you have not withheld your son, your only son Isaac, from Me.'

With racing pulse and beating heart, the old gentleman quickly released his son from the altar upon which he was bound. Lifting his eyes and looking around, he saw behind him a ram caught in a thicket by his horns; this ram became the burnt offering, the substitute lamb for Isaac.

This mountain top of Mount Moriah would henceforth be called *Jehovah Jireh*, meaning 'the Lord provides.'

This dramatic story is not quite finished until we remember that there was heard a second voice from heaven that day. God's own father-heart fully understood the magnitude, the depth of Abraham's obedience. He was looking down through the centuries to that point in time when His own beloved Son would be the sacrifice for all men of all time. There would be no substitute then as there had been for Isaac; He was, is, and ever will be '*The Lamb of God* slain from before the foundation of the world.'

Abraham's heavenly Father was moved by the expression of devotion from this earthly father, and God took this opportunity to reconfirm His covenant with Abraham. 'In thy seed shall all the nations of the earth be blessed; because thou hast obeyed my voice.'

And so The Lamb of God, the Lord of glory, accepted the substitute lamb as a proper and adequate provision for both the patriarch and his son. The ram lamb caught in the thicket at the right time, in the right place, for the right believers was a superb foreshadowing of the perfect provision of God's own suffering for His people.

This indeed the Lord had done – He himself was that Lamb.

This indeed Abraham believed – he took and trusted.

This indeed was counted to him for righteousness – he accepted God's substitute for his son.

CHAPTER 4

༄

The Passover Lamb

The Saving of the Firstborn

The blood shall be to you for a token upon the houses where ye are: and when I see the blood, I will pass over you ...

(Exodus 12:13)

The Old Testament has been the stage setting in our unfolding drama of the Lamb of God. Act One in this divine drama took place in the Garden of Eden. Act Two was performed in the pasturelands around the rich Euphrates Delta. We saw Act Three on Mount Moriah. We have now come to one of the most gripping of the Old Testament scenes: Act Four occurs in the fertile lowlands of Egypt in the Delta of the Nile.

Nearly four hundred years have passed since that moving reprieve for Isaac on the mountain by Jehovah-Jireh himself The Great Provider of a substitute for Abraham's child of promise had also provided a place of refuge for His people in the land of Egypt. I have considered with awe that area of land at the mouth of the Nile where the Hebrews made their homes. Approximately 100 miles long and 150 miles wide, it is a region of immense fertility. Even today this section of

Egypt is a major factor to the nation in terms of crop production and livestock production.

The nation of Israel had been special, invited guests of the Pharaoh, probably Rameses II, to whom Joseph had been Vice Consul. Jacob's family, seventy strong, had come to make their home with Joseph during the famine. With some disdain, because they were livestock keepers, Pharaoh had generously assigned the Hebrews their own section of the country – the land of Goshen, the most fertile area of the whole of Egypt. It is no wonder that 'the children of Israel were fruitful, and increased abundantly, and multiplied, and waxed exceeding mighty; and the *land was filled with them*.'

The status of these people had gradually deteriorated during the centuries after they left their homeland. 'The king who knew not Joseph' was jealous and afraid of these 'foreigners' whom God had so obviously blessed. He decided to use them for forced labour in his city-building projects. This only made them stronger, and their numbers increased further.

Eventually God's time for the great exodus of Israel from Egypt had come. The cruel Pharaoh, hating the Hebrews, yet greedy for their slave labour, was reluctant to release them. Plague upon plague was unleashed by God against the land of Egypt. Finally there would be a slaying of all the favourite, firstborn sons of every family. This was to be the last drastic judgment that would free Israel from their Egyptian slave masters. This great tragic event would signal the triumphal exodus of a whole nation, some two million people, from their bondage.

In order for God's special people, the Israelis, to be preserved from the awful peril of that night, each family was carefully instructed to offer a lamb or kid of the first year, flawless and unblemished, as a sacrifice. This lamb was to be known as the special 'Passover Lamb.' The laying down of its life, the shedding of its blood, the substitution of its flesh, would replace the death of each family's firstborn son.

Imagine the bustle and activity throughout the Nile Delta that day! The very best lambs of the Hebrew flocks were selected. Some families who were too few in number to use a whole lamb by themselves joined with neighbours and friends for the Passover celebration. The children were under watchful care that day. The firstborn son, particularly, was made to understand that his very life was being ransomed by the Passover Lamb. The mothers in each household prepared roasted flat cakes (Japatis) of unleavened flour. They prepared vegetables, the 'bitter herbs,' to be eaten with the roast lamb.

The lamb's blood was carefully collected in a bowl, then each Hebrew mother held the bowl as the father dipped a stalk of hyssop in the blood and applied it to the entrance of their home. The three applications on lintels and door jamb were symbolic of the cross. No doubt the oldest son watched this ceremony with great intensity and concern so every detail was in order. He probably checked several times later in the day to be sure that the blood was still clearly visible. The death of their own substitute lamb assured each family that the destroying angel would *pass over* that home. The lamb's blood sprinkled upon the doorposts and head crosspiece of the entrance way declared the immunity of the entire family within from the dire judgment without.

As evening came, every member of the family was

carefully accounted for and kept indoors. They gathered around the table in travelling clothes, staves in hand, shoes on their feet. Quickly they ate the roasted lamb, herbs and bread. They were ready to leave in haste in the night.

As the hour of midnight came, the Hebrew families looked at each other in wonderment and awe as the Mid-eastern wails of mourning began to arise from the Egyptian households. 'There was not a house where there was not one dead.'

It was enough! God's predicted judgment was upon Egypt. Pharaoh could not wait to get the Israelis out of the land. 'The Egyptians were urgent upon the people, that they might send them out of the land in haste; for, they said, We be all dead men' (Exodus 12:33).

God decreed that this Passover should be a memorial service, in memory of Israel's flight from Egypt – symbolic of The Passover Lamb Who was to come. There are three powerful emblematic elements in this service. The unleavened bread represented the haste with which the Hebrews left Egypt; it is also a picture of the sinless Christ, His body broken for us, of which we partake as members of His family. The bitter herbs represent the slavery, the misery which the Hebrews were leaving behind; these herbs also represent the bitter cup of suffering which our Lord drank on our behalf. The Passover Lamb was the substitute, a sacrifice of shed blood providing protection from death for each Hebrew firstborn; this spotless lamb represented God's own firstborn, only begotten Son whose shed blood and laid-down life bears the death sentence for the whole world.

So, once more, in simple language and unmistakable

symbolism, the lamb slain in Israeli homes in Egypt at that first Passover feast portrayed The Lamb of God, slain from the foundation of the world – the One Who 1,500 years later would be offered in death at the Passover feast in Jerusalem.

The authenticity and accuracy of this portrayal comes with special impact to those of us who through force of circumstances or choice of profession have had to slaughter sheep. During my own years as a sheep rancher, the so-called 'killing season' was a time of personal anguish and remorse. Yet the slaughter of lambs was absolutely essential to the success of the ranch operation itself; some lambs simply had to be sacrificed every year in order for the rest of the flock to flourish and thrive. The flock had to be kept to a size that the ranch could support in terms of optimum nourishment, shelter and disease control. My own survival as a shepherd depended directly upon the substitute death of my own lambs.

This was no easy thing for me – no light task; no careless, casual incident. The little creatures are so silent in the hands of their owner. They do not bleat or scream in protest. It is almost as if they quietly acquiesce to their own death. As the killing knife severs the jugular vein from which the warm lifeblood flows, there is not a sound. The little, innocent life, lived so briefly, so fleetingly, for a few months, is poured out in but a few brief moments.

They are born to die!

They came briefly but for this one purpose.

Out of their death springs life for others!

A profound principle little understood by most Christians and seldom explained, because it is never fully grasped, is the law of the so-called 'energy conversion cycle,' a term used in scientific circles. If I am able to explain this in understandable terms, it will enable the reader to recognize how authentic and realistic is the divine revelation of God's Word.

Once death had entered into the dimension of life upon planet Earth, it began to condition all of its activities. This was not God's original intention. Our federal parents, Adam and Eve, were endowed with the same enduring, eternal life as God himself. But this was short-circuited and grounded to earth because of their submission to Satan. They believed his insinuation that wilful disobedience to God was really of no grave consequence or significance.

When Adam and Eve set their own selfish wills in direct opposition to that of their loving Heavenly Father – this Creator who had given them a wonderful environment, fulfilling occupation, His own friendship, His very life – an incredible separation occurred.

The self-centredness of man was set against the selflessness of God. Evil and good, death and life, despair and love – the darkness of man's dilemma and the light of God's salvation were set in direct opposition one to the other. Because of this death, because of this separation, God's best plans were perverted. The sentence of death had been passed on man and all other forms of life. Life no longer came from God directly to His creation; life would now come through death.

Allow me to explain. Rather than our first parents partaking freely and fully of abundant resources provided for them directly from the hand of God, they now had to turn and till the soil and husband livestock. Every crop they produced, whether from their little garden or their little flock, would have to forfeit its life in order to feed and sustain man.

Life could now come to them only through death – the death of grain, vegetables, fruit, flesh or food of any sort that once possessed life.

In short, one life had to be laid down for another life. One needed to die in order for another not to die.

This principle prevails to this very moment. Every erg of energy we possess, every ounce of weight our bodies carry, every element of life we own is ours only by virtue of the death of other living forms.

God instantly saw and knew all this the moment Adam and Eve sinned. He recognized at once the rupture of His own wondrous original design and intentions for man. And God immediately initiated His own intervention, the plan He had already prepared, to redeem us from this human dilemma. The first innocent lambs were slain, and their pelts provided the first couple with protection from the elements, flesh for survival, and atonement for their sin.

Even further, this substitutionary sacrifice was a signal from God to man that He knew all life on earth was henceforth conditioned and dependent on death. The energy conversion cycle was already underway. All life thereafter would come only through death.

God knew that ultimately only the forfeiture of His own divine life could possibly provide the eternal life essential to man's survival. Only from His divine death could come our hope of immortal life. The Creator had given life once; now, through death, He was giving it again. This is why every lamb ever offered, every sacrifice ever made, every life of an animal forfeited was a special symbol of God's own redemptive purposes.

True, these animals were offered as a substitute for the owner himself but, beyond this, they depicted this profound principle that governs and pervades the entire human race – that life comes only through death.

The liberal theologians who look with disdain upon what they refer to as the 'butcher-shop' gospel show an enormous naiveté in failing to understand this combined scientific and spiritual principle at work in the universe.

It is noteworthy that in giving the clearly defined instructions to the Hebrews for their preparation of the Passover Lamb, God emphatically told them to consume its flesh in entirety that night. Not only would the blood of the lamb sprinkled on the doorposts provide them with protection from judgment, but the flesh of the lamb eaten that night would energize them to escape from Egypt and 'pass over' the Red Sea to freedom.

Some 1,500 years later, *The Passover Lamb* arrived in Jerusalem at the time of the Passover Feast. He wished to celebrate this special memorial service with His friends.

On that night, the twelve young men little knew the enormous significance of their simple meal together with the Master. They were still quarrelling and wrangling over personal position. They were still at odds over jealous rivalries. One of them, a ruthless and selfish thief, was totally oblivious to the Passover supper as either a memorial or a sacrament.

As Judas took the broken bread and poured-out wine from His Saviour's hands, he had no idea those same hands would soon be nailed to a cross. Preconceived ideas of power and wealth had blinded his view of

Christ as *God's Lamb*. The rest of the group were really not much better. Those who did meditate on the first Passover celebration were ignorant of *The Passover Lamb* in their midst. They did not realize that in a few short hours, Jesus would be offering himself as the supreme sacrifice for all men of all time. They did not know that as every lamb offered on ten million altars had looked forward to this point in history, so from then on every Communion service held, every Last Supper celebrated, would look back to it. But there was One at that table who knew, who fully understood what was facing Him as if it had already taken place.

Not only would that life laid down in our behalf provide a substitute for our sins, but also that body broken and spilled blood shared with us would provide the very life essential to our eternal survival.

This was the issue to which Christ addressed himself so emphatically in John 6 and the one which even His closest disciples had difficulty accepting: 'Except ye eat the flesh of the Son of man, and drink his blood, ye have no life in you. Whoso eateth my flesh, and drinketh my blood, hath eternal life; and I will raise him up at the last day' (John 6:53, 54).

The Lamb of God, *The Passover Lamb* slain in our stead, was a spotless Lamb. He was not stained with His own wrongs. He was not contaminated by His own self-ishness, His own wilfulness.

It was our sin, our selfishness, which He took upon himself. He, who knew no sin at all, condescended to be made sin for us that we might be made right and clean and pure with the righteousness of God.

It is significant that in the original ordinance estab-lished by God for the sacrifice of the Passover Lamb, clear, unmistakable details were given for the total disposal of the animal. Its blood was to be sprinkled on the doorposts, its flesh was to be eaten, and all the rest – the pelt, fleece, wool, and offal – were to be consumed by fire before dawn.

This fire represents divine retribution and judgment upon the parts of the animal not consumed by the family. At Calvary that same inviolate judgment fell upon our sins, our selfishness, our wrongs, our pride – all borne in the person of our suffering Saviour. In appalling agony and spiritual separation from God himself, our Lord endured the awesome ignominy of hell in order that we might be spared, saved ... *passed over* ... by the irrevocable judgment of our righteous God.

CHAPTER 5

❧

The Sin-Bearing Lamb

The Scapegoat in the Wilderness

The goat, on which the lot fell to be the scapegoat, shall be presented alive before the Lord, to make an atonement with him, and to let him go for a scapegoat into the wilderness.

(Leviticus 16:10)

History moves on. Israel has celebrated the first Passover and has left Egypt *en masse*. The great exodus of an entire nation, at least two million strong, has taken them across the upper reaches of the Red Sea into the desert wastes of Sinai – the Mount of God. And here we come to Act Five. Three months after Act Four has taken place in Egypt, Act Five in the divine drama is performed in the wilderness.

It is difficult to describe in words the forbidding solitude but majestic grandeur of this desolate setting. Certainly there would be no distractions of civilization as God prepared to speak directly and personally to His special servant Moses and, through him, to His people. Imagine the numbing awe of the children of Israel, after their careful ceremonial cleansing and after the fearful warnings against untimely approach to the mountain, to see their leader, their father-figure, Moses, disappearing into the thunderous cloud.

On this gaunt and dreadful mountain, God gave to Moses not only the Ten Commandments, the basic structure for the moral and ethical conduct of God's special people, but also detailed instructions as to how these Ten Commandments should be lived out in their daily lives. At this point in time, these instructions were bound up with symbolic ceremonies and specific sacrifices which were important to the whole nation. With their limited spiritual understanding and without a written Word of God, they needed these visual ceremonies.

Though God chose to speak to His people through these graphic celebrations, He never intended the symbol to replace personal faith and wholehearted obedience to His commands. 'This people honoureth me with their lips, but their heart is far from me ... for laying aside the *commandment* of God, ye hold the *tradition* of men, as the washing of pots and cups: and many other such like things ye do' (Mark 7:6–8).

Among the instructions given to Moses on Mount Sinai were details for a special ceremony to be included with the burnt offering. It would be a dramatic visual presentation to Israel of God's unique work in atonement. Combined with the sin offering described in Leviticus 16, there was to be a second animal 'presented alive before the Lord' which would bear away the sin of the people.

The two kid goats were necessary to fully describe the two aspects of the work which Christ would complete on the cross. The High Priest, Aaron, had specific instructions concerning his ceremonial cleansing and attire. Then he was to select from the flock of Israel two matched kids, healthy and unblemished. Aaron was to cast lots on the two, selecting one for a sacrifice to God and the other for a scapegoat. The first animal symbolized the atonement for sin which was needed in order for Israel to have fellowship with God; the second one represented that which the sin-bearing Lamb of God would do at Calvary: *bear in His own body* the sins of the whole human race, taking them away, to be remembered against us no longer.

Again, the symbolism of this sacrifice and ceremony was a clear reflection to the whole nation of their atonement. In subsequent centuries, the millions of lambs, kids, and bullocks slaughtered and sacrificed on the altars of Israel were speaking of God in Christ, The Lamb suffering in their stead and bearing away their sins.

These sacrifices of blood certainly looked forward to the culmination of all such offerings when Christ himself would fulfil the picture; but they looked back, as well, to all that had been accomplished already by God for them in His suffering and agony on their behalf. Even thousands of years before the fact, Christ's death was a *fait accompli*; God suffered through every animal sacrifice as if He were suffering on the Cross already.

This peculiar people, chosen to carry out God's special plan for the world, had grieved and wounded Him beyond our ability to comprehend. Their parting comment as Moses left them to talk face to face with God was, 'All that the Lord has spoken, we will do.' Yet when Moses returned to the people from the mountain, he faced a scene of lawlessness and lewdness beyond imagination. Again and again throughout their history, rebellion, stubborness, waywardness and perverseness cost Him enormous pain and suffering.

The great poets and prophets of Israel spoke often of the suffering Saviour. David, the ancient shepherd king of Israel, spoke both poetically and prophetically of God's Son enduring great shame and suffering.

In his magnificent Psalm 22, speaking under the inspiration of God's own Spirit, he portrays in clear and power passages the suffering of God, very God in Christ – *The Lamb of God*. In moving stanzas, David looking down the years, was quoting Christ 'before the fact': 'My God, my God, why hast thou forsaken me?' What a shattering, sobering thought that Christ himself should be forsaken! That, for no sin on His own part, He should endure such terrible separation from His Father.

The hymnwriter of a past century has caught the drama and pathos of this sin-bearing Lamb so well:

O Lamb of God! Thou wonderful sinbearer;
Hard after Thee my soul doth follow on;
As pants the hart for streams in desert dreary,
So pants my soul for Thee, O Thou life-giving One.

I mourn, I mourn, the sin that drove Thee from me,
And blackest darkness brought into my soul;
Now, I renounce th' accursed thing that hindered,
And come once more to Thee, to be made fully whole.

Descend the heavens, Thou whom my soul adoreth!
Exchange Thy throne for my poor longing heart,
For thee, for Thee, I watch as for the morning;
No rest or peace is mine from my Saviour apart.

Come, Holy Ghost, Thy mighty aid bestowing,
Destroy the works of sin, the self, the pride;
Burn, burn in me, my idols overthrowing,
Prepare my heart for Him – for my Lord crucified.

At Thy feet I fall, yield Thee up my all,
To suffer, live, or die for my Lord crucified.

The powerful portrait of the sacrificial lamb is not one which appeals to our human vanity and pride. Mankind shuns suffering. We abhor humiliation. We flee from sorrow of any sort. Degradation and despair are conditions we resist.

And yet the human condition, despite all our fancy pretence at success and splendour, is shot through with pathos and pain. Life itself, as C. S. Lewis so provocatively points out, carries much more pain than pleasure. The tapestry of our days is coloured more strongly with stress than with singing, it is woven through with dark threads of despair and grief more than with strands of glory and light.

The human mind rejects the implications of God himself suffering for our salvation; yet if *God* suffers, how can puny man escape it? In all our frantic efforts to escape suffering, do we realize that our own sin and selfishness are the cause of so much suffering in this life and in the hereafter?

In chapter 59 of his prophecy, Isaiah gives a graphic description of the human condition with this opening statement: 'Your iniquities have separated between you and your God, and your sins have hid his face from you, that he will not hear.' And the prophet goes on to describe man in his folly and childish reactions, shaking his puny fist at his Maker. Cynical and sceptical, he tries to cover his inner despair and soul sickness with a smirk or a smile. He pretends all is well when, in fact, all is wrong within.

His are the symptoms of a grief that eats away his

soul like an insidious gangrene. He is out of touch with God, out of joint with his fellowman, and, even more often, alienated from himself. In anguish he wanders on, sometimes longing for light, more often preferring the darkness of his own evil deeds. We resent and resist this disclosure of our own undone condition. We insist in our selfish pride that 'mankind is not so bad.' We cling to the false hope that mankind is getting better and better.

It is no wonder that Isaiah concluded, 'there was no man [to help], and wondered that there was no inter-cessor' (Isaiah 59:16). But the prophet did not stop there: '*therefore HIS arm brought salvation. ....*'

There was no help for man, except God himself step into our time and space. Before ever a race of men set foot on this planet, The Lamb of God was prepared, in case it was necessary, to come and bear away their total grief and sorrow, these outer symptoms of the inner illness of sin and selfishness which is the bottomless chasm separating us from God and from our fellowman.

Somehow, somewhere, someone must build a bridge across that appalling chasm. We cannot save ourselves, try as we may. We cannot cleanse our own conscience. We cannot shrug off our own sin. There must be a sinbearer apart from ourselves.

This God has always seen and clearly understood. *Man has not!*

And so here in the wilderness at Mount Sinai, God added a bold, fresh stroke to the portrait of The Lamb of God. The two young animals before the High Priest represented another piece in the unfolding picture of God's atonement. After the lot was cast and the one was chosen for the sacrifice, its blood was carefully brought into the innermost holy place of the tabernacle to be sprinkled on the mercy seat where God met with man. Instead of suffering for their own sins, absolution and atonement were made through the death of the lamb for the entire nation.

The eternal law, the inviolate principle, that 'the soul that sinneth, it shall die,' had been fully exonerated. In the substitute death of another, the law was satisfied and the guilty sinners set free.

Further evidence and illustration of this incredible transaction was now ready for public manifestation with the second sacrificial kid. This was to be a public demonstration to the rest of the nation, barred from entrance to the holy of holies, that their sins had in fact been forgiven. This was public assurance that their God had met them in mercy. They could now know beyond doubt that their guilt was gone and their future was free.

His hands already stained with the lifeblood of the first animal, the High Priest now laid them upon the head of the second little innocent creature, symbolic of the transfer to it of all the sins of Israel.

This sacrificial animal, too, would pay with its life. The sinbearer scapegoat would carry away the sins of the nation into the oblivion and obscurity of the wilderness. Led away by a 'fit man,' representative of the only One truly appropriate for this task, this little animal would never be seen again.

This was an annual rite, a symbolic and visual demonstration once each year to the nation of Israel of the two messages inherent in the atonement.

Years later in Israel's history, the Spirit of God

speaking through the inspired writer to the Hebrews declared categorically that the blood of goats and lambs could never take away sin, 'for the law *having a shadow* of good things to come, and not the very image of the things, can never with those sacrifices which they offered year by year continually make the comers thereunto perfect ... But *this man,* after he had offered one sacrifice for sins for ever, sat down on the right hand of God' (Hebrews 10:1, 12).

Christ fulfilled all the parts of this ceremony when He died on the cross – He himself is the great High Priest, the sacrificial Lamb, the 'fit Man' and the Scapegoat bearing away our sins into the immensity of God's generous forgetfulness!

In turn, for all He has borne on my behalf, He asks only that I reach out my hands in faith and lay them in quiet trust upon His person. Just as the priest in faith placed his hands on the living animal which would be led away into the wilderness, so now I can rely upon my divine Sinbearer to act for me. Christ's assurance to me is that if I do so, my sins will be borne away, never more to be remembered against me. 'I will put my laws into their hearts, and in their minds will I write them; and their sins and iniquities *will I remember no more*' (Hebrews 10:16, 17). What deliverance! What freedom!

Even beyond His wonderful forgiveness and acceptance, the Father invites us to enter now *with boldness* into the holiest by the blood of Jesus. A child of God can have this confidence because of the ministry of the divine Scapegoat. Under the protection of God's divine forgetfulness, we can in turn forgive and accept others; and we can even forgive ourselves. We then know what it is to walk in the light, the wonderous brightness of

His presence. Our days have meaning. Our years have purpose. Our despair has turned into the laughter of a joyous love – love for God; love for other followers of the Lamb; love for the lost.

CHAPTER 6

ℭ

The Suffering Lamb

Isaiah's Word Pictures of the Lamb of God

Surely he hath borne our griefs, and carried our sorrows; yet we did esteem him stricken, smitten of God, and afflicted. But he was wounded for our transgressions, he was bruised for our iniquities: the chastisement of our peace was upon him, and with his stripes we are healed. All we like sheep have gone astray; we have turned every one to his own way; and the Lord hath laid on him the iniquity of us all. He was oppressed, and he was afflicted, yet he opened not his mouth: he is brought as a lamb to the slaughter, and as a sheep before her shearers is dumb, so he openeth not his mouth.

(Isaiah 53:4–7)

This is an appropriate point in this study of the Lamb of God to reflect on the historical sequence of Isaiah's special revelation. Much of the enormous impact of this passage from Isaiah lies in its prophetic accuracy. Not only does the prophet picture the ritualistic rites of the Passover Lamb slain on ten million Israeli altars for the preceding 700 years, but also he depicts under the inspiration of God's Spirit the suffering of God's own Passover Lamb some 700 years in the future.

We have come to the sixth sublime Act in the ongoing pageantry of God's revelation of himself as our Saviour. The suspense, the drama, has been building with each new presentation of the Lamb of God. The first five gave to God's people important aspects of what the Lamb of God does. Now, Isaiah, seven centuries before the fact, paints in stirring language, which only God himself could have inspired, a vivid description of The Lamb of God himself.

Now we see lifted up, for all men of all time, the Lamb slain, not only for His own chosen people but for the *whole human race*. '*All* we like sheep have gone astray; we have turned everyone to his own way; and the Lord hath laid on him the iniquity of us *all*' (Isaiah 53:6). It is with the sheep who have gone astray that The Lamb of God, though spotless and having never strayed himself, is so strongly identified. The blind, selfish, groping sheep can be brought into the fold only by The Lamb of God.

God has never left man in ignorance or confusion concerning His purposes. All through the long prelude of centuries prior to His own appearance, The Lamb of God acted decisively, deliberately to reveal in unmistakable terms that every move He made, every action He took was for His lost sheep, His lost people.

Who Believes Our Report?

The simple, clear answer to the prophet's rhetorical question is, *almost no one!*

The reason, of course, is obvious. We do not believe the prophet's presentation of the problem nor the solution to our human dilemma. We assume rather naively that most of us are a rather respectable lot. How quickly do we forget the appalling atrocities which man has perpetrated against man, and against God, all down through human history.

We deliberately close our eyes to the never-ending tragic tale of death, murder, greed, cruelty, theft, rape, torture and war which have marked man's footsteps from the murder of Abel to the killing of millions of the unborn today. We tend to believe for the most part that human beings are noble, grand and glorious individuals, intent only on lofty ideals and righteous aspirations.

Too often in our western culture, with its history of Judeo-Christian influence, we forget the ferocious pagan conduct of the hidden peoples who have known nothing of God and His incredible love. Modern humanists with their secular philosophies often hold forth on the 'essential goodness of man' – as if primitive societies are happy, free, innocent children at heart. This is in spite of the evidence of cruel, heartless cultures and cults; the atrocities of inter-tribal wars and vendettas; the casual attitude toward human life; the human sacrifices; the torture of children – the list could go on and on and should stab us wide awake to the dilemma of those who grope about in the darkness of unbelief.

But, no, mankind does not believe the prophet's report about the human condition; neither do we believe the prophet's report concerning God's way out of man's dilemma. That God himself should take on a body 'marred more than any man,' to be despised and rejected by the very ones to whom He came, take more than human understanding to comprehend. We are still hiding our faces from Him.

Is it any wonder, then, that when God came among us in human guise, He was tortured to death – offered as a human sacrifice, the final horror of our human degradation?

We dare not look with righteous disdain upon those contemporaries of Jesus who crucified Him so long ago. Cruelty and hatred and injustice and flaming fury are not the special hallmark of a certain passionate race of another generation. Twentieth-century man, with his sophisticated, smooth, cynical veneer of civilization, is no less a part of that roaring mob which led Him away to be crucified.

This deeply moving proclamation by Isaiah is not one man's view of the human dilemma, but God's. Whether Isaiah's report is believed or not changes not one iota of its truth.

For reasons not clearly understood by Bible scholars, Isaiah's prophetic utterances regarding Christ's sufferings have been broken arbitrarily in two at the beginning of chapter 53. Some translators from the past have actually incorporated Isaiah 52:13–15 into chapter 53. At the very least, the last verses of chapter 52 should be looked upon as the preamble and overture to this magnificent portrayal of the suffering Lamb.

Isaiah cries out that the eternal God comes disguised as the suffering Servant. He will succeed in His magnificent mission of seeking and salvaging lost sheep. By the incredible exchange of laying down His life for ours, He is able to raise us from our ruin.

Oh, that we could grasp the import of that phrase, 'laying down his life'! In our beautiful sanctuaries and comfortable pews, we tend to forget that His royal visage is marred and contorted beyond recognition. He who has never known even a moment's fleeting whisper of personal guilt carries the guilt of every man, woman, and child who has ever lived ... – 'the Lord hath laid on him *the iniquity of us all.*'

Evil men mocked and jeered at his death. Satan and his cohorts laughed fiendishly at their seemingly successful conspiracy. They thought they had killed God! They thought they had thwarted His best plan. They concluded for a moment that the King's Representative was no longer a factor to be dealt with.

But the presumptuous victory orgy turned to terrified silence as indications of divine wrath were unleashed upon the earth. The three hours of darkness at noonday were sobering enough; but the veil of the temple rent from top to bottom; the earthquake; the exploding rocks; the opened graves; and appearances of those long dead caused even the godless soldiers to conclude, 'Truly this was the Son of God!'

Hand-in-hand with evil men, the father of evil had had only a fleeting moment of triumph. From before time began, *God had planned* for the death of His Son. The forces of darkness had actually cooperated in their own undoing! Because the cross is not the culmination of God's redemption plan. Beyond it lay a royal mausoleum. Christ's death was but a step towards the Resurrection morning That which to the onlookers appeared as a total tragedy was and is a perpetual triumph in the economy of eternity.

Isaiah caught a glimpse of that triumph in the closing refrain of Isaiah 52: 'Many nations will marvel at him. Kings will be speechless with amazement' (Isaiah 52:15, GNB).

Yet in spite of all the foregoing good news, most men

and women simply will not believe in Him, the One who made intercession for the transgressors.

The word *believe* is commonly bandied about in Christian circles. We use the phrase 'believe in Christ' very casually and sometimes carelessly. We speak glibly about thousands, if not millions, of so-called believers.

What does the word 'believe' as used in Scripture really mean? Giving mental assent? Accepting an idea as true? Giving credence to the concept of an historical Christ?

To simply accept that He was born in Bethlehem, lived and ministered among men for thirty-three years, then died a dreadful death on a cruel Roman gibbet is not *believing*, in the spiritual dimension of the word. Even millions of Moslems believe in Jesus Christ this way.

Our Lord himself when He was here on earth had trouble getting people to really believe. He decried the fact that though He spoke to them about himself, though He taught them truth clearly, though He performed mighty miracles, they still did not truly believe (John 10:24–38).

To believe means that one has a deep inner passion (thirst) for Jesus Christ which can be satisfied only by partaking of His own life and Spirit. 'Jesus said unto them, I am the bread of life; he that cometh to me shall never hunger; and he that believeth on me shall never thirst' (John 6:35, 36). In the next chapter of John, on the last day of the great feast, 'Jesus stood and cried, saying, If any man thirst, let him come unto me, and drink. He that *believeth* on me, as the scripture has said, out of his belly shall flow rivers of living water' (7:37, 38).

In the realm of our physical well-being, if we thirst, we must drink water. Our bodies are roughly 70 per cent liquid. In order to maintain cell turgidity and for body metabolism to proceed normally in good health, water must be assimilated into our systems daily, water is essential in order to sustain the chemical and physical exchanges of nutrition as planned. Likewise, in the spiritual sense, to believe implies that the very life of God in Christ must be assimilated into our spirits, into our souls. We must actually open our innermost being to receive Him. We then become partakers of the very nature of God himself.

The result of this kind of *believing* will be a diametric change in us. We are no longer just men and women who know about an historical Jesus. We are no longer those who merely discuss a doctrinal Christ in a casual, clinical way. We will no longer regard God as a distant diety, detached and far away from us in the immensity of outer space. Christ becomes the very source of our life, our constant companion. His presence by His Spirit is a living, dynamic reality. His will, His wishes, His intentions, His purposes become ours. He is the confidante for all our decisions. We know Him, and we are acutely, serenely aware that He knows us. In brief, *to believe* in Christ is to have Him as part of every moment, waking or sleeping.

'God gave us eternal life, and this life is in his Son. He who possesses the Son has that life; he who does not possess the Son of God does not have that life' (1 John 5:11, 12, AMP).

A moment's reflection will make abundantly clear to us that the number who have believed the prophet's report this way are remarkably few – perhaps less than

5 per cent of the earth's total population. Our Lord warned us that it would be so. Few there be who find this life, this truth, this way to live. But it is to this tiny handful that the arm of the Lord is revealed. It is to them that God in Christ becomes a powerful person. The Spirit of God becomes their companion, their counsellor, their comrade-in-arms for their sojourn here on earth.

It is the one who is prepared to accept God's evaluation and verdict regarding his own undone condition who will turn to Christ. No longer holding God at arm's length, and now seeing himself in his own sin and despair, he will open himself to Christ's entry into his life. To this one the Saviour comes, revealing himself in all of His winsome compassion, understanding and strength. With forgiveness, acceptance, love and serenity, He becomes our dearest friend, our fondest companion. It should not be difficult then to concede quickly to His lordship of our lives. He deserves to be sovereign. He is entitled to hold pre-eminence in our affairs.

This is to recognize, 'O Christ, you are God, very God.' This is to respond, 'O Christ, your wish is my command.' This is to reply, 'O Christ, whatever You wish, I shall do it.' Herein lies peace – Christ in us. Herein lies power – Christ through us.

The Lambkin's Tender Years

Under the inspiration of God's own gracious spirit, the prophet Isaiah proclaims in the second verse of this remarkable chapter that the coming one, the Christ, the suffering one, would grow up as a 'suckling,' a 'tender shoot,' a 'tiny lambkin.'

The Hebrew expression used here is YONEQ, derived from the verb YANAQ, which in its most profound intent refers to a small, nursing infant or a suckling, newborn offspring.

Most ancient translators have represented this term as a tender young shoot, a frail sprig of new growth emerging from a stump growing in a waste piece of desert land.

But it can also mean a little lambkin whose heel marks – hoofprints – are made in dry, dusty ground. For the Hebrew term SHORESH, generally interpreted as 'root,' can also mean 'heel.' Both word pictures are valid, though the second is more in keeping with the over-all theme of this magnificent pronouncement. Nor does it change the metaphor.

This Lamb would grow up before the Lord, not in lush surroundings befitting His origins, but in the 'desert' – in very humble, ordinary circumstances. His family had only the most meagre of material possessions; His education paralleled that of an ordinary Jewish boy. His occupation was that of a carpenter, working with His hands to fashion things for others to use.

This tender Lambkin did not gambol through verdant green pastures divided by a sparkling mountain stream; his heelprint was found in the desert places, unlikely surroundings to produce and nurture the very Son of God.

This one took upon himself the form of a servant, made himself of no reputation, and was made in the likeness of men (Philippians 2:7). Born in a sheepfold to a carpenter's wife and raised in the hot, dusty market town of Nazareth in the province of Galilee which was looked upon with disdain by the rest of the country, the Eternal One, the Mighty God, the Prince of Peace became in fact God's tender Lambkin. He it is who would become a suffering servant but also our sinless substitute.

Our Suffering Substitute

It is proper and appropriate at this point to remind the reader that this One who stooped down to become the suffering substitute Lamb of God for our sakes will one day also stand before us in unbelievable splendour, majesty and light as the supreme Judge of all the earth.

We do well to remember that sin, particularly our own sins, are not easily set aside by God. Sin is totally abhorrent to Him. He does not casually 'sweep them under the carpet.' The immutable law of God has been broken; a penalty must be paid. When God pays that penalty, and we accept His substitutionary death as our own, we are brought into a new relationship: the judge has become our father.

This is the reason that to reject the great Judge's offer is such a heinous crime. This is why those who cling to their sins, their own way, rejecting God's gracious offer, are 'crucifying the son of God afresh.'

Some years ago a young woman was arraigned before a California court for a misdemeanour. When the charge was read, she pleaded guilty. All the evidence and her own conscience pointed to a verdict of guilty.

It was no surprise when the judge, in sonorous tones,

read out the verdict against her. She had to either pay a fine of $100 or spend ten days in jail.

Unfortunately, the youthful offender did not have the money to discharge her debt. She was helpless to free herself from the judgment against her.

The judge looked down at her in the prisoner's dock. There she stood, totally guilty before the law. Her own waywardness had led her into this awkward predicament.

Slowly, surely, with great dignity, the judge slipped his robes from his broad shoulders. In a gesture of momentous consequence, he stepped from behind the bar and came down the steps to stand beside his own daughter in the dock.

Reaching into his own pocket, he withdrew the amount of money needed to cancel her debt, paying the price to set her free.

He who had been her judicial magistrate had also been her loving father. It was he who paid the full penalty of her crime, and it was he who stamped 'Paid in full' across her fine. It was he who set her free.

Her father was wounded for her transgression. Her father was bruised for her iniquities. Her father was grieved with her guilt. Her father bore the cost of her acquittal. By his substitutionary sacrifice on her behalf, she was set free, restored, made whole again as a member of his family and a member of society.

This little story is a true account of a single, sublime incident in the annals of a California courtroom. In the stirring saga of human history and God's sovereign dealing with the human race, we see the same precise principle at work.

The Lamb of God Gathers the Strays

The sixth verse of this regal chapter of Isaiah is without question one of the best known and most familiar in the whole of the New Testament. Millions have glibly quoted it across the centuries. Yet few pause long enough to seriously consider its enormous implications.

'All we like sheep have gone astray.'

What does it mean to be like sheep?

What is it to go astray?

If the simile were truly understood, most men and women would be deeply offended. In our western culture, most people blithely assume that sheep are sweet, soft, white, innocent, harmless creatures dotting far-off hillsides, looking so inviting and cuddly in their woolly coats.

How far from reality! The harsh, unhappy truth is that sheep just aren't that beautiful – except at a distance and in the poetic imagery of the viewer's imagination.

Sheep are very, very stupid! They are incredibly stubborn! They have a very offensive odour. They are prone to sickness, susceptible to innumerable parasites and diseases. Timid, helpless, fearful creatures, they move under blind compulsion of the mob instinct. Under improper management when left to their own devices, they can be most destructive of the land and its resources. They are, when unattended, harsh and hard-headed with one another. They have a natural predilection to wander away, ending up in difficulties of a dozen kinds. They are easy prey for predators. They are a perpetual worry to their owners. No other class of livestock demands so much constant, meticulous care and attention.

No, sheep are not naturally attractive animals; and neither are we!

Man in his pride, arrogance and haughty intellectualism proclaims himself to be 'homo sapiens' – the wise man. In the blindness and folly of his own supposed wisdom and philosophy, he insists that he is the ultimate product of the evolutionary process. This chance system, he argues, began purely by accident and proceeds by fits and starts with no specific design or direction. In ignorance, stupidity, and incredible perversion, man has gone on to proclaim that there is no God. He declares vehemently that because he is the product of pure happenstance, he need not answer to anyone for his conduct or behaviour. Man, he insists, is but a molecular entity with chemical and physical responses to external stimuli. Ultimately, he states, each one is entitled to go where he may choose; to behave as he may wish; to do his own thing in his own way no matter what the consequences. 'And every man did that which was right in his own eyes,' could be our modern lament.

Are we surprised by the chaos and corruption of our society?

Are we surprised when Isaiah cried out in anguish, 'We have *all* gone astray!'

In the realm of science and technology, men will respectfully submit to the disciplines of certain standards. An inch is an inch, whether it be in the Bureau of Standards in Washington, Tokyo or London. A pound is a pound, be it in Ottawa, Hong Kong or Canberra. Only as engineers, technicians, and tradesmen work and live by these basic standards can there be any sort of general cohesion of commerce and industry.

Yet in the realm of human conduct and personal behaviour, men strongly resist any thought of a final absolute standard for their welfare and life. 'Tolerance' is the watchword. It is believed that a person should be perfectly free to indulge any chosen lifestyle. The secularists claim that it is our inherent privilege to play life's little game by any set of rules we may devise or design.

Yes, Isaiah, we have gone astray!

We are astray not only collectively as a society, but we are astray as individuals within the family of man. To use the simple terminology of our Lord, the great Good Shepherd, we are 'lost sheep.'

Most of the men and women who turn their backs upon God, who ignore the call of Christ, who spurn the gentle overtures of His Spirit, do not realize the remorse and anguish they bring upon Him. In despising and rejecting Him, not only do they rupture their relationship with Him but also go on to ruin their own lives.

To turn to one's own way is really nothing less than to repudiate God.

Adding insult to injury, many behave as though God could be abandoned at will. We will just do our own thing and He will leave us alone.

Fortunately, is spite of the insistence of some that they have shaken Him off, it simply is not so. 'Whither shall I go from thy Spirit?' asks the Psalmist. 'Or whither shall I flee from thy Presence? If I ascend up into heaven, thou art there: if I make my bed in hell, behold thou art there. If I take the wings of the morning, and dwell in the uttermost parts of the sea; even there shall thy hand lead me, and thy right hand shall hold me. If I say, Surely the darkness shall cover me; even the night shall be light about me. Yea, the darkness hideth not from thee; but the night shineth as the day: the darkness and the light are both light to thee' (Psalm 139:7–12).

The whole question of being 'near' or 'far' from God, of being 'lost' or 'found,' of being 'astray' or 'coming home,' is not a matter of miles or distance in terms of spacial or physical measurement. Rather, it is a concept of closeness in which there is communion, agreement, harmony, mutual understanding and good-will between ourselves and God.

Two people may be sitting in the same room on the same couch together. If there is animosity, estrangement, ill will and misunderstanding between them, in truth they are 'miles apart' even if they are within arm's reach of each other. So it is with us and Christ. The measure of our 'closeness,' our communion, our compatibility is not one of distance but of unity, agreement, love and mutual acceptance.

Incredible as it may sound, the responsibility for establishing this bond of affection and oneness between God and a sheep gone astray has been laid upon The Lamb of God. He it is who comes to seek and save the lost strays, to draw them back.

In the traditional life of the eastern shepherds, the stray sheep were always retrieved and gathered up by the shepherd's pet lamb. Every shepherd owned a special, hand-reared pet lamb who was considered almost as affectionately as his own children.

Like a veritable shadow, wherever the shepherd went, the pet lamb followed. Wherever he walked, the pet lamb walked. And whenever the shepherd set out into the wild pastures, the upland range or rough hill country to gather his stray stragglers, full responsibility for their safe return rested on the pet lamb.

It was the pet lamb who came alongside the lost ones, who fed side by side with them, who called to them, who influenced them to follow him gently back to the master's fold. It was the pet lamb, who, at the close of day as the sun set over the western hills, came home in the master's footprints, faithfully bringing the strays with him.

The term 'bellwether' refers to this special lamb (who often wears a bell), bringing the stray sheep back to the fold, back to the shepherd. The divine Bellwether is The Lamb of God, Jesus Christ. Even out of the most difficult circumstances to which our own waywardness and selfishness have brought us, He gently but firmly nudges us in the right direction. In love and compassion and care, He comes to call us back to God our Father and home where we belong.

The Lamb of God in Silence

We westerners take great pride in our freedom to expound, propound, advocate, and articulate every thought, every cause which crosses our path. Thus the concept of a thorn-crowned Saviour standing silent before His accusers seems totally absurd to the modern mind.

This aspect is emphasized by the prophet as he likens The Lamb of God to a sheep struck dumb before its shearer.

Shearing sheep is not a sweet, romantic task It is

terribly hard work It is done at the hottest time of the summer season. Then the wool 'rises' from the sheep's skin, allowing the shears to move swiftly and deftly through the outstretched strands, separating the fleece from the pelt.

Sheep hate to be sheared. They are terror-stricken but silent in their fear and apprehension of the ordeal. When taken in hand they rigidly stiffen their bodies, arch their necks, then bury their heads in the midriff of the one who bends over to shear them.

In its natural state, raw wool is not the shining, snowy-white soft substance that most people imagine. Instead, it is usually very dark and dirty, stained with soil, mud and manure. In some cases it will be caked with several pounds of dung from the sheep itself. The fleece is full of sticks, bits of weeds, burrs and assorted grass seeds that cling to the fibres. Often it is infested with ticks, mites, and other parasites that prey on sheep. The fleece is greasy and oily with lanolin, which, when it is hot, emits a most disagreeable and repulsive odour.

Only after the wool has been removed from the sheep, then thoroughly washed and cleansed from foreign matter, does it have the attractive appearance commonly held in our mind's eye. Raw wool in Scripture represents the outward expression of the inner life. In its natural state it stands for *self*; and as such it was never allowed to be worn by any of the priests who entered the holy place or offered special sacrifices of sin offerings (see Ezekiel 44:15–18).

When Isaiah in his first chapter compared sin to scarlet and crimson, contrasting them with snow and wool, he was referring to wool which had been washed, thoroughly cleansed and made ready for the spinning wheel. One of the great paradoxes of Scripture is the exhortation to bring our sins to the blood of Christ for washing white as newly cleansed wool.

The Lamb of God in Humiliation

After our Lord had celebrated the last Passover supper with His companions, and after He had shared with them the wonderful truths recorded in John chapters 13–17, He led them out to the garden of Gethsemane where His ultimate humiliation was to begin. Because all the dreadful details of that despicable ordeal have been recounted in my book *Rabboni*, they will not be elaborated on here. Sufficient to say that in His lynching, abuse, mock trial, torture, flogging, and in the desertion of those closest to Him, we see not only the bestiality of human behaviour, but we see also the grandeur of God.

The reasons for saying this are twofold. The first is because Jesus' contemporaries, bent on His destruction, thought only that they were dealing with a man, some carpenter from Nazareth. They had set themselves to silence Him. They cared not about the methods they used to finally crucify Him. They resorted to all the intrigue, falsehoods, deception and evil of which human beings; are capable.

What they did not know, and most men still do not know, was that 'Jesus of Nazareth' was 'God of Heaven.' They did not recognize Him as The Messiah, The Anointed One, The Christ who had come to save them – God himself: They refuse to see His deity demonstrated in what He did and what He said.

Even to this day, some who consider themselves Christians draw back from the concept that Jesus Christ is none other than God. The world out-and-out denies His deity. Every attack made upon His person, every charge levied against His credentials by the false cults of the world, every falsehood perpetrated against Him by the opposing forces of darkness are ongoing evidences of His eternal verity, His timeless truth.

If Jesus were not the Christ of God, He would long ago have been lost in the hazy mists of man's memory. Like false pretenders and crazy imposters across the ages, His record would have blown away in the winds of time.

But that did not happen! Despite the most concerted attempts of human society, human philosophy, human governments and human ignorance to obliterate His presence and power, He has become the dearest person in all of life to a hundred million hearts from centuries past to the present. His deity goes unchallenged by those who know Him as Saviour and Redeemer.

Isaiah declared that He would be taken from prison and from judgment – that He would be cut off out of the land of the living, stricken for the transgression of His people. Here was His remarkable willingness – even beyond that, His *intention* – to be made captive in our human condition, to be humiliated and falsely accused, incarcerated in the narrow confines of our humanity. This He did, not by compulsion or constraint from without, but by His own choice: 'It *pleased* the Lord to bruise him …'

Jesus Christ was not a martyr. He who was subjected to such gross humiliation by His contemporaries was not merely caught in the toils and terror of fickle fate. He was, rather, God deliberately setting aside His honour, prestige, and splendour. The Eternal One quietly stripped himself of His own power to take upon himself the mantle of a man in human flesh and form. The everlasting *I Am* set aside His endless immortality to enter the captivity of an earthbound body subject to death. The Supreme Sovereign of the universe *made himself* of no reputation to become a suffering servant, The Lamb slain for our sins (Philippians 2:1–8).

It was not men who bound Him against His will – it was He who chose to be made captive in our stead.
It was not for His own wrongs that He suffered – it was for our sins that He was shackled.
It was not His condemnation that took Him to the cross – it was our conviction that caused His death.

Even Pilate, looking at Jesus through the narrow, secularist view of a Roman official, could see this fact. He insisted, 'I find no fault in Him.' And the Roman governor's wife was fully aware that 'this is an innocent man.' The rough, tough, battle-hardened centurion who crucified Jesus exclaimed in awe, 'Truly, this was the Son of God.'

This willing Captive could proclaim liberty to the captives and the opening of the prison to them that are bound. He had been there!

He who made His grave with the wicked could forgive the wicked. The one whose body was bruised and beaten could bring healing to all mankind. In bearing the grief of His separation from God that day, He could bring comfort to those who sorrow. This One who carried the guilt of the whole world could bring forgiveness and reconciliation to all who would receive it. His captors shouted at him in derision, 'He saved others, himself he cannot save!' Himself he *would not* save. If He had, all the rest of us would have perished. Yes, He was willing to be made captive, willing to be condemned, willing to be crucified in order that you and I could be set free, pardoned, and given eternal life.

Unshackled from bondage to Satan, sin, and selfishness, we are free to become His own humble 'loveslaves,' followers of The Lamb.

🦗

PART II

The Lamb of God
in Person

CHAPTER 7

C

The Lamb of God Incarnate

The Redeemer Comes

When the fullness of the time was come, God sent forth his Son, made of a woman, made under the law, to redeem them that were under the law ...

(Galatians 4:4,5)

When Christ came, born of a virgin – the Eternal One, the Prince of Peace, the Mighty God, the Everlasting Father, the Wonderful Counsellor – He set aside His supernatural splendour. In unutterable condescension He humbled himself, took upon His impeccable person the form of a man. God himself entered the human family as a babe born at Bethlehem (Isaiah 9:6; Philippians 2:1–11).

Here was the supreme Seventh Act.

For some thirty-three years He would play His divine role upon the planet garbed in human guise. Most of His contemporaries were totally oblivious to His origin. They understood even less of His purposes in this performance.

Even His so-called earthly 'parents,' in reality but His boyhood guardians, scarcely seemed to grasp the fact it was not only the Son of Man who had come into their care but also the Son of God. His behaviour as a boy baffled them. At the age of twelve, He stunned even the teachers and scholars steeped in the traditions and ancient truths of Israel.

This little lad who ran and played and laughed and cried and asked a score of searching, stabbing questions of His mentors was no ordinary child. He was *The Lamb of God* moving among ordinary men in mufti. He grew in grace with both God and man. But His family and friends really knew Him not. Though maturing in favour with His fellows, still He stood among them as a stranger from another sphere.

The days of His youth and early manhood were busy with boyhood exploits and the usual achievements of human adolescence. He was not a difficult teenager, given to tantrums and sullenness. Rather, He honoured His lowly peasant parents, taking on the trade of a simple, small-town carpenter.

Working with wood; sawing planks; shaping slabs of timber; smoothing yokes; building boxes; making ploughs; hammering spikes and chopping chunks of tough olive wood or handling heavy acacia were part and parcel of His earthly drama and youthful days.

The pungent aroma of fresh cedar sawdust, the smooth feel of oak shavings curling over His big brown hands, the beautiful grain of freshly smoothed wood were the greater portion of His few short years, so simply spent in the carpenter shop.

Though He was The Lamb of God, the Everlasting One, His neighbours were the rough-and-tumble tradesmen of Nazareth, a tough trading town. It stood on the crossroads of commerce that criss-crossed the country. Here shepherds and farmers and camel drivers and common city people came to Christ, not to have their souls and spirits mended but broken beds and worn-out ploughs and cracked yokes.

He knew all about making candlesticks and ox stalls and shepherd crooks and farmer's forks. He was God, very God, in close touch with man, very man. Out of all these personal, private contacts came the great parables, the timeless truths, the pungent, powerful teaching of His later public ministry.

Then one day the whole scene changed. He set down His saw; hung up His hammer; put the plane on its shelf; dusted off the sawdust from His hands and headed for the distant Jordan River.

As He moved down the slope leading to the water's edge where John, the flaming desert firebrand, stood shouting to the masses around him, Jesus was noticed. For the first time in almost thirty years of quiet obscurity, His true identity was recognized. John, the most powerful prophet ever to appear in Israel, shouted aloud for all to hear and see – 'Behold, look, there is The Lamb of God!'

John's dramatic announcement seemed, for the most part, to be lost on the careless crowd. A tiny handful of his own disciples eventually felt drawn to follow Christ. But out of the multitudes of thousands whom John baptised, never more than about a hundred ever felt the personal compulsion of Jesus of Nazareth. Even at that, almost all of these eventually deserted Him. Ultimately, only a faithful band of dozen tough, young teenagers were in His regular retinue. Of these the oldest was the blustery, big fisherman, Simon Peter, whose forceful personality eclipsed most of his mates.

For nearly three years the little band of thirteen men roamed and ranged like wandering sheep across the length and breadth of Palestine. Their Bellwether was Jesus of Nazareth. Though the rambunctious young roustabouts scarcely realized it, they were following God in human guise.

Awe-struck, sometimes startled, other times deeply dismayed, they imagined somehow their hero would usher in a powerful new empire of which they would be an important part. His constant reference to His new and unique 'Kingdom of God' was a theme that fired their youthful zeal and charged their latent ambitions to break out from the bondage of Rome. They would be glad to get rid of the Caesar's legions. They would be happy to see Pilate sent packing.

Yet His way of going about such grand schemes puzzled and perplexed them. He never established a power base for himself. He never formed any political party. He never forged any links with the ecclesiastical heirarchy of the day. He never made any attempt to manipulate people. No committees were commissioned to make a study of the current economic climate. He never used any subtlety or diplomacy to try and ingratiate himself with those in positions of power or prestige.

On the contrary, this Christ was a loner. He was an enigma to His contemporaries. He was a scourge to the so-called spiritual leaders of His day. He was a menace to the status quo of His society.

Wherever He went, the impact of His person and the dynamic of His teaching attracted enormous public interest. Men and women by the multitudes came to Him for healing of body, for cleansing from disease, for delivery from demons, for restoration of sight, for uplift of spirit, for refreshment of soul, for forgiveness of sins.

The lives He touched were turned around. The eyes He looked into, with such enormous love, beheld the beauty of God in this One, yet most of them knew Him not. He was The Lamb of God moving amongst the lost sheep of the nation of Israel, bringing back a few strays from their self-willed wandering.

Repeatedly and emphatically He stated that He had come to seek and to search and to save the lost sheep that had strayed.

The way an eastern shepherd did this was always by using his own pet lamb to lead the wanderers home. Here was The Lamb of God playing this very role amid lost and weary men and women. He had come unto His own, but most of His own had not received Him, much less responded to His overtures of compassion.

Often He looked out on the careless, milling multi-tudes around Him. 'Oh,' He cried from the depths of His sorrowing spirit, 'they are like sheep that have gone astray, lost and bewildered without a shepherd' (See Matthew 9:35–38).

Not only did He do His utmost to gather up a few, but He sent out His twelve young companions in pairs to do the same. 'I am sending you out to the lost sheep of Israel,' He told them. 'You will be as sheep among wolves, terribly vulnerable, dreadfully endangered; but be of good courage, I shall be with you' (Matthew 10).

It was all very exciting, very blood-tingling, very daring and dramatic. They too, like their leader, healed the sick, restored sight to the blind, cast out demons, and even considered burning up whole communities with celestial fire if they failed to grant them a proper reception.

Sometimes their short-sighted and impetuous

tactics did not mesh with The Master's way of doing things. They were looking for fireworks, action, and visible results. He seemed intent only on quiet service and utter self-sacrifice.

In fact, some of them became incensed with His attitude of love and concern in ministering to the endless needs of men and women. It mattered not what their demands might be, whether for food or forgiveness or teaching or healing. Jesus was always ready to give and give and *give* of himself. In contrast, His companions complained that the crowds should just simply be sent off home; there was a limit to how much a man could endure.

What they did not seem to know was that this 'man' with whom they tramped over the dusty trails of their tough land was 'The Man of Sorrows' – God himself touched with the feelings of human infirmity. He was moved by the sin and pain of struggling mankind.

And as He himself moved steadily, surely, with unshaken step toward an almost inevitable confrontation with His enemies, His disciples were utterly bewildered. Stormy, sullen, passionate Peter even tried to prevent it happening. In frustration he shouted at Jesus that this should never take place.

But it was for the cross that He had come! The horrible hounding of His footsteps; the cruel, relentless attacks on His person and teaching; the final explosive confrontations with the ecclesiastical hierarchy of the day; the stirring triumphal entry into Jerusalem; the moving last supper with His men; the agony of Gethsemane; the bestial betrayal; the mock trial by those in power – these were all but a dramatic prelude to the cataclysm at Golgotha.

In all of this anguish, Christ moved with quiet strength and calm serenity. Nothing, nothing, took Him by surprise. Though He was 'the Man of Sorrows,' acquainted with grief – both ours and His – He was also 'The Lamb of God,' moving in might and majesty.

It was for the cross that He had come. It was for the sins of the whole world that He was to suffer. He was The Passover Lamb, slain, suffering from before the foundation of the world, absorbing the penalty for us all. It was our perversity, our pride which would take Him to the tree. In this perfect Being there was no fault. He was The Lamb of God, blameless, harmless, impeccable in conversation and action. He, the faultless One, the sinless One, the innocent One, alone could stand and suffer and die in our stead, without a blemish.

Here was God in Christ, reconciling the whole world unto himself. Here was He who knew no stain or shame of sin, being made sin for us blighted mortals, that we might be made righteous with His very own righteousness (2 Corinthians 5:18–21).

Yes, at this Passover feast, celebrated with such strong and emotional ardour by the unknowing multitudes, God acted to intervene on their behalf. He saved others; but in order to do so, himself he could not, dare not, save. The very essence of His character; the very make-up of His divine Person, demanded that He share His own life; lay down His own body; spill His own blood; give up His own Spirit in order to save us from our sins.

This was God's way. This was His Son's way. This was eternity's way. This was love's way. This is the way of the cross.

Those who stood and looked upon His dying could not understand. Nor do most of us!

In utter blindness, ignorance and folly the society of the day laid cruel hands upon The Lamb of God, offering Him as a substitute for subversive Barabbas, a man given to violence and intrigue. The mob thought it a joke of sorts. They screamed for the innocent blood of an innocent man, little knowing how desperately their depraved souls needed that blood to cleanse and purge them from their own poisonous iniquity.

In their shame and stupidity men have ever crucified God to assuage their own conscience. Always, ever, they insist it is God who is wrong, God is at fault, God is to blame for their own wicked behaviour. It is God who is nailed to the cross of their sinful conduct while evil wears the crown in all of their affairs.

As Christ hung on the cross, the crowds clapped their hands in glee. They jeered at His plight and pain. They scoffed as though He were nothing more than a scarecrow suspended on a hill between heaven and earth. Little did they know that as His Spirit was given up, He entered the hell of separation from His own righteousness in order that they might be clothed in His own holiness.

It was a dramatic, earth-shaking transaction.

It was translated into terms of sorrow and suffering for all the world to see ... but beyond human comprehension.

For sin and cynicism had blinded those who looked on with contempt.

Only the rough, battle-hardened Roman Centurion and his élite guard looked upon The Lamb of God in brokenness of heart and contrition of spirit. They cried out from the depths of their spirits:

'Surely this was the Son of God!'

Only God could lay down His life with such royal dignity for such contemptible humanity.

Such amazing condescension is almost beyond my puny ability to grasp. Such incredible humility is beyond my capacity to understand. Such awesome compassion for lost sheep like myself is beyond my hard heart to resist. From out of the depths of my innermost being there is wrung the cry, 'You came, Christ, You came because You cared!'

It is this One who grew up in Galilee. It is this One who for so many years toiled in the relative obscurity of a dusty carpenter's shop in Nazareth. It is this one who as a tender lambkin ran errands for Mary and Joseph, leaving little footprints in the the dusty paths of His hillside town and in the hearts of His family and friends.

The Scriptures are very meagre in their record of these early years of Our Lord's life. But in the brief and abrupt statements that are made there is a precise endorsement of the ancient prophet's pronouncement. He, The Lamb of God, would and did grow up in favour both with God and man. He matured in both wisdom and stature. His teenage years and adolescence were not marred, not marked by hostility, arrogance or tempestuous rebellion. He was a well-adjusted youth.

Yet, in spite of all this, His contemporaries saw nothing of unusual or special significance in Jesus the carpenter, son of Joseph. His fellow townsmen from Nazareth looked upon Him as one of their excellent craftsmen. He learned His trade well from Joseph. He did careful, meticulous work, with skill and expertise of the highest calibre. Any yoke He made or chest He built was bound to wear well and last for years.

In the process of time, He came to be well known as the carpenter's son. He was commonly called Son of Joseph. He was considered, after His father's untimely death, as 'The Carpenter.' If one wanted first-class workmanship at fair prices, delivered on time, done with dignity, Jesus was the 'man' to do it.

Before His Galilean neighbours and associates Jesus was a pleasant, quiet, unostentatious bachelor whom children loved and adults were content to regard as their friend. But beyond this He had no special or unusual magnetism that marked Him out as one of God's special appointment.

Before God, however, this One living out His early years in the degradation of Nazareth was His Son, His Lamb, garbed in the guise of a carpenter.

If ever there was a town in the hills of Galilee greedy for gain, it was Nazareth. It was to Galilee what Las Vegas is to the USA or Havana is to Cuba. Nazareth was where the fierce passions of foreign traders crossed with the deceitfulness of crafty merchants.

It was a town notorious for its pimps, prostitutes and evil of a hundred sorts. Here there were imported all the lewd practices of Phoenicia, Persia, Rome and the pagan tribes of Palestine.

Amid such sordid surroundings, this veritable wasteland of wickedness, the Lamb of God left His first footprints in the dust of time.

His contemporaries had no special respect for this 'suffering Servant' who toiled at His common trade among them. But God did. He saw Him as His only begotten Son, the first among many brethren.

Few of us ever fully comprehend the soul anguish of the sinless Son of God during His dreadful years in

Nazareth. What torment of spirit, what anguish of heart, what suffering of soul He endured as He grew up before God amid such evil! It is indeed astonishing that the divine record is so silent on this span of time in which He endured such contradictions of sinners.

The whole atmosphere of Nazareth, its environment, its life-style, must have been a horrible affront to His impeccable person. Perhaps it is well for us that the shades of silence have been drawn across these formative years of Christ's early manhood.

Certainly during His youth He was never singled out as someone very special by His fellow Galileans. In His early manhood He was never lionized as a potential leader. He was never elected to any position of prominence. He was simply regarded as 'one of us' – 'the carpenter of Nazareth.'

Apparently only His mother, Mary, knew and hid away in the depths of her own spirit the special knowledge that this, her firstborn son, was also God's special Son. She sensed that her lamb was also God's Lamb.

And when, after thirty long years of waiting in the wings, the day finally came that He stepped for the first time into public view, John the Baptist shouted – 'Behold, The Lamb of God!' When He rose from the Jordan waters a voice from Heaven declared – 'Thou art my Beloved Son; in thee I am well pleased!'

This is the One of whom the prophet Isaiah 700 years earlier had declared:

> *For unto us a child is born,*
> *unto us a Son is given;*
> *And the government shall be upon His shoulder:*
> *And His name shall be called:*

Wonderful,
Counsellor,
The Mighty God,
The everlasting Father,
The Prince of Peace

(Isaiah 9:6).

Here was God himself, bearing all the splendour, all the attributes, all the titles of the Triune Godhead, stepping out in the public manifestation of His own Person, yet in the form of a perfect man. This is a concept which escapes most of us to this day, even with the full benefit of our historical hindsight and increased illumination.

This tender, unpretentious, unostentatious 'Lamb of God,' declared so fearlessly and forthrightly by John to have come taking away the sin of the world, was no less than God the Father, God the Son, God the Holy Spirit – in His completeness, in His might, in His majesty.

Yet to His contemporaries, Jesus the Christ remained but another mendicant without any special magnificence, without any unusual magnetism, without any unique material attributes that would attract others to Him.

It is true, as we shall see subsequently, that He often had crowds of people pressing in upon Him. Yet this was never because of His personal appeal or charming charisma. Children, it is said, were attracted to Him because of the integrity of His character and gentleness of spirit. But the massed multitudes came either to be fed, to be healed, to see the miracles or to have their hope of an earthly empire ignited by His teaching concerning the Kingdom of God, which few ever understood.

This was proven by the manner in which gradually His public life slowly sank into obscurity, until at the end He was forsaken by all.

All of this entailed enormous suffering for the Saviour. Anything worthwhile in the world always costs a great deal. Our deliverance, our redemption from our own despair, our liberation from our own dilemma have been paid for at the appalling price of God's own terrible reproach by men.

Let us never delude ourselves into thinking that The Man of Sorrows shared our sorrows lightly or bore our grief with gaiety. He was not just a jolly good fellow. He was not participating in a pantomime.

He was, instead, shot through with the pain and pathos or our human tragedy. He entered fully and completely into the trauma of His times. Not only did He bare the slings and stones of adversity hurled at Him by His antagonists, but in a second deep dimension He drank to the dregs the despair of our human condition.

Unlike the God of any other world religions concocted by the contrivance of man's imagination, this One came among us in total identification. He walked where we walk. He stood where we stand. He lived at our level. He was tested at all points as we are tempted. He made himself one of us. He understood us completely. He who knew no sin was made sin with our pollution that we in turn might be made right with His righteousness (2 Corinthians 5:19–21).

He had never known such ignominy in the realms of Glory whence He came. For there He had moved in an environment free from the stress, the sin, the darkness and despair of our human condition. Yet let it never be forgotten that there, too, He had been fully aware that

He must share our sorrows and be fully cognizant of our grief

Otherwise He could never be our God.

Otherwise He could never be our Strong Deliverer.

Otherwise He could never be The Lamb of God that takes away the sin of the world.

Yet, strange as it may seem, impossible as it may sound, despite all He has done on our behalf we turn our faces from Him, not wishing to be identified with Him.

It is well nigh incredible.

It is so true it can hardly be taken in!

It is the most incongruous ingratitude known on earth.

The world as a whole does not honour or esteem Christ as someone special or worthy of acclaim. He is regarded with disdain as someone meek and weak. He is put down as someone pathetic. He is made of no account with ridicule, jests, and cruel jeers.

His name is bandied about by millions in profuse profanity and loathsome oaths. His dignity is dragged in the dust by thousands who think it great sport and very cunning to hold Him in contempt and scorn. Blatant books and scandalous films are produced to portray Him as a pervert or false pretender.

No other god in all the world is attacked with such vehemence or vituperation. He is the object of an on-going lampoon by those whose own lives are sordid and sunk in debauchery. The assaults of man against this One have never abated. And it will be seen that they will be accentuated. He is not esteemed except by those few who have learned to know Him and love Him.

Yet, let me remind the reader, that though men have

done such dreadful despite to The Lamb of God, He in turn has never turned against us. He has never returned railing for railing. He has never reciprocated in anger against those who rejected Him.

Rather, His response has ever been, 'Father, forgive them, for they know not what they do!' What an incredible attitude of generous grace! What a great God!

Dare we do less than quietly contemplate such compassion, such care, such concern; then, in turn, declare boldly, gladly: 'I am one of His, I too shall share His suffering in this world.'

The Lamb of God – Our Suffering Substitute

It is the man or woman who, through the illumination and conviction of God's own Gracious Spirit, sees themselves as a 'sinner' who will seek His mercy. Because of the inherent pride of the human spirit, because of the innate perverseness of the soul, because of the incredible pollution of mankind most of us react violently against any mention that we may have wronged God.

The suggestion that we are surely sinners – that our selfish, self-centred behaviour is diametrically opposite to the gracious, self-giving, self-less character of Christ – eludes most of us. Our excuse is, 'that is how *everybody* thinks. This is how *everybody* behaves. That is how *everybody* lives.'

It has not dawned on the consciences of most men and women that their whole life-style is an affront to God. It has not become apparent that both their inner attitudes as well as their outer actions have alienated them from the close companionship of a loving Father who longs to establish an open, intimate, joyous relationship with us as His children.

'Your iniquities have separated between you and your God, and your sins have hid his face far from you …' (Isaiah 59:3).

Perhaps if we put this problem into the perspective of an inter-personal human relationship, we can grasp what it is that we are doing to God.

Have you ever tried to live in the same home where one person was a proverbial liar? You discovered that this individual distorted the truth at every turn. You found nothing that was said could be relied upon with confidence. You learned that this one was usually deliberately misleading you.

Obviously an overwhelming alienation and separation would set in between the two of you. The other could not be trusted. His or her conduct and character would become a source of intense irritation. You would be injured, grieved and hurt by this behaviour. The other person would perpetrate lies about you; cast doubt upon your good character; circulate falsehood about your family; destroy your peace of mind; ruin your relationship with others; enmesh you in constant controversy.

All of this because this individual was given to lying and deception. This one defect alone would be enough to destroy any hope you might have of establishing a noble, wholesome relationship.

And yet there really is one hope for healing between you. There does remain one way of restoring harmony. A path of painful restoration is open to you.

It is the formidable force of forgiveness.

If you are the person great enough in spirit, generous enough in soul, good enough in heart to absorb these hurts; to take this abuse; to suffer these insults without rancour or recrimination, in time a bridge can be built between you and the offender.

The cost of such forgiveness is enormous. The suffering you must endure to extend forgiveness to your antagonist is heart-wrenching.

The hurts you personally must handle and the abuse you must absorb at the hands of your adversary are awful and awesome.

Yet this is the path of peace. This is the route to total restoration. This is the highway to healing and wholeness – both for you and for the one who wrongs you.

Forgiveness, whether between man and man; man and woman; man and God, entails immeasurable cost. One must pay the price of personal humiliation.

This God has done, always does, ever will do in His loving, caring dealings with us.

May I remind you, dear friend, that our Father God does not reside 'away out there' in the immensity of inter-stellar space. He is not some remote deity, isolated from our human condition, insulated from the sins and suffering which our human behaviour imposes upon Him.

He is here.

He is present upon planet earth.

He is in immediate proximity to you as a Person at this point in time.

He is the One ever wounded with your terrible transgressions. He is the One bruised and broken by your wicked behaviour, with your unbelievable craftiness.

He is the One ever absorbing the blind and brutal outrages of your guilt.

This is The Suffering Lamb of God.

This is the One who instead of wreaking vengeance upon us for our vile behaviour, absorbs the gross injustice of our conduct and extends to us the generosity of His own gracious forgiveness.

This is the One who, in the person of Christ, came among us, laying aside the power, splendour, and authority of His divine position, to make himself of no reputation; to stand all the abuse heaped upon Him; to absorb all the insults and degradation hurled at Him, in order to extend forgiveness to us fallen men.

Someone had to accept the death sentence for fallen man.

That One was God our Father himself, Judge of all the earth, Saviour of all lost men, who saw there was no other way to deliver us.

In the person of His Own Son, in the guise of human form, having set aside His glory in the eternal dimension of the heavenlies, the suffering Saviour stripped himself, stepped down to our place, and as The Suffering Substitute paid the price of the sin charged against us in order to deliver us.

No wonder total forgiveness has been granted to us.

No wonder complete reparation has been made for our wrongs.

No wonder utter reconciliation has been accomplished for us in the overwhelming, loving generosity of our Gracious God ... Our Father in Heaven.

The Father and His Sons

During His short earthly sojourn among us in human form, Christ recounted the story of the father and his two sons. Though often titled 'The Prodigal Son,' its purpose was, and is, to portray the remarkable character of God. In ways more poignant and profound than any other parable it reveals what the forgiveness of God really is (Luke 15:11–32).

The young prodigal demanded his full share of his father's estate. This he promptly proceeded to waste and squander in total abandon. Flinging off all restraint, he 'lived it up' without any sense of responsibility to his loving benefactor. That he debased himself in debauchery and drunkenness mattered not. His self-centred preoccupation with sensual indulgence ultimately plunged him to the animal-like level of a boar in a pig pen.

In all of this it was his father who bore the burden of his behaviour. His father knew full well what his son was doing. His father felt the anguish of his son's folly. He saw his own reputation dragged into the mud by his son's misdeeds. He suffered the excruciating pain of personal heartbreak over his boy's behaviour. He endured the loss of much of his estate in his son's stupidity. He absorbed the personal humiliation of the prodigal's perversity. The dear man died a thousand deaths in suffering and sorrow for his wilful, wayward son.

Yet never once did he turn away from him in disgust.

His tear-filled eyes searched that lonely, empty road leading home, waiting for his boy's return.

In his great, generous heart, forgiveness waited to be extended. It was always there. The price for this forgiveness had been paid. Its cost had been carried. All of its suffering had been endured long before ever the boy came back.

So, when at last, the crucial day came that the son dragged his sin-stained, selfish soul back to his father's home, it was to be greeted not with reprimands and rebuke but with hugs, kisses, joy and delight.

This is forgiveness, the great forgiveness of God!

It was the father who had suffered and suffered and suffered in the place of the prodigal. It was he who had stood the shame. It was he who endured the loss. It was he who absorbed the humiliation.

But because of all this it was he and he alone who could extend healing to his boy. He alone could grant pardon. He alone could assure his boy of absolute acceptance again.

There was no re-hashing of the past. There was no going back into the mud and murk of his debauchery. There was no digging up of his degradation.

This is God's gracious, generous, great-hearted forgiveness.

Instead, the father flung a glistening white cloak around the shoulders of his son, completely covering the slime and shame of the pigpen. He thrust a new ring of gold on the hand that had squandered his estate. Here was total acceptance despite the worst his son had done to him. He placed new sandals on the mud-stained feet. From now on those feet would walk in new paths of peace and right conduct.

This is total forgiveness. This is total absolution. This is total acceptance. This is total healing between God and man, between heaven and hell, between Christ and me.

No wonder the fatted calf was butchered! No wonder

a hilarious homecoming was celebrated with singing, dancing, and joyous music!

The one sad note in this startling story is that the elder, self-righteous, self-assured son never came in to join the festivities. His pride prevented this. He proved to be even more lost than his prodigal brother. He showed that his own selfish arrogance had alienated him from his father even more effectively than his brother's sinful behaviour. Sin comes in many guises. Its most insidious form is selfish self-merit.

To both of his sons the father extended full forgiveness, full acceptance, full love. The prodigal son accepted this; but the elder brother would not.

When Christ told this story he was telling the story of His own love and forgiveness for us fallen men. Do you understand?

The Lamb of God in His Death

The death our Lord died was one of enormous depravity and indignity. It was part of the appalling humiliation to which He had subjected himself from the time of His entry into our human form.

From the crude, filthy manger to the cruel, ignominious cross, God in Christ had descended to the lowest depths to become identified with the lowest dregs of humanity. Many people are not prepared to face the appalling abuse heaped upon this One by the intransigence of His human contemporaries. They try, instead, to draw a deceptive veil of respectability over the record of man's violent treatment of God.

In some cases cranks and cynics even portray Him as

an imposter; a pretender; a charlatan who contrived His own crucifixion. All of which only proves the point even more dramatically of man's perversion and wickedness.

The truth – the terrible truth, the irrevocable truth – is that The Lamb of God, this One who suffered from before ever the earth was shaped and flung into space, was fulfilling in human flesh and form all that had been foretold for uncounted centuries. The dreadful, bestial abuse He underwent did not come as any surprise to Christ.

When He was betrayed by one of His closest friends and companions for thirty pieces of silver, He had been sold for the literal price of a slave; thirty shekels was the going price for a scrawny, black prisoner dragged to Jerusalem across the desert wastes from the Sudan, Ethiopia or East Africa. These wretched, weary, heart-broken fragments of the human family who had fallen into the terrible clutches of the slave traders were bartered away for thirty pieces of the bright metal. They were among the most forlorn of the earth's entire human community. Yet God in Christ reached down to their level.

His mutilated form was manacled and beaten by His captors, and subjected to gruesome, ugly indecency. The ruffians off the streets of that fierce city of Jerusalem, the city that had always slain and tortured its prophets, pounced upon this One like hyenas and jackals dismembering a hapless victim.

He was stripped; He was spat upon; He was beaten; He was flogged with cruel whips bearing slugs of iron that gouged and tore His flesh; He was punctured with cruel thorns plucked from the desert and rammed down hard upon His head – all this evil was man's violent reaction against God's own unsullied righteousness.

It was the hatred of evil toward good.

It was the attack of depravity on truth.

It was the response of vileness to purity.

It was the reaction of sinful man against a righteous God.

His butchers came dressed in many guises. Some were the sophisticated scribes and scholars of the Sanhedrin. Others were the Pharisees, the High Priests and powerful ecclesiastical élite. Some who took part in slaying the spotless Lamb of God were ruffians off the dusty streets and side roads of this dreadful city. Some were royalty, garbed in robes of high office and supposed nobility. Still others were rough Roman soldiers, hardened in battle, tough in their games of human suffering The conspirators came from every strata of society; they represented every segment of the world, the wretched, wicked world He had come to save.

Supposedly they had had their last laugh; when at last they were done with jeering and leering at Him; when finally they had wearied of their own terrible atrocities, they sat down to watch Him die.

This forlorn, forsaken Being hanging in appalling agony upon the tree was bearing not the burden of His own misdeeds but the incredible calumny of their own despicable misconduct.

It was not just the flaming, burning pain of spikes through His hands and feet; it was not just the loss of blood from gaping wounds in His brow, His back, His abused body; it was not just the tormenting thirst of dying by slow degrees beneath the burning sun that brought death.

It was the terrible, terrible load of sin that stained His sinless Person. This pure One, this sacred Lamb, suspended betwixt heaven and earth as the supreme sacrifice for all men of all time, was subjected to the shame of being made utter sin in our place.

From ancient times such an one was accursed of God. From the days of Moses, no greater indignity could be levied against any living soul than to be hung upon a tree. To be so degraded was to be despised and abhorred by both God and man. Such a death was considered to be so awful it even contaminated the countryside and defiled the very ground upon which the atrocity took place (see Deuteronomy 21:22–23).

Under Roman rule, such spiritual observances were often set aside. Instead, the crows and ravens, vultures and carrion-eaters were allowed to consume the carcasses which hung on crosses. If any fragments fell to the ground, hyenas, dogs and jackals would scavenge them.

When soldiers came to check and see if the three victims were dead, it surprised them to find that The Lamb of God had already expired; His Spirit had departed. So there was no need to shatter His shin bones as was the normal custom, that final awful shock used to terminate what little life might still flicker.

No, no bones were broken in the body of God's own Passover Lamb. And this too was precisely in accord with the divine edict of old. For in the institution of the Passover sacrifice, it was declared categorically that not a single bone should be broken. (Read Exodus 12:43–47; Numbers 9:12).

In the gathering gloom of this horrendous day, two

of Jesus' friends requested permission from Pilate, the Roman Governor, to take down the body. Their request was immediately granted – both because Hebrew custom demanded it, and also because it was Pilate's political stance to try to placate the religious leaders.

Previously that day he had made the ignominious exchange with them of Barabbas for the brave 'King of the Jews.' But such grim exchanges are not uncommon among the children of men. People still play their ghastly little games with God. They still exchange life for death; light for darkness; love for despair – simply because their penchant for the evil things in life overrides any desire for decency ... much less divinity.

To this very hour in human history men still shout, 'Give us Barabbas, give us knavery, give us violence, give us lawlessness! Away with Christ, away with honesty, away with righteousness, away with purity!'

Joseph and Nicodemus both were sure, as were His other disciples and the humble, heartbroken women who watched Him die, that this was the end of their friend and Master. The cross, they were sure, was the end of His career. His death meant the demise of their hopes and plans for the Kingdom of God.

How little any of them understood the events of the hour.

How few of us comprehend the triumph of Golgotha.

How few ever grasp the victory of God in His death!

It was not a man who gave his life on that cross. It was God, the Eternal One – *Love* himself.

That He tasted death there for every man is true.

But that death and decay could not constrain Him is seldom understood.

From the instant He declared triumphantly, 'It is

finished!' and volitionally freed His own Spirit from its imprisonment in human flesh and form, a path of utter freedom was fashioned for all men to follow.

For death could not hold Him!

For decay could not touch Him!

From birth up to His death He had been subject to the terrible degradation of our human condition. But at the moment of His resurrection He took to himself again all the splendour, power, majesty, dominion, glory and dignity of the Godhead.

When His friends wrapped His body in fine linen and special spices, these gestures were but human screen for the majestic movements of God in the unseen world.

He was alive! He was active. He was ministering to the multitudes of human spirits imprisoned prior to this hour. He was setting them free to follow Him, just as in subsequent centuries other imprisoned spirits, including yours and mine, could be freed to follow The Lamb of God, no longer bound by the shackles of death which He shattered for all time. (See 1 Peter 3:18–20).

This One whom His friends thought they had interred in such a beautiful tomb was not wrapped in death. 'He is not here!' the angel declared. 'He is risen!' He whom men had treated with such violence and deceit had broken the bands of death. He had destroyed the fear of death. And now all men could pass through it ... and beyond it, into the glorious realm of our God.

Surely, death was now but the doorway through which men could step into that new dimension of life with Christ.

He, The Lamb of God, had come; He had tasted death for every man; He had conquered; He had finished His earth work.

The resurrection of Christ has been an oft-neglected theme in the church. Yet at the time it happened, it transformed and galvanized a cringing, fearful little band as no other event could. The sudden, unmistakable, undeniable presence of the Risen Lord was the tremendous thrust and divine dynamic of the early church.

No other human being in all of history has ever experienced a resurrection like this. It is true, men and women have been raised from death and returned to their previous pattern of mortal life. Jesus himself raised Jairus' daughter from death; He restored the son of the widow of Nain to his mother; He brought back Lazarus, His special friend, from the grave. And earlier in history, Elijah had restored the son of the widow of Zarephath to life.

Each of these and others like them have been resurrected from death. But here is the difference: each was still subject to death, still limited by time/space, still bearing a mortal body which would eventually fall under the power of death.

At Christ's resurrection, no man unwrapped His linen winding; no man commanded Him to rise again; no man removed the stone at His grave door; no man led Him forth from the grave.

When in majesty, might and splendour He stepped out of the human limitations of the form in which He had deliberately imprisoned himself for thirty-three years, it was to take on the resurrection form of *The Victorious Lamb of God*. No longer limited by time, space, matter, or human body, He could appear and disappear at will, moving with the unbelievable speed of light.

He could appear to the veiled eyes of His friends as a total stranger, a gardener, a companion on the road, a fellow fisherman on the beach. He could likewise be seen as their dearly beloved Master, Rabboni, their dearest Friend, the living embodiment of the One wounded with nails, punctured with thorns, pierced with a Roman spear – eating bread, tasting honey, relishing fish.

For forty days and nights He moved among His friends and followers in His wonderful glorified body. Eventually more than five hundred people saw Him. Here was The Lamb of God slain from before the foundation of the earth now appearing in resplendent resurrection form, understandable to human senses yet not restrained by the human condition.

'I am the resurrection and the life,' He told Martha. The resurrection life which transformed His own body was the final stamp which validated and vindicated His life and death. This transformation more than any other single event brought His followers to a belief in Him that they had never had before.

One look into the empty grave, one moment's recognition of Rabboni's voice, one touch of His nail-pierced hands, one instant's breaking of bread, one breakfast by the beloved Galilee, and they all knew 'it is The Master.'

Everything now had fallen into place for them. All that He had said had been so, everything He told them had come true; The Lamb of God had indeed proven himself to be totally trustworthy, absolutely believable, utterly reliable.

Now all the splendid pageantry of His earthly sojourn was complete – every detail of its perfect execution carried out in accord with the sublime will and generous wish of God.

He had not resorted to violence to vindicate himself. He had not returned railing for railing to justify His own innocence. He had not tried to use His powers as the Potentate of heaven to manipulate men on earth. Not once had He deviated from the grand design to deliver us from our awful dilemma.

The Lamb of God had fulfilled and fully accomplished every prediction made about Him. All the ancient prophesies spoken of old by men, seers, priests and prophets under the unction of God's Spirit had been carried out to the most minute detail. He had totally verified all of the forecasts about His birth, life, death and resurrection amid the human race.

Now all of that was over. Now the splendid pageantry of His earthly sojourn was completed. Now the drama of His humanity was done. Every detail of its perfect execution had been carried out in accord with the sublime will and generous wish of God.

All of it was for our redemption, for our forgiveness, for our reconciliation to himself. All of this was stamped, sealed, and finalized by His remarkable resurrection.

By His perfect doing and by His perfect dying all the demands of the ancient, irrevocable, inviolate law of God were fully met. By His total, gracious, generous self-giving all the demands of a great, loving God were totally satisfied. By His magnificent substitution of himself in our stead, standing and suffering in our place, absorbing the penalty for our pride and rebellion He so brought us peace; and so our searching spirits and souls, too, are satisfied.

All He accomplished was achieved in utter perfection. All He did was in accord with the gracious, good, and generous will of God. He came. He conquered. He looked upon the terrible travail of His own soul, and He, too, was satisfied.

In all of this there was enormous glory, honour, and splendour surpassing what His friends could fully comprehend in those cataclysmic days. The rapidity of the events and the magnitude of the divine momentum left them almost aghast.

The giant, immaculate, shining linen curtain that had protected the privacy of the holy place in the Temple had been torn from top to bottom. No longer was the mercy seat of God an inviolate inner sanctum accessible only to the high priest once a year, even then only under the protection of the lamb's blood he bore in his hands. Now The Lamb of God himself had entered once for all into the most holy place. He had met man at the divine mercy seat. Now an open entrance for all men to come before the very throne of God without fear or apprehension had been made. The One who had been tempted in all points as we are, yet without sin, who had been touched with the feelings of our infirmities, now stood in power, majesty and splendour as our supreme Intercessor, our great High Priest. Even more wondrous, more startling, was the fact that The Lamb of God in resurrection assured a new relationship with himself. He called His followers His brothers. He told Mary to 'go to my brethren, and say unto them, I ascend to my Father and your Father; and to my God, and your God.'

The Lamb of God saw His humble, stumbling, unbelieving earth friends as 'brothers.' They had been brought into the family of God. They had been 'adopted into the beloved.' They had become heirs and joint heirs with Him. They were sons and daughters who had been lost and astray but now were in the fold. The Lamb of God had brought the wanderer's home. Some of the lost sheep were safe. He had brought sons to glory.

That Christ saw himself still active in this role is borne out by the last breakfast He shared with His brothers beside the lake. Though He helped them take in the largest catch of fish the young fellows had ever netted, their conversation did not centre on fishing. Instead Jesus quickly turned to the topic of sheep.

Three times He questioned Peter closely whether or not he really did love Him. And three times the Lord instructed Peter carefully to care for His sheep and lambs. The joyous, hearty, happy days on the dear, old Lake of Galilee were over for all of them.

This was the beginning of a new era, a new age, a new dimension of responsibility. From now on The Lamb of God in glory would intrust to His brethren on earth the care and concern for other lost sheep. 'As the Father sent me into the world, so send I you!'

The Lamb of God in His Ascended Majesty

An intense awe, a grand sense of wonder, a still, profound touch of majesty attends our Lord's ascension. His return to the splendour and magnificence of the unseen realm was, on earth, but a momentary parting with His faithful followers.

One instant He was here: the next He was gone. There was no fanfare of trumpets to herald His departure. There was but the cloud overhead into which He was caught up to the heavens. Then came the simple, straightforward angelic announcement that one day He would return just as He had gone.

But what of the interim?

What transpired beyond the screen that separates the natural from the supernatural world?

We are told explicitly that He was crowned with glory and great honour. There was celebrated in the expanses of eternity a coronation that transcends anything man can imagine.

The Conqueror had come home!

The crown of command now rested on His thorn-pierced brow. The sceptre of divine power was placed in His nail-pierced hands. His bruised body now reposed upon the throne of majesty on High. His pierced feet were placed on the footstool of His fame.

He who justified many and bore the guilt of multitudes now sits supreme in the realm of our God. As Paul put it so eloquently in his powerful epistle to the Philippian Church,

Wherefore God also hath highly exalted Him, and given Him a name which is above every name: That at the name of Jesus every knee should bow, of things, in heaven, and things in earth, and things under the earth; And that every tongue should confess that Jesus Christ is Lord, to the glory of God the Father

(Philippians 2:9–11).

Well may we ask ourselves why we are not given greater details, further information? Simply because we could not possibly comprehend the magnificence of His might and majesty with our finite minds.

Sufficient for us to know that the glory and honour He set aside in order to take on himself our humanity, He now fully reclaimed and repossessed. The power and prestige which were previously His, He now re-assumed. He became again in very truth *King of Kings and Lord of Lords.*

Proof that this had taken place was the gift of His own power to His Church at the day of Pentecost. There came upon them the Mantle of His own gracious Spirit. Directly from Him by His own royal decree, they received the Paraclete who would empower the occupants of the Upper Room to go out and turn the world upside down.

The Lamb of God now reinstated in the heavenly places in great glory was the One worthy of all acclaim. It was because of Him and through Him and in Him that men and women drawn from every nation, tribe and tongue upon the earth would be formed into one family.

And their endless chant of praise throughout all of eternity would be, 'Worthy is The Lamb that was slain to receive power, and riches, and wisdom, and strength, and honour, and glory, and blessing' (Revelation 5:12).

He it is who now holds in His hand the lives of His own saints. He it is who keeps them from the evil one. He it is who grants to them the strength to overcome evil. He it is who empowers them to prevail against their own destructive self-nature.

To such His special sublime assurance ever remains:

To him that overcometh will I grant to sit with me in my throne, Even as I also overcame, and am set down with my Father in his throne

(Revelation 3:21).

It is the *person* of The Lamb of God in heaven which guarantees that there shall never again be any night there. Gone forever are the sorrows which comprise so great a part of our earth days. He, The Man of Sorrows, has long since borne them all away. Instead He now wipes away every tear, dries every eye, gives to His own the oil of gladness in the place of mourning

It is in the *presence* of The Lamb of God in glory that all separation ceases. Never again will we be torn by the painful tugs of parting or the deep wounds of distance that so often distress us here.

The *power* of The Lamb of God guarantees the total extinction of all evil in His domain. Never, ever again shall sin or selfishness or evil hold sway. He has conquered all of these. He has subdued them to His sovereign purposes. His followers are set free in a new dimension of divine delight.

The *purity* of The Lamb of God assures us for all time that there can be no curse there. Nothing that defiles, deceives or diverts us from himself can enter there. Never again will His people have to contend with the wiles of the wicked one. The enemy of our souls will be banished forever, while the blood-bought children of The Lamb clap their hands with joy, giving glory, honour and adoration to Him who lives forever and forever.

He who is Potentate of the eternal ages will be seen at last as *The Lamb of God, The Alpha and the Omega, the one from everlasting to everlasting, who ever lives to make sublime intercession for us.*

In gratitude, awe and wonder His redeemed shall praise Him forever and serve Him with loyal devotion. *He is Lord of Lords, King of Kings, God very God!*

Amen and Amen!

Reflections

It is with awe and wonder that we reflect quietly again upon the divine drama unfolded by The Lamb of God – Our Suffering Saviour.

Act 1 – The personal intervention of Our Loving God to provide a proper covering for the wilful wrongdoing of the first man and woman, our federal forebears, Adam and Eve – Genesis 3

Act 2 – The substitute sacrifice of a lamb slain for the life of a single soul, Abel – Genesis 4

Act 3 – The divine provision of a suitable ram as a satisfactory sin offering for both father and son, Abraham and Isaac – Genesis 22

Act 4 – The arrangement by God for a passover lamb to provide protection for a whole household, a family and first-born son – Exodus 12

Act 5 – The sacrifice of a wilderness lamb, the scape-goat sin-bearer, to atone for the sins of an entire nation, Israel – Leviticus 16

Act 6 – The moving revelation to Isaiah of The Lamb

of God suffering in the stead of all of us who have gone astray, each turning to his own way – Isaiah 53

Act 7 – The actual arrival, in human form, of The Lamb of God, God in Christ, to take away the sin of the whole world – Jew and Gentile – all men of all time – Luke 2, John 1–3

GLORY BE TO THE LAMB!
– REVELATION 5

We want to hear from you. Please send your comments about this book to us in care of the address below. Thank you.

ZONDERVAN™

GRAND RAPIDS, MICHIGAN 49530 USA

WWW.ZONDERVAN.COM